THE
HISTORY OF
POLAND

ADVISORY BOARD

THE HISTORY OF POLAND

M. B. Biskupski

The Greenwood Histories of the Modern Nations
Frank W. Thackeray and John E. Findling, Series Editors

Greenwood Press
Westport, Connecticut • London

Library of Congress Cataloging-in-Publication Data

Biskupski, Mieczysław B.
    The history of Poland / M.B. Biskupski.
      p. cm. — (The Greenwood histories of the modern nations, ISSN 1096–2905)
    Includes bibliographical references and index.
    ISBN 0–313–30571–4 (alk. paper)
    1. Poland—History. I. Title. II. Series.
  DK4140.B57 2000
  943.821—dc21   99–043162

British Library Cataloguing in Publication Data is available.

Library of Congress Catalog Card Number: 99–043162
ISBN: 0–313–30571–4
ISSN: 1096–2905

First published in 2000

Greenwood Press, 88 Post Road West, Westport, CT 06881
An imprint of Greenwood Publishing Group, Inc.
www.greenwood.com

Printed in the United States of America

∞™

The paper used in this book complies with the
Permanent Paper Standard issued by the National'
Information Standards Organization (Z39.48–1984).

10 9 8 7 6 5 4 3 2

For Virginia

Contents

Series Foreword

The Greenwood Histories of the Modern Nations series is intended to provide students and interested laypeople with up-to-date, concise, and analytical histories of many of the nations of the contemporary world. Not since the 1960s has there been a systematic attempt to publish a series of national histories, and, as series editors, we believe that this series will prove to be a valuable contribution to our understanding of other countries in our increasingly interdependent world.

Over thirty years ago, at the end of the 1960s, the Cold War was an accepted reality of global politics, the process of decolonization was still in progress, the idea of a unified Europe with a single currency was unheard of, the United States was mired in a war in Vietnam, and the economic boom of Asia was still years in the future. Richard Nixon was president of the United States, Mao Tse-tung (not yet Mao Zedong) ruled China, Leonid Brezhnev guided the Soviet Union, and Harold Wilson was prime minister of the United Kingdom. Authoritarian dictators still ruled most of Latin America, the Middle East was reeling in the wake of the Six-Day War, and Shah Reza Pahlavi was at the height of his power in Iran. Clearly, the past thirty years have been witness to a great deal of historical change, and it is to this change that this series is primarily addressed.

With the help of a distinguished advisory board, we have selected nations whose political, economic, and social affairs mark them as among the most important in the waning years of the twentieth century, and for each nation we have found an author who is recognized as specialist in the history of that nation. These authors have worked most cooperatively with us and with Greenwood Press to produce volumes that reflect current research on their nation and that are interesting and informative to their prospective readers.

The importance of a series such as this cannot be overestimated. As a superpower whose influence is felt all over the world, the United States can claim a "special" relationship with almost every other nation. Yet many Americans know very little about the histories of the nations with which the United States relates. How did they get to be the way they are? What kind of political systems have evolved there? What kind of influence do they have in their own region? What are the dominant political, religious, and cultural forces that move their leaders? These and many other questions are answered in the volumes of this series.

The authors who have contributed to this series have written comprehensive histories of their nations, dating back to prehistoric time in some cases. Each of them, however, has devoted a significant portion of the book to events of the past thirty years, because the modern era has contributed the most to contemporary issues that have an impact on U.S. policy. Authors have made an effort to be as up-to-date as possible so that readers can benefit from the most recent scholarship and a narrative that includes very recent events.

In addition to the historical narrative, each volume in this series contains an introductory overview of the country's geography, political institutions, economic structure, and cultural attributes. This is designed to give readers a picture of the nation as it exists in the contemporary world. Each volume also contains additional chapters that add interesting and useful detail to the historical narrative. One chapter is a thorough chronology of important historical events, making it easy for readers to follow the flow of a particular nation's history. Another chapter features biographical sketches of the nation's most important figures in order to humanize some of the individuals who have contributed to the historical development of their nation. Each volume also contains a comprehensive bibliography, so that those readers whose interest has been sparked may find out more about the nation and its history. Finally, there is a carefully prepared topic and person index.

Readers of these volumes will find them fascinating to read and useful in understanding the contemporary world and the nations that comprise it. As series editors, it is our hope that this series will contribute to a heightened sense of global understanding as we enter a new century.

Frank W. Thackeray and John E. Findling
Indiana University Southeast

Preface

This is a particularly opportune moment to make a new attempt at interpreting the Polish past. With the fall of communism, the collapse of the Soviet Empire, the reunification of Germany, and the restructuring of the security and economic architecture of Europe, the world is strikingly different from what it was just a few years ago. Poland, which has re-emerged as an independent nation after nearly half a century of communism and Russian control, is within this altered context both a new and restored country. Hence the relationship of today's Poland to the country's previous incarnations is a serious and challenging question. Historians, like everyone else, are inclined to a Whiggish view of affairs, seeing the present as the inevitable product of the past. When Poland was a rather pitiable member of the Warsaw Pact, its economy perpetually in shambles, it was almost unavoidable to see in the past a kind of attenuated prologue to modern national tragedy or at least to national inconsequentiality. Now, with Poland returning to play a lively role in the world, we are well moved to rummage about the past again, this time with a happier mission, seeing failure as variation not theme.

This volume on the history of Poland concentrates on developments in the last century, especially the last several decades. As a result, events of the distant past, even if of great moment, are relatively slighted in comparison to more recent episodes. The condensed introduction merely indicates the major themes in Poland's historical evolution that have played a fundamental role in shaping the nation's modern life, and the relatively more generous coverage of the years from 1795 to 1914 merely prepares the ground for the discussion of twentieth-century developments.

Whereas this work is intended for the general reader and high school and college students, the author has tried to avoid presenting a mere annotated chronology, but has striven to provide a critical and interpretive account of Poland's history. Thus, many controversial problems are raised, and some interpretations may not yet enjoy general acceptance in the academic canon. This is, therefore, as much an interpretation of the Polish past as a recounting. It is the profoundest hope of the author that specialists on Central Europe, or Eastern Europe, or whatever region in which Poland is located in the intellectual world of the day, will read the book with interest and profit from it even though not always agree with it.

In conclusion, I should like to thank three colleagues who have read and offered many valuable comments on various chapters: Stanislaus A. Blejwas, holder of the Endowed Chair in Polish and Polish American Studies at Central Connecticut State University; Robert Szymczak of Pennsylvania State University; and Virginia R. Mitchell of the University of Rochester. The text is doubtless the better for their advice, and the poorer where it was rejected. Of course, I accept the final responsibility for any errors of fact or follies of judgment which mar the presentation. I must also acknowledge, with deep gratitude, the contributions of Frank Thackeray, of Indiana University-Southeast, who first suggested this assignment to me and subsequently endured my delays and idiosyncrasies; and Barbara Rader, of Greenwood Press, who supported my efforts even when she must have been exasperated by their tardiness. I hope their patience has not been betrayed by the result. My children, Aleksandra, Jadwiga, and Mieczysław, endured their father's long withdrawal and constant arcane mumblings with forbearance, even charity. Finally, I should like to dedicate this volume to my beloved wife, Virginia, who has had more faith in me than I have deserved.

Timeline of Historical Events

10th Century	Proto-Polish state organizes in Central Europe
966	Poland adopts Roman Catholic Christianity
1000	First Polish Archepiscopal See formed at Gniezno
1025	Bolesław I ("Chrobry") crowned as first king
1228	Konrad of Mazovia invites Teutonic Knights to Poland
1241	Mongols invade; battle of Legnica fought
1264	Act of Kalisz makes Poland sanctuary for Jews
1364	University of Kraków founded
1374	Act of Koszyce grants broad powers to local parliaments
1385	Union of Krewo is first step in Polish-Lithuanian union
1386	Polish-Lithuanian union begun when Jadwiga of Poland marries Jagiełło of Lithuania; Lithuania adopts Christianity, and Jagiełło becomes king of Poland

1410	Polish-Lithuanian Commonwealth defeats Teutonic Knights at Grünwald
1413	Union of Horodło reorganizes joint realm; Polish noble clans adopt Lithuanian counterparts
1425	*Neminem captivabimus* law enacted, which guarantees due process—a precocious constitutional development
1454	Act of Nieszawa creates powerful role for the national parliament; the "Republic of Nobles" begins
1505	*Nihil Novi* statute makes parliament the effective locus of political power
1569	Union of Lublin reorganizes the Commonwealth
1573	Elective monarchy begins and Poland is a Royal Republic; Warsaw Confederation regarding religious toleration issued
1596	Union of Brześć creates the Uniate Church; capital moved from Kraków to Warsaw
1648	Cossack rebellion begins
1654	Cossacks ally with Muscovy
1658	Treaty of Hadziacz makes the Ukraine an equal third part of the Commonwealth, with Poland and Lithuania, but act never effectuated
1667	Treaty of Andruszów with Russia divides the Ukraine
1673	Turks defeated in battle of Chocim
1683	Sobieski leads relief of Vienna and defeats the Turks
1699	Treaty of Karlowitz ends the war with Turks
1768–1772	Confederation of Bar leads to war with Russia
1772	First partition occurs
1789–1792	The four-year *sejm* is an era of reform
1791	May third Constitution adopted
1792	Traitorous Confederation of Targowica is formed
1793	Second partition occurs

1794	Kościuszko insurrection takes place and Połaniec manifesto frees serfs
1795	Third partition occurs; last king, Stanisław August, abdicates
1797–1803	Polish Legions serve in the Napoleonic Wars
1807	Duchy of Warsaw established
1815	Congress of Vienna establishes Congress Kingdom and Kraków Free State
1830–1831	November Rising occurs
1846	Galician peasants revolt
1863–1864	January Rising occurs
1867	Galicia given autonomy within Austria-Hungary
1871–1878	*Kulturkampf* (German persecution of Roman Catholic and ethnic minorities) begins in German Poland
1886	Colonization Commission established in German Poland
1892	Polish Socialist Party and Social Democratic Party founded
1894	The so-called HKT Society (named after its founders, Hansemann; Kennemann; and Tiedemann) is formed in German Poland
1895	Polish Populist Party established in Galicia
1897	National Democratic Party (*endecja*) founded
1905–1907	Revolution in Russian Empire includes Poland
1912	KTSSN (The Provisional Commission of Confederated Independence Parties) established
1914	World War I erupts; NKN (Supreme National Committee) founded
1915	Polish Victims Relief Fund created in Switzerland
1916	November 5: Central Powers issue a proclamation establishing the Kingdom of Poland
1917	KNP (The Polish National Committee) established

1918	Second Republic established; Józef Piłsudski is head of state
1919	Ignacy Jan Paderewski is first premier
1919–1922	Silesian Risings occur
1919–1921	Polish-Russian War fought
1920	Poles victorious at battle of Warsaw and battle of Niemen and Russia is forced to terms; plebiscite in East Prussia held
1921	Peace of Riga signed
1922	Upper Silesian plebiscite held; president Gabriel Narutowicz assassinated
1923	Piłsudski leaves government; Polish borders recognized internationally
1926	Piłsudski's coup takes place in May
1930	Opposition arrested and Ukrainians "pacified"
1932	Nonaggression pact signed with the Soviet Union
1934	Nonaggression pact signed with Germany
1935	March constitution enacted with expanded presidential powers; Piłsudski dies
1937	OZON (The Camp of National Unity) founded
1938	Poland occupies Teschen; restrictions against Jews enacted at Polish universities
1939	August 23: Hitler-Stalin Pact signed; September 1: Germany invades, September campaign takes place; September 17: Soviet Union invades; Władysław Sikorski heads government in exile
1940	Katyń massacre occurs
1941	Sikorski-Maisky Treaty reestablishes Polish-Soviet relations
1942	Mass extermination of Polish Jews begins; *Żegota*, the cryptonym for the *Rada Pomocy Żydom* (Council for Aid to the Jews), formed
1943	Sikorski dies; Allies betray Poland at Teheran Conference; Stanisław Mikołajczyk becomes head of exile

	government; Warsaw ghetto rising takes place; Union of Polish Patriots formed
1944	Warsaw rising occurs; provisional government established
1945	Government of National Unity established in Warsaw
1948	PZPR (the Polish United Workers' Party) formed
1951	Władysław Gomułka arrested for "nationalist deviation" Światło disclosures occur
1956	Poznań riots take place; Polish October occurs; Gomułka returns to power
1965	Polish episcopate sends letter to German bishops
1968	Student riots; anti-semitic campaign
1970	Germany recognizes Odra-Nysa line; riots in Baltic cities bring down Gomułka; Edward Gierek comes to power
1976	Riots take place at Ursus and Radom; KOR (the Committee of Workers' Defense) established
1978	Karol Wojtyła elected Pope John Paul II
1979	First Papal visit made to Poland
1980	Strikes occur; Solidarity formed
1981	Martial law drives Solidarity underground
1989	The Roundtable negotiations take place; elections see Solidarity victory; Wojciech Jaruzelski elected president; Tadeusz Mazowiecki becomes first non-Communist premier since World War II; Leszek Balcerowicz initiates "shock therapy" economic restructuring
1990	Lech Wałęsa elected president
1991	First free elections to parliament held
1993	New election allows coalition of SLD (Democratic Left Alliance) and PSL (Polish Populist Party); Hanna Suchocka's government falls; Waldemar Pawlak becomes premier
1995	Aleksander Kwaśniewski defeats Wałęsa for presidency

1997   Center-right electoral triumph: Jerzy Buzek becomes premier and Balcerowicz returns to lead Finance Ministry

1999   Poland admitted to the North Atlantic Treaty Organization (NATO)

1

Poland Today

GEOGRAPHY, TOPOGRAPHY, AND CLIMATE

Poland's total surface area, 120,725 square miles (312,683 sq. km.), is about equal to that of the British Isles. Although Poland today ranks sixth in size on the European continent, it was once Europe's largest country covering a million square kilometers. Many major locations in Poland's history, therefore, now lie outside its current borders.

Poland is bordered by Germany in the west (where the border is formed by the Odra and Nysa rivers), and the Carpathian mountains separate Poland from the Czech and Slovak republics in the south. In the east, Poland has a long border with Ukraine and Belarus which corresponds largely to the so-called Curzon Line which was imposed on Poland by the Soviet Union during World War II and later accepted by the Western powers. The northeastern corner of Poland abuts Lithuania, and the northern boundary is formed by the Baltic Sea, in the west, and the bizarre Russian enclave known as the Kaliningrad oblast in the east.

Poland, reflecting its name derived from *field* in Polish, is predominantly flat. The most significant topographical features are in the south where the Sudety (Sudeten) and Karpaty (Carpathian) and a small portion of the Bieszczady mountain ranges are found. The central portion of the Carpathian range, known as the High Tatry mountains, are the tallest in Poland, and their rugged, forbidding character makes them appear far higher than their peaks—which do not exceed 8,000 feet—would suggest. These mountains are dotted with numerous stunning lakes, and the whole area is renowned for its beauty. Abundant snow makes the area ideal for winter sports, and it is widely hoped that the winter Olympics will be held in Poland early in the twenty-first century.

There are a number of notable forest areas in Poland, the most famous of which is the unique Bialowieża region of the northeast which Poland shares with Belarus. These extraordinary forests, the largest of their type in Europe, are home to 5,000 species of flora, including 500-year-old oaks, and 10,000 species of fauna, including the last of the rare European bison and many other exotic species. Poland is pursuing a program of reforestation which is gradually allowing the country to reach European Union (EU) standards while repairing many decades of environmental damage and neglect resulting from Communist rule. Northern Poland is famous for its lakes which dot Pomerania and Mazuria. The long Baltic coast gives Poland a number of superb beaches as well as economically important commercial fishing possibilities. The best-known major ports are the striking Hanseatic city of Gdańsk (the former Danzig), Szczecin, and the modern city of Gdynia, as well as the resort area of Sopot.

Poland's climate is temperate with moderately warm summers—the average July temperature is 76°F—and rather cold, snowy winters. The mountains of the south and the northeastern corner of the county have the most severe winters.

POPULATION AND DEMOGRAPHY

Poland's population is approximately forty million, making it fifth in Europe. It is the only major European state to exhibit recent demographic vigor, and though its annual increase is just a shadow of the astonishing rate of a generation ago, it is still growing. Poland's neighbors, in contrast, are experiencing steady, and in some cases, stunning, population declines. Poland's relative demographic health has allowed it to remain a "young" country with obvious economic consequences. Of the former Communist states west of Russia, only Ukraine, which is demographically unhealthy, and Poland have significant populations; many of the others are very small.

Poland is one of the most nationally homogeneous countries in Europe. More than 95 percent of the population is ethnically Polish, and there are only tiny minorities of Germans, Ukrainians, and Belarussians—each about 1 percent of the population. The country is almost uniformly Roman Catholic, with very small Protestant, Orthodox, and Uniate communities, and a handful of Jews, the post-Holocaust remnant of a very large minority.

The capital and the largest city, with almost 1.8 million people, is Warsaw which is undergoing tremendous development. Other major centers are Łódź, a nineteenth-century manufacturing center that is being converted to high-technology production, with almost 900,000 people; and several other metropolises of approximately half a million or more: Kraków, the ancient capital deemed by the United Nations Educational, Scientific, and Cultural Organization (UNESCO) a "world cultural treasure"; Poznań, the dynamic capital of western Poland; Wrocław, in beautiful Lower Silesia; Gdańsk and Szczecin, the Baltic ports; Katowice, the manufacturing center of industrial Upper Silesia; and Lublin, the historic city near the eastern border. Each is home to at least one major university.

THE POLITICAL SYSTEM

The Polish Third Republic emerged in the wake of the failure of Communist Poland, the so-called Polish People's Republic or PRL. After two years of transition, a new governing system was organized which is essentially parliamentary with a reasonably strong executive branch. A new constitution was adopted in 1997. The president is elected every five years by popular vote. In 1995 Aleksander Kwaśniewski, a former Communist belonging to the Democratic Left Union (SLD), was elected defeating the famous Solidarity leader Lech Wałęsa. The next election is scheduled for the year 2000.

Real power resides in the two-house parliament. The upper house, the *Senat*, with about one hundred seats, has relatively little power. The lower house, the *sejm*, contains over four hundred seats and is elected every two years. A very large number of prominent parties and coalitions have emerged since the fall of the PRL, and one of the major political difficulties of the Third Republic has been to create a stable system with a manageable number of broadly based parties.

Currently, no party is close to enjoying majority support in the electorate. The SLD, is essentially a post-Communist coalition. Well-organized, the SLD has eschewed its Communist heritage and has adopted a moderate progressive line in favor of a democratic political system, market capitalism, and full integration into European economic and defense alliances including the North Atlantic Treaty Organization (NATO) and the European Community (EC). The SLD is the only essentially leftist party in the Third Republic and therefore is able to focus that segment of the electorate quite efficiently.

The moderate Freedom Union (Unia Wolności), or UW, is socially progressive and economically supports the free market. Led by economist Leszek Balcerowicz, the party contains many of the most impressive political figures of the Third Republic, including attorney Hanna Suchocka, a former prime minister, and historian Bronisław Geremek, who is currently the foreign minister. The party appeals chiefly to urban intellectuals and the new class of capitalist entrepreneurs.

The revived Polish Populist Party (PSL) has proven a major political failure in the Third Republic. Like its historic predecessors, the PSL has presented a narrow, class-based program which has made it unpopular outside of rural Poland. Its uninspired leadership has failed to broaden the party's base, and its performance in elections has been dismal and declining. This situation is a serious problem for Poland, which has economic and social as well as political dimensions, because Poland's rural population proportionately is one of the largest in Europe. The economic surge of the 1990s has done little to improve the enduring economic hardship of the farms and villages. With the PSL floundering, the rural Polish population is increasingly without effective leadership or a significant voice in national politics.

The political right in Poland has been characterized by divisiveness, which has led to political impotence. In 1996 a new coalition, the Solidarity Election Alliance (AWS), based on the former Solidarity movement, temporarily organized a powerful center-right block. This alliance probably will not be a lasting one, however, because it unites fundamentally different factions. One of the major challenges of the next century will be for Poland to create a viable party of the right.

There are also innumerable smaller parties, and many of the creations of the early 1990s proved ephemeral. Of the national minorities, only the Germans regularly elect representatives to the *sejm*. There is no minority voting bloc as such.

In 1999 Poland joined NATO with profound consequences for the nation's international position, but it is still too early to discern them fully. Poland is already closely associated with the EC and is preparing rapidly for full membership early in the twenty-first century. This will involve Poland in so-called Euroland, which, along with North America and

China, will be one of the three major economic concentrations of the world.

CULTURAL LIFE

Although Polish culture is one of the most vibrant and distinctive in Europe, it does not enjoy the prestige or recognition many Poles believe it merits. This is true even though there have been numerous Polish winners of the Nobel Prize in the field of literature, including Henryk Sienkiewicz, Władysław Reymont, Czesław Miłosz, Isaac Bashevis Singer, and Wisława Szymborska, and even though few countries have produced as many major musical figures in this century, including Ignacy Jan Paderewski, Karol Szymanowski, Grażyna Bacewicz, Krzysztof Penderecki, Witold Lutosławski, Tadeusz Baird, and Henryk Górecki. The situation is the result of Poland's long foreign occupation, during which Polish artists, writers, and composers were placed under enormous pressure to bear witness to the national tradition, to be essentially "Polish" in their creative endeavors. This situation has given Polish culture a profoundly national flavor, which accounts for the close relationship between intellectual culture and politics in Polish history. On the other hand, this preoccupation with national themes has rendered Polish culture unusually insular, perhaps even provincial, and has prevented it from attracting a broader world audience. Hence, history has conspired to make Polish intellectual culture both profoundly part of the national tradition and unusually resistant to easy appreciation by an international audience. The poet Cyprian Norwid's intonation, "Neither a sword nor a shield are the nation's weapon; but a masterpiece is!" may be an inspiration but it is also a burden. This explains why many of the works considered by Poles to be of the highest artistic value are little known outside Poland and, if known, underappreciated. Perhaps only the Hungarians have experienced the same phenomenon, but Poland is a much larger country and hence the situation appears the more anomalous. The poet Jan Lechoń's lament, "And in the Spring let me see Spring, and not Poland!," captures the obligation history has placed on the Polish artist who, in having served Poland the better, may have served art the poorer.

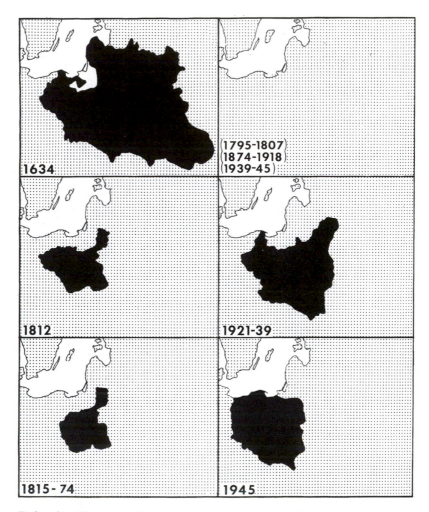

1634

(1795-1807)
(1874-1918)
(1939-45)

1812

1921-39

1815-74

1945

Poland's Changing Territory. *Source*: Norman Davies, *Heart of Europe: A Short History of Poland* (Oxford: Oxford University Press, 1984). Reprinted by permission of Oxford University Press.

2

The Heritage of Old Poland

Late in the eighteenth century, the numerous elite of Poland "felt a sense of national power, greatness, and inexhaustible strength. They believed Poland to be the best state in Europe."[1] Within twenty years, their country, one of the continent's largest, would disappear from the map. Poland would not again emerge until the twentieth century. What caused these people to be so profoundly deluded regarding their country? Obviously, they assumed that the long national existence of Poland; its large role in international affairs over many centuries; its achievements in politics, culture, and arms had entitled it to significance, certainly, at least, to existence. What had transpired over the many years before the eighteenth-century disaster that had convinced the Polish people of the country's essential worthiness? What was, in sum, the historic experience of Poland? Let us consider the shaping influences of Poland's historic evolution, tarrying only over those that left an indelible mark on the nation's formation.

Poland arose as a distinct political entity late in the tenth century, although some form of rudimentary political organization had been developing long before then. The first historically identifiable dynasty, that of Piast, controlled a territory stretching from the Odra river valley in the west—approximately today's border with Germany—eastward until the western Slavic-speaking Poles became intermingled with the eastern Slavic ancestors of the Ukrainians and Belarussians, somewhere between the San and Dnieper rivers.

Poland arose on the margins of old Roman Europe. This had a number of profound consequences. First, it meant that the new Slavic state was at a more primitive level of economic and cultural development than those territories south and west which had benefited from direct contact with Rome and the Christian religion that had developed within it. Thus the integrating elements of medieval European culture came to Poland late and from the outside. Second, Poland's geographical position in the northeast put it at the frontier between Roman and Catholic civilization, and the quite distinctly different world expanding from Constantinople: Orthodox in its Christianity and Byzantine in its political and cultural tradition.

In 966 Poland opted for conversion from Rome, not Constantinople, thus choosing the western over the eastern variant of European culture. This placed Poland between the two great sibling civilizations of medieval Christian Europe. The Russians, to Poland's east, chose Orthodoxy a little later. The Ukrainians, Lithuanians, and other peoples between the Polish and Russian cultural worlds were influenced and dominated alternatively by both with fundamental consequences for the history of Europe.

Poland's choice of conversion joined it to the family of European Christendom, but it immediately raised the question of whether Poland would also join the Holy Roman Empire, that amorphous political structure created by Charlemagne in 800 as an attempt to create a Christian commonwealth in Europe. The empire was universal in pretension, but it was effectively confined to the German-speaking portion of Europe. For the first centuries of its existence, Poland struggled to assert its independence from the empire as a politically and culturally distinct entity. Its success in establishing an archepiscopal see, directly under Rome (in 1000), and in elevating its ruler Bolesław I to the status of king in 1025 effectively underscored Poland's rights to a separate existence. By comparison, the Czechs, Poland's immediate neighbor to the south, despite their precocious political and cultural development, were unable to loose the bonds of domination in their formative centuries and gradually became absorbed into the Holy Roman Empire.

Poland's gradually established sovereignty was severely compromised by internal disunion which plagued the country for much of the eleventh to thirteenth centuries when Poland came close to following the path of the Czechs. However, under the vigorous leadership of the last two Piast rulers, Władysław Łokietek (who ruled from 1306 to 1333) and Kazimierz III "The Great" (who ruled from 1333 to 1370), Poland emerged as a powerful central European state controlling a considerable territory and playing the dominant role in the region. Nonetheless, two enormous geopolitical challenges were clouding Poland's future by this era.

In the north, the Teutonic Knights had arrived on the shores of the Baltic, ironically at Polish invitation, as a crusading order to convert the still pagan population of the area to Christianity and to protect Poland's open frontier to the northeast. Waxing dramatically in wealth and power, the Knights became an enormous military force and controlled a good portion of the Baltic coastal region and dominated the trade into the Polish interior. There developed, inevitably, a struggle between the Knights and Poland for control of the region later known as East Prussia in which each saw its most vital interests at stake.

The Knights were largely, though not exclusively, German in origin, as their name would imply, and later observers interpreted Poland's many wars with the Knights as a vast ethnic clash. This is both an exaggeration and a misrepresentation. Neither the Knights nor the Holy Roman Empire earlier regarded themselves or functioned as a German state in anything like the modern meaning of those words. To see these as episodes of a fated race war pitting Poles against Germans is to engage in an anachronistic simplification and to reduce complicated phenomena to caricatures.

The strategic threat represented by the Knights in the north was matched by a vast problem along the eastern frontier. In 1240 the Mongols (also known as the Tatars) had smashed the Eastern Slavic state of Kievan Rus and had subjected all of its people, the ancestors of today's Russians, Ukrainians, and Belarussians, to its control. Mongol armies, having consolidated the Kievan realm, surged westward, ravaged much of Hungary south of the Carpathians, and visited destruction upon Poland north of the mountains. Though a combined Polish-German army was able to stop the Mongols at Legnica, near today's Wrocław, in 1241, the Mongols remained a constant threat to Poland from the east.

The picture was further complicated by the meteoric rise to prominence of Lithuania. From its rather narrow confines along the Baltic, the Lithuanians, under a series of gifted soldiers, expanded rapidly in the thirteenth and fourteenth centuries, pushed the Mongols back, and brought much of Eastern Slavic territory under their control. This resulted in the establishment of a large, rather ramshackle state, the Grand Duchy of Lithuania, on Poland's eastern border. Composed of a pagan

Lithuanian ruling elite and a population largely eastern Slavic and Orthodox, this state was, like Poland, hard pressed by both the Teutonic Knights and the Mongols.

At the end of the fourteenth century, Poland was fundamentally transformed when the heiress to the Piast dynasty, Jadwiga, was betrothed to the Grand Duke of Lithuania, Jagiełło. The dynastic link, which was concluded by a series of accords begun with the Union of Krewo in 1385, resulted in joining Poland with the far larger Lithuania, thus forming the largest state in Europe. The true nature of this union which is still very controversial, formed a fundamental problem for much of Polish history. In the modern era, Lithuanian nationalists have insisted that the union was little more than an alliance in which the contracting parties retained a high degree of individuality, only coordinating foreign and military police for mutual benefit. The traditional Polish interpretation, in contrast, has emphasized the increasingly close and multiform nature of the union which evolved quite independently of the original intentions of its negotiators and resulted in the transformation of the east of Europe. Poland, already long Christian, converted Lithuania and brought the Church, with all its political, cultural, as well as theological significance, to the east. Poland was also a far more developed administrative entity, and its population was considerably larger. Polish practices, customs, and nomenclature gradually penetrated the Lithuanian Grand Duchy, beginning with the Union of Horodło of 1413, when the joint realm was reorganized, at both official and unofficial levels, and Poles moved eastward in large numbers. By 1569 the dynastic union of two centuries earlier had been much transformed, but whether it was one country of two parts, or two countries with considerable cooperation at many levels, is still debated.

More controversial is the meaning of this union for Polish history and culture. There are, essentially, two diametrically different conceptions of the meaning of this era for Poland (the modern consequence is discussed in subsequent chapters). The Polish-Lithuanian union changed Poland into a large, multinational, multilingual, and multidenominational state in the east of Europe, from what had been a compact central European realm of Polish Catholics. The immediate surge in strength was demonstrated by the joint state's victory over the formidable Teutonic Knights at the battle of Grünwald in 1410, one of the great battles of the age. Did this change constitute the stage upon which the great days of the country were played out as Poland shaped a unique and vigorous culture, of diverse origins, into a powerful and attractive national culture, or did this constitute a misdirection of Poland's historic vector bringing into it alien territories far from vital interests farther west? Did Poland lose its way and become dissolved in a sea of foreign influences and traditions and thus condemn itself to disunity, weakness, and eventual destruction? These fundamental questions of the Polish national experience have never been answered decisively.

With Jagiełło came a new dynasty which was to rule the joint state, called originally Poland-Lithuania but gradually simply Poland, for almost two centuries. These were great centuries for Poland, which saw the creation of the first national university (the Jagiellonian in Kraków) established in 1364, which boasts among its alumni Copernicus (1473–1543), the great scientist. An impressive vernacular literature arose featuring such figures as Mikołaj Rej (1505–69) and especially Jan Kochanowski (1530–84), probably the greatest Slavic poet of the pre-modern era.

These centuries also brought about a profound reorientation of Polish history. Poland ceased to be a Central European state and became an Eastern European one instead or, at least, in addition. Poland, or the Commonwealth as it was usually called, became involved in the question of who would control the bulk of eastern Slavic territory. This inevitably plunged Poland into a contest with Muscovy, the new power center of the Eastern Slavs which arose in the fourteenth century, over who would control the lands separating ethnic Poles from ethnic Russians. Much was at stake here. Poland represented an essentially western orientation, including the Latin alphabet, Catholicism, and later Protestantism as well; Muscovy's Orthodox civilization was quite distinct if not altogether divorced from that of Europe. Whether the centuries of integration into the Polish state made the people of the borderlands—Lithuanians, Belarussians, and Ukrainians—more oriented culturally and politically westward toward Poland or eastward toward Muscovy has been a basic question in the history of Europe. This much is clear. From the mid-fourteenth century, Poland dominated its eastern borderlands for centuries and in doing so transformed itself into a significant actor on the European stage. The loss of the eastern borderlands, or *kresy* as the Poles call them, doomed Poland to increasing strategic inferiority and prepared the way for the state's eventual destruction.

By 1572 the last Jagiellonian had died, and Poland again faced an era of profound transformation. The two centuries of Jagiellonian rule had seen Poland rise to play a major role on the continent and bid fair repeatedly to a yet greater position when members of the house of Jagiełło sat on the thrones of Hungary and Bohemia and the so-called Jagiełłonian system controlled much of Europe from the Baltic to the Adriatic. Even though the most gigantic of these visions proved ephemeral, what remained was vast enough, and Poland by 1572 was at the pinnacle of its power and influence with impressive achievements in culture and the arts to match its renown in military triumphs. Domestic politics developed according to an unusual pattern. Effective power gradually devolved to the huge gentry class (the *szlachta*) and the parliamentary system in which their influence was exerted. In a series of acts (Koszyce, 1374; *Neminem captivabimus*, 1425; Nieszawa, 1454; and *Nihil Novi*, 1505, to name the most obvious), Poland was gradually transformed into a decentralized state with enormous power vested in regional assemblies—the *sejmiki*—as well as the national parliament, the *sejm*. Although certainly not a modern democracy, this was a unique constitutional evolution of great significance for later history.

However, with the extinction of the Jagiellonian dynasty, Poland took a bold step which again has become the subject of continuing debate. Poland reconceived itself after 1572 as an elective monarchy, a royal republic, in which the subsequent monarchs would be elected by a vote of the numerous *szlachta*, the ruling class of Poland.[2] Once chosen, the prospective monarch would be required to sign a contract, the *pacta conventa*, which would curtail his ruling prerogatives in advance and protect the rights and privileges of the gentry. The elected king, though certainly no figurehead, would have his power limited by various structures and restrictions, and he would be unable to designate his successor. His death would necessitate a new election. This unusual system, whose main architect was Andrzej Zamoyski, was inspired by the model of the Roman Republic, but it incorporated many long-developing traditional Polish constitutional practices, and it preserved the decentralized Poland that had evolved by the end of the sixteenth century. This is the more noteworthy as much of the continent was well on the road to establishing increasingly centralized monarchical authority and laying the ground for the absolutist regimes of the eighteenth century.

Post–1572 Poland was perhaps Europe's most complex polity with large communities of Poles, Ruthenians (today's Ukrainians), Lithuanians, Germans, Jews, Armenians, Tatars, and others. Ethnic Poles were probably a scant majority. Poland became a huge experiment in unity from diversity by which heterogeneous elements were integrated by an essentially Polish state culture. To be sure, this national culture was confined to the elite, perhaps a tenth of the total; how far it had penetrated the consciousness of society is not easily determined. Whether this would have become an integrating national culture embracing the bulk of the population is an open question as it would require us to rerun history with Poland surviving future partitions and having a chance, like France, to create a mass national culture within historic borders not ethnographically determined.

This system Poland established after 1572 has been variously hailed as an extraordinary experiment on broadly based politics—one of history's three great experiments in at least quasi-republican governance, along with Rome and the United States, according to the American historian Robert Howard Lord—or condemned as a prescription for the enfeeblement of the central government and hence the gradual withering of Poland's ability to compete in the international arena. This, in turn, raises another question. Do we look at the authors of this system, the gentry, whose interests were so scrupulously protected, as a selfish minority to whom civic virtue was little more than class interest and who, in their short-sighted vanity, doomed their country to ruin, or do we see them as enlightened and magnanimous pioneers of a precocious quasi-republicanism, whose essential sin was being ahead of their time?

Again, a central question in the Polish historical experience has not been answered with any clear consensus. In this case, however, we must be wary of two quite distinct tendencies to draw extreme conclusions. The first is characteristic of much of western historiography concerning Poland which anachronistically interprets Poland's past from the perspective of the partitions and the destruction of the state at the end of the eighteenth century, often citing such peculiarities as the constitutional requirement for unanimity (the *liberum veto*) as proof that the structure was erected on flawed foundations and hence doomed. By this logic, Poland ended in failure leaving us to trace the origins of disaster. This predetermines us to find in the constitutional innovations of the sixteenth century a kind of national suicide pact by which the Poles created the vehicle of their own destruction. This nonsense reflects the western historical profession's ignorance of the details of Polish history. Equally nonsensical and equally productive of much misunderstanding is the Polish tradition of regarding their country's history as an unalloyed saga of liberty, too precious to be maintained in a squalid continent dominated by rapacious powers. For all of its handsome elements, the Royal Republic dangerously allowed one class, the *szlachta*, to dominate the country to such an extent that the rise of a middle class was grossly retarded, diverting and delaying the economic development of Poland and gradually making it incapable of competing with economically more vigorous states. Hence, the Royal Republic was a complex phenomenon the consequences of which should be approached with caution. This much, at least, seems clear: while Poland remained militarily powerful, its experiment in quasi-republicanism was allowed to appear as essentially harmless and even admirable. Once the country entered on a disastrous decline, after the mid-seventeenth century, the system seemed ever more pernicious and damnable. To what degree, however, the system either prompted Polish success, or determined Polish decline, is a larger and still conjectural question.

The whole issue of the relative merits of this constitutional innovation is further complicated by the matter of religious toleration, which is intimately involved. By the time of the creation of the Royal Republic in 1572, the Protestant Reformation had attracted many adherents in Poland, particularly among the *szlachta*. In 1573 the Warsaw Confederation "for the first time in European history wrote the principle of religious toleration into a nation's constitutional law."[3] Hence, the religious heterogeneity of the *szlachta* is at least partly responsible for their efforts to establish, constitutionally, a decentralized and religiously tolerant state.

It is important to remember that, unlike, Western Europe, Poland had long existed as a denominationally diverse land, with a huge Orthodox population as well as much of Europe's Jewry within its borders. Protestantism was functionally less a challenge to Poland than it was to Western European states. This also explains why old Polish patriotism is fundamentally different from the ethnic nationalism of the modern era. Polish religious toleration, which contrasted strikingly with the sectarian violence of the bulk of the continent, lasted as long as the state's security allowed it to maintain a magnanimous domestic order.

The first elected monarchs did not provide a clear answer as to whether the new system would work well. Among them were the briefly reigning and rather ridiculous Henryk Walezy (Henri Valois of France) and the vigorous Transylvanian soldier Stefan Batory whose victory over the Russians in the Livonian wars (1576–1586) secured Polish power in the northeast. The most disastrous selection was certainly Zygmunt III (1587–1632), scion of the Swedish house of Vasa, whose election led directly to a series of wars between Sweden and Poland from which the only victor was Muscovy, which gradually established itself on the ruin of the other two.

By the beginning of the seventeenth century, Poland occupied a paradoxical position. Its international standing had never been stronger: military victories over Sweden and Russia brought the country supremacy in the east, and Polish troops had even occupied the Kremlin after crushing the Russians at the battle of Kłuszyn in 1610. The 1596 Union of Brześć, a religious compact by which the Orthodox population of Poland accepted union with Rome and thus created the Uniate Church, promised the increased "Polonization" of the realm as the major religious barrier to the spread of Polish culture had been bridged. This integrating state culture, indeed, seemed to be enjoying an era of unparalleled vigor, and the Poles were convinced that their country was in every respect the model of modern civilization. However, the threats outbalanced the promise. Though the Russians and Swedes had repeatedly been routed, neither was crushed, and the great days of military power for both still lay in the future. Security was not permanently established. Moreover, the rapidly expanding Ottoman Turkish empire was eying the Black Sea coastal region as an area for future expansion. Initial tests of arms in Bukowina (where a Turkish victory at Cecora in 1620 was avenged by a huge Polish victory at Chocim the following year), where the Commonwealth abutted the Turks, portended serious problems ahead.

Domestically, the Union of Brześć raised as many problems as it settled. It caused the rapid spread of the Uniate Church and Polish culture and, soon after, direct conversion to the Roman faith among the upper classes of the formerly Orthodox territories of the Commonwealth; however, the bulk of the population was little affected, perhaps even alienated, by the defection of its former co-religionists who adopted Roman Catholicism, the "Polish faith," to obtain more easily political power and social advancement.

The population of the southeast, primarily eastern Slavic and Orthodox, had reason to protest. Ever since the Union of Lublin brought Polish rather than Lithuanian administration to the Ukraine, the result had been the rapid socioeconomic transformation of the land. It was ceasing to be a frontier province of provisional and infrequent administration and more a regular part of the Commonwealth with regular taxes and onerous serfdom. In 1648 the Cossacks, an almost impossible to define collection of frontiersmen living according to their own laws on the borderlands of the Commonwealth, rose up in rebellion against the encroachment of the Polish, Catholic, or, worse, Polonized and Uniate, administration and its Jewish agents. In many ways, a classical frontier revolt against the forces of state uniformity, the Cossack rising was far more formidable because it focused a series of overlapping grievances: religious (Orthodox against Catholic and especially against Uniate converts), ethnic (Ukrainian against Pole or against Polonized Ukrainian), and class (the poor masses against the upwardly mobile minority who saw in the Commonwealth both their fatherland and their personal future). The Cossack wars were a massive social, religious, and ethnic rebellion of the southeast of the Commonwealth. Though no match for the regular troops of the country, the rebels and their Tatar allies caused enormous destruction and huge population losses; the Jewish population of the southeast were their especial victims.

Ironically, the poor prospects of the revolt led to its disastrous expansion. In 1654 the leader of the Cossacks, Bohdan Khmelnytsky, sought Russian aid against his Polish masters, and the rebellion was transformed into an international conflict. Once at war with the Russians, Poland's position quickly deteriorated. Sweden, Brandenburg, and even distant Transylvania all fell upon the country in a series of incredibly confusing wars which dominated the last half of the century, an era understandably called "The Deluge." By 1667 Poland was forced to a strategically ruinous peace with Russia (the Treaty of Andruszów) in which it lost all of the eastern Ukraine beyond the river Dnieper.[4] A few years later, in 1672, a new war with Turkey erupted and lasted intermittently until 1699. By the end of the century, Poland had lost perhaps a third of its population and was in economic ruins. Even World War II did not cause such wholesale destruction.

These wars unraveled the whole structure of the Commonwealth and had an incalculable effect on the country and all of Eastern Europe. Some historians have argued that 1648 was a turning point in European history, making the east of the continent weaker and poorer than the west ever after. Not only was Poland wasted, but the sectarian viciousness of the wars did much to destroy the long-nurtured principles of ethnic and religious toleration which had been the hallmark of old Poland. By the beginning of the eighteenth century, Poland was not only smaller, poorer, and weaker than it had been in previous centuries, but it was a meaner and less generous land as well.

This brings us to the last era in the history of old Poland, another one filled with controversy over its meaning. Jan Sobieski (who ruled from 1674 to 1696), the warrior king whose famous victory over the Turks saved Vienna and perhaps much more in 1683, was unsuccessful at invigorating the monarchy and securing Poland's international position. His successors, the so-called Saxon monarchs, saw Poland fall increasingly under Russian influence, and, though nominally independent, Warsaw gradually lost control of its own foreign policy. To be sure, large factors were at work: the ruination of the wars of the preceding century, the economic enfeeblement that made Poland the weakest large state in Europe, and the constitutional system which, by preventing vigorous action by the monarch, militated against reform and, by reposing effective power in the gentry, prevented Poland from taking any concentrated action. In other words, the constitutional system that had made Poland precociously republican now made it dangerously weak. So determined was the nobility to protect its rights that it now regarded virtually any action by the government as an infringement on traditional liberties, and appeals to old Polish virtue were often a cover for protecting the private greed and personal vanity of one class against the needs of the country. Paralysis punctuated by anarchy became the stuff of Polish politics. Moreover, by the eighteenth century, Poland was not well positioned to profit from the rapid development of commerce nor the revolution in military technology which were transforming the west. Poland was, in short, an anachronism which was rapidly failing in the race for a secure position in a rapidly evolving continent. By late in the eighteenth century, a reform movement appeared, and the next decades were essentially a contest between the effectiveness of that movement and the fatal weakening of the state.

The reform movement split the gentry between those who saw fundamental transformation as necessary to save the nation and the most powerful nobles who believed that traditional Polish decentralization and weak governance enabled them to pursue power and position. The defense of traditional Polish practices of course, was not always an insincere defense of position, and the reformers, often drawn from the lower *szlachta*, were conversely guilty of wishing to exploit patriotic appeals to mount changes that would benefit them at the expense of their more powerful fellow nobles. Nonetheless, the obvious weakening of the country in comparison to its neighbors clearly undermines the argument of the defenders of the status quo that they were acting solely for patriotic reasons.

Whatever doubt there may have been of the desperate need for radical change in Poland's condition was dispelled when, in 1768, a national protest against overt Russian influence in Poland led to a virtual national insurrection, the Confederation of Bar. One of the leaders, Kazimierz Puɫaski, later died fighting in the American Revolution. Crushed by Russian forces, the Confederation dramatized the impotence into which the Commonwealth had declined and stimulated the reformers to make an all-out effort. However, before they could accomplish anything, disaster struck. Fearing that their success in Poland would embolden the Russians to seize control of the country, Frederick II of Prussia proposed to Catherine II of Russia a partial despoilment of Poland which would eventually include Austria as well among the beneficiaries. The result was the first partition of Poland (1772) which reduced the country by almost a third: Russia gained 93,000 square kilometers in the east; Austria, 81,900 square kilometers in the south; and Prussia, 36,300 square kilometers is the strategically and economically vital northwest of Poland.[5] It was an unprecedented catastrophe and demonstrated Poland's helplessness.

This set the stage for the reformers to make a great effort to save a fast disintegrating situation. By 1788 they had captured a sufficient hold on power to control the agenda of parliament, and they maintained, in almost continuous session, the so-called four-year *Sejm* which enacted many sweeping changes. This movement culminated in the abolition of the *liberum veto* (to many the symbol of Poland's constitutional paralysis), other major reforms, and the adoption with the reluctant and belated support of the king, the feckless Stanisław August Poniatowski, of the May Third Constitution in 1791, Europe's first written constitution. This impressive document went far toward redressing many of the constitutional impediments to national revival.

Indeed, the constitution so concerned Russia and Prussia that they combined to partition Poland once again. The Second partition of Poland, in 1793 was so gigantic an amputation of territory that what remained was incapable of independent existence. In the second partition, Poland lost more than 300,000 square kilometers, 80 percent of which went to Russia and the remainder to Prussia. Austria did not participate. Polish territorial losses in this partition were larger than the size of today's Italy. This sparked a final armed protest, the Kościuszko rising led by the celebrated soldier of the American Revolution, Tadeusz Kościuszko. Proclaiming himself "national leader" (*naczelnik*), Kościuszko freed all serfs who joined the insurrection and improved the conditions of even those who did not in the 1794 Połaniec manifesto. An all-Jewish volunteer regiment joined the rising under Berek Joselewicz. Though he rallied immense forces, Kościuszko had neither the time nor the money to arm and train them. His military effort was thus doomed. In 1794 Kościuszko was briefly able to maintain a military advantage and won the important battle of Racławice, but he was defeated decisively at Maciejowice where he was wounded and captured. With the rising crushed, three partitioners joined in a final act of extermination, and Poland disappeared from the map of Europe in the third partition of 1795. The third partition netted Austria 47,000 square kilometers; Prussia, 48,000; and Russia,

120,000. Between 1772 and 1795, Polish territorial losses amounted to more than 733,000 square kilometers.

The fact that Poland did not exist for more than a century helps explain why its voice has been absent from many arenas, including the recreation of the European past by historians. When Poland reemerged in the twentieth century, many traditions had become solidified in recounting the European story, and Poland was conspicuous by its absence. Since that time, reintegrating Poland into the story of Europe has been a slow process. Now, at the beginning of the twenty-first century, with Poland an established and increasingly significant member of the world community, one of the anticipated changes is the gradual reemergence of Poland, retroactively, to a worthy role in history.

NOTES

1. Daniel Stone, *Polish Politics and National Reform, 1775–1788* (New York, 1976), 1.

2. Traditionally the *szlachta* was reckoned as constituting 10 percent of the entire population of the country and an even higher percentage of certain provinces. The most recent research, however, has reduced this by about a third. Nonetheless, this would still make the Polish gentry a uniquely huge element of the population in comparison to the social structure of the rest of Europe.

3. James Miller, "The Sixteenth Century Roots of the Polish Democratic Tradition," in *Polish Democratic Thought from the Renaissance to the Great Emigration*, ed. M. B. Biskupski and James S. Pula (New York, 1990), 21.

4. Andruszów was later confirmed by the 1686 Treaty of Grzymułtowski, which made the Commonwealth's losses of 1667 permanent.

5. Some idea of the magnitude of these territorial losses can be gained from realizing that the Prussian share, the smallest, comprised a territory considerably larger than today's Belgium. The Austrian share was approximately equal to contemporary Austria, and Russia's to Hungary. In total, in the first partition, Poland lost an area not much smaller than all of Great Britain.

3

Poland's Long Century, 1795–1914

The extinction of Poland in 1795 was one of the decisive developments in the creation of modern Europe. For two centuries the structuring of the continent has been profoundly affected by the disappearance of the Polish Commonwealth. Only now, at the third millennium, shall we witness a European world whose geopolitics are not formed in the shadow of the partitions.

The demise of Poland moved Russia into the heart of Europe. Within a few years of Poland's fall, Russian troops fought the French in Switzerland and marched in triumph in Paris. The era of Russia as a major factor in Europe had begun. The borders of the tsarist empire, after 1795, included more than three-quarters of a million square kilometers of territory—an expanse approximately equal to all of today's France plus all of Great Britain—wrested from Poland over the preceding 150 years. The map and structure of the east of Europe had been dramatically, and permanently, recast.

The demise of Poland also launched the modern history of Germany. Prussia, which had been a Polish vassal, gained so much of its former master's land that almost as many Prussian subjects were Poles as Germans. The partitions, which enlarged and consolidated Prussian holdings, laid the base for the erection of the German Empire under Prince

Otto von Bismarck, the first chancellor of the German Empire. If the twentieth century in Europe was essentially a struggle between the Germans and the Russians for mastery of the continent, then it was the partitions of Poland that first raised the question, which would be answered by two world wars.

Whether the partitions were inevitable, the result, variously, of Polish constitutional weaknesses, or the rapacious ill-will of its neighbors, has been a central questions intriguing historians and haunting Poles for two centuries. This much, at least, is incontrovertible, the survival of Poland would have had momentous consequences. A British historian has speculated that, absent the partitions, the whole notion of "backward" Eastern Europe may well never have arisen; an "eastern France" may have restructured the modern map of the continent.

The partitions were so central to the national experience of the Poles that few parallels exist in the history of other lands. In 1795 a nation once the largest in Europe, more than eight centuries old, led by a class confident, indeed recklessly confident, of the virtues of their culture and attainments, had disappeared. Could there be a Poland without a state? How could the Poles maintain their culture and national unity while being absorbed into different realms? Could they regain their independence? Upon what forces could the nation rely for its regeneration? Could a multinational, multiconfessional, multilingual community survive without the borders and common institutions of sovereignty, or would historic Poland simply disintegrate under the stress of time? If the Poland of pre-1795 disappeared, what would replace it? How could one define Poland other than by what had been? How could one define a Pole other than by a citizenship now irrelevant? The "Polish question" faced the stunned and dispirited population of the ruined Commonwealth at the end of the eighteenth century.

The old Europe ended with the French Revolution of 1789, and the balance of the continent was revolutionized by the collapse of Poland at nearly the same time, this beginning "a long nineteenth century" that lasted until World War I in which the European state system collapsed, only to be rebuilt along different lines following the war. These lines included a new and radically different Poland.

For Poland the essential challenge of the long nineteenth century was not the recapture of independence, though this seemed to be so obviously the goal to so many. Rather the problem was simpler yet more profound: how to survive as a definable community, linked to a historic tradition, without the benefit of sovereignty. Of all the obstacles that stood in the way of the restoration of sovereignty, in whatever form and by whatever strategy, the most significant was the fact that to the great majority of the population of the Commonwealth these questions were virtually meaningless. Poland had lost its independence in the age immediately preceding the democratic revolution. The nationally conscious *szlachta* were a small minority in a state of poor peasants; serfdom still existed until long after the partitions. Indeed, even the integrating elements of Polish language and Roman Catholicism were foreign to many and were utterly alien to the great majority in the vast eastern lands. The restriction of national consciousness to a relatively small elite of a heterogeneous state was not a condition unique to Poland; indeed, it was the rule rather than the exception in Europe. The nineteenth century would redefine nations, as the masses decided who they were and what significance that decision had. As a state, Poland "missed" the nineteenth century and had to improvise its national definitions, with profound consequences. In 1789, after all, one Frenchman in three could not speak French, but by 1914 France was a unified national state. A similar evolution could well have occurred in Poland if it had not been partitioned.

Polish history in this era exhibits three structuring themes: the rise and fall of political programs offering strategies for national survival, the evolution of national self-definition, and the economic and demographic trends of the continent.

The final agonies of the Commonwealth coincided with the wars of the French Revolution (1789–1815). For the first time, the Poles would be faced with the difficult choice of how to exploit an international conflict to Polish ends. Napoleon, whose enemies included all of the partitioning powers, was welcomed by many Poles, who believed that his military genius would bring low the Commonwealth's murderers and restore the Polish state. Hence, many Poles flocked to Napoleon's banners, and Polish legions were formed as distinct units in French service in 1797 during the French campaign in Italy. Polish battlefield exploits—which were frequent and conspicuous—were, Poles hoped, to be repaid by French championship of Poland's political restoration. Polish legions fought in the Italian campaign, played a dramatic role in the Peninsular War (1807–1814), and fought with unequaled sacrifice in the ill-fated 1812 invasion of Russia. Poles remained with Napoleon when his fortunes fell; they fought at Waterloo and even accompanied him into his final exile on remote St. Helena. So profound an impression did the legions make upon the Polish imagination that the national anthem, *Jeszcze Polska nie zginęła* (Poland will never die), specifically implored Polish soldiers from Italy to liberate the homeland.

Napoleon, however, did not make Polish restoration a major element in his wartime strategy. His Polish policy reached its apogee when he created, in 1807, the truncated Duchy of Warsaw a small, pseudo-Poland carved out from Prussia's swag in the partitions. It lasted only as long as Napoleon's military star was in the ascendant. When Napoleon was defeated in 1815, Polish dreams of regaining their independence, "taking back with the sword what the enemy has stolen,"[1] celebrated in the song of the Polish legions, collapsed. Those who had doubted Napoleon's commitment to the Polish cause, like the brilliant Adam Prince Czartoryski who served the Czar, were ruefully vindicated.

The immediate result of Polish infatuation with Napoleon was defeat and failure. However, with the rise of the European Romantic movement, which stressed heroism, sacrifice, defying the odds, matching indomitable spirit against implacable reality, the Poles' recent wartime efforts induced a cult of Romantic Polish patriotism. In song, in art, and in lore, Polish battlefield prodigies became welded into a cult of Polish self-definition. Poland was no longer to be explained by the ignominy of the partitions, but was to be represented by the bravura patriotism of the legions, throwing all on the altar of an exalted love of country. Thus was born the Romantic Poland which, though periodically rejected as outmoded, or even suicidal, retained enormous power over the Poles for more than a century and has not been wholly abandoned even now. The cult of martial patriotism, with Polish independence as the ultimate good, became perpetually renewed throughout the nineteenth century as each failed effort produced new martyrs and made the goal, by its very elusiveness, all the more precious.

In 1815 the Congress of Vienna (a conference of the four major victor states, Russia, Austria, Prussia and Great Britain, plus France), reassembled Europe after nearly a quarter century of warfare but did not see fit to restore Poland. The partitioning powers were united in the realization that any resurfacing of Poland would ultimately put into question their gains from the Commonwealth's destruction. As for the remaining major powers, France was defeated and lacked both the ability and inclination to involve itself in the east. The British were even less disposed to activity in so distant a part of the continent as long as the major powers could be kept in balance. Thus, with a few platitudinous remarks of solicitude, the congress reburied Poland after insignificantly reapportioning the pieces; Russia gained and Prussia lost, reflecting their contributions to the defeat of Napoleon. The only change of importance was the curious creation of the Congress Kingdom of Poland. A truncated Duchy of Warsaw, this fragment of historic Poland was given a separate administration under Russian rule and allowed a considerable measure of autonomy, including a constitution, a parliament, and a separate army. The influence of Prince Adam Czartoryski, who had served Alexander I of Russia in opposition to Napoleon, was everywhere apparent. The ruler of the Congress Kingdom was the Russian tsar who locally was deemed the king of Poland. This curiosity, far from being a reborn Poland, but certainly not just a piece of Russia, was doomed from its inception, whatever the motivation for its creation.

Even the limited autonomy of the Congress Kingdom, however, stimulated Polish desire for true independence and the expansion of the borders to include the lands of the historic Commonwealth. This restiveness made the kingdom increasingly odious to the Russians who resented Polish ingratitude for liberties, including a constitution, that the Russians themselves did not enjoy. Inevitably, the experiment exploded and the kingdom rose up in revolt: one of the most tragic of Poland's many insurrections. In November 1830, young Poles nurtured in the tradition of the Romantic cult of risk and sacrifice rebelled. The result was a catastrophe for the Poles on many levels.

Politically, the cautious military strategy of the Poles was suicidal. The well-trained, highly motivated army of the Congress Kingdom was more than a match for the nearby Russian forces, but unrealistic hopes for the support of the western powers, especially France, caused the Poles to avoid bold military strokes. This hesitancy was increased by the diffidence of the senior officers who never believed their small forces could unseat Russia, the conqueror of Napoleon. Hence, what little chance the November Rising had for success was squandered at the outset. Eventually, overpowering Russian forces, and the indifference of Europe, crushed the Poles despite prodigies of valor. Politically unimaginative, the Polish leaders squandered the opportunity to garner a mass following by failing to emancipate the peasants, fearing that the *szlachta* would have been economically ruined.

Russian reprisals were horrifying: tens of thousands of Poles were forced to emigrate; many were executed; far more were sent into exile in Siberia. The most fundamental change, however, was the systematic extermination of the Polish presence in the east. The tsarist authorities began the wholesale "de-polonizing" of the *kresy*, the old eastern territories of the country. Fifty-thousand *szlachta* families were dispossessed and deported. The process of reducing the Polish presence in Europe continued until 1945. For the Poles, the long nineteenth century was to see the reduction of their country. Polish schools, learned societies, and libraries were closed and systematically looted, especially in the east. The liberties of the Congress Kingdom, along with the name, vanished. After 1831 a vindictive and harsh rule reigned over the defeated land, which remained quiescent and stagnant for a generation.

Austria had not particularly wanted the portion of Poland it had gained in the partitions. It added yet more minorities to an ethnic crazy quilt, and the broad arc of land beyond the Carpathians only complicated the unity of the empire. For a generation, Vienna tried to barter Galicia—as its Polish lands were called—for something else, perhaps a portion of Saxony—but to no avail. Galicia was economically exploited by Vienna but otherwise neglected. Its burgeoning population made it increasingly poor and beset. In 1831 the Galicians sent volunteers to their compatriots in the Congress Kingdom, and in 1846 they planned to stage a complex national rising in several parts of the partitioned country. The effort misfired disastrously, and the Austrian authorities either encouraged or at least tolerated a ferocious peasant's revolt, a rising that devastated the province and sowed class war in the place of Polish dreams of national union. Two years later, when much of Europe was rocked by the 1848 "Springtime of Nations," Galicia was passive and badly divided. For the Poles of Galicia, the situation was doubly perilous: class warfare between the desperate peasants and the landowning *szlachta* split the nation, whilst the large Ruthenian population, perhaps half the total, threatened Polish control of the province as well. Even the tiny Republic of Kraków, a reasonably prosperous island of partial autonomy created by the Congress of Vienna, lost its special status as a symbolical vestige of the former Poland and was made an undifferentiated part of Galicia. "Galician misery," a byword for wrenching poverty, well reflected the political hopeless of Austrian Poland, as well, after 1848.

In Prussian Poland, the situation was scarcely better. Berlin had divided its gains from the partitions into West Prussia and the Grand Duchy of Poznań. The latter was allowed some concessions to its Polish population; the former none. In 1848 the Poles and Germans of Poznania rose up as part of the revolutionary wave, cooperating in favor of local rights and constitutional reform. However, after a few months, the liberal impulses of the revolution were overwhelmed by nationalism on both sides and the result was hostility and eventually warfare in which the

Poles were overcome by the Prussian army. The long tradition of strained but functioning German-Polish cohabitation in Poznania began its descent into unforgiving national conflict, worsening by the generation, and culminating in the mutual slaughter of the twentieth century.

In the last third of the nineteenth century, everything altered. So profound were the changes in Poland that we may regard the era as the birth of the modern Polish nation; or at the least the death of the historic Poland that had lingered evanescently beyond the grave since the partitions.

The most obvious transformations were political, and every portion of the country was affected. In Russian Poland, another insurrection, beginning in January 1863, was crushed after protracted fighting. In order to preempt Polish efforts to rally the peasantry, the Russians liberated the Polish serfs in the midst of the struggle, hoping to isolate the *szlachta* and, in the long run, to gain the loyalty of the emancipated peasantry, thus shattering the basis for any future Polish opposition. Further, the Russians again concentrated their reprisals on the Polish east, eliminating with extraordinary efforts the cultural and economic presence of Polish civilization from the borderlands. This was ominous for the Poles because in 1863 many of the non-Polish population of the east had been deaf to the blandishments of the insurgents, especially in Ukraine. In 1831 Commonwealth patriotism had still maintained a powerful, ingrained hold on the multiethnic population. A generation later, however, the national movements of the Lithuanians, Belarussians, and Ukrainians, combined with decades of systematic Russian destruction of the Polish cultural and economic presence, took their toll: the unity of the Commonwealth died, replaced by increasingly intolerant, nationally defined communities, the Poles included.

Serf emancipation immediately preceded the final, long-delayed appearance of the industrial revolution in Polish lands. In the late nineteenth century, Warsaw, Łódź, Piotrków, Zagłębia Dąbrowska, and countless smaller towns rapidly became major manufacturing centers, with a huge proletariat and a rapidly developing bourgeoisie. The Jewish community of Poland, largely urban, witnessed a surge of assimiliationist sentiment, many even converting to Catholicism. The old social basis of Polish politics—a nationally conscious *szlachta* and a nationally definable, if not fully nationally conscious, peasant mass—was disappearing. If there was to be a new politics in Poland it would have to be erected on an entirely different socioeconomic base.

The changes in Galicia were equally significant. In 1866 Bismarck's Prussia stunningly defeated the Habsburgs, shaking the Austrian Empire to its foundations.[2] Hoping to avoid disintegration, Austria decided to buy off its most recalcitrant subjects. The Hungarians were given coequal status in the renamed Austro-Hungarian Empire; the Poles, less numerous than the Hungarians, failed in their bid for the creation of a three-part state and had to settle for virtual autonomy in Galicia and considerable influence at both court and parliament. Galicia, still poor and backward, was nonetheless transformed into a miniature Poland. Its educational system, including two major universities (the Jagiellonian in Kraków and the Jan Kazimierz University in Lwów), became Polish cultural engines—its press, stage, and galleries became the avenues for the dissemination of the Polish language. Though mandatory support for the Habsburgs undergirded everything, the post-1867 world gave the Poles their first open politics in generations. So many Poles became prominent in the congenial Catholic and aristocratic circles of Vienna that Austria alone among the partitioning powers could count on the loyalty, if not affection, of most of its Poles at the close of the nineteenth century. Within a few decades, Poles served in the highest ranks of the Austrian government and military, and Galicia had become the only part of historic Poland where Polish politics could be practiced almost openly.

Less happy for the Poles, but no less influential, were the changes that took place in Prussian Poland. The unification of Germany in 1871 became the prelude to an increasingly ugly struggle between Berlin and its Polish subjects when Bismarck decided to consolidate the new empire by conducting a ruthless campaign against religious and ethnic minorities, known as the *Kulturkampf*. Because the Poles were both, the *Kulturkampf* fell especially hard on them. Official persecution, begun in 1872, was followed by government-funded economic discrimination with the establishment of the Colonization Commission in 1886. Eight years later, state policy was supplemented by private initiative when the openly chauvinist Deutscher Ostmark Verein (popularly known by the initials of its founders [Hansemann, Kennemann, and Tiedemann] as the H-K-T Society) began a campaign to promote the active Germanization of the east by anti-Polish propaganda and the encouragement of ethnic rivalries.

German persecution had a paradoxical result. On the one hand, the systematic discrimination and crude propaganda alienated the Polish population of Germany irretrievably. However, for all its discrimination, Germany was still a state of laws and considerable civic freedom. These

circumstances the Poles used to organize—socially, politically, and economically—to withstand the German onslaught. The rapid economic development of Germany included the Polish territories which became the
most modern, productive, and educated portion of historic Poland. Of
equal importance, the anti-Catholic crudity of the *Kulturkampf*, plus the
increasingly hysterical race baiting by the Germans, proved a remarkable
stimulus to the national consciousness of the Poles of Silesia and Prussia.
These territories had been lost by the Commonwealth centuries before
the partitions, and their Polish population had gradually become sub-
merged. In the last part of the nineteenth century, these Poles, peasants
and industrial workers with few bourgeois elements, almost devoid of a
landowning class or intelligentsia, began to assert a Polish identity. Ironically this reanimation of western Polish lands was simultaneous with
the loss of the Polish east to the Russians. Poland was thus being reshaped quite apart from its will or control.

The defeats and disappointments of the century inevitably undermined Polish self-confidence, debased the traditional status of the *szlachta*
as preemptive leaders of the national movement, and cast doubt on the
appeal of insurrection and martial patriotism as appropriate responses
to the reality of partition. In response, new attitudes and ideas began to
call for a reexamination of Polish history, a reevaluation of Polish politics, and a new, more realistic program for the future. These new approaches are known as the Kraków school, positivism, organic work, and
tri-loyalism. These approaches were separate but mutually reinforcing
features of a general trend away from the obviously unsuccessful efforts
made in earlier decades.

The historians of the Kraków school criticized the Polish past, citing
weak central authority as the recipe for disaster that overtook Poland in
the partitions. Rejecting the revolutionary tradition as a pointless squan-
dering of national energies, these historians emphasized order, realism,
and civic responsibility. This, in turn, required the establishment of a
practical compromise with the partitioning powers. The realization that
the Poles were so weak that some truce was required with the partitioners, a tri-loyalism, was a compromise by which the Poles, by agreeing to
be loyal, though not necessarily patriotic, citizens, would lessen if not
eliminate suspicion and harassment. This trade-off would allow the Poles
to devote themselves to the undramatic but necessary tasks required to
maintain and develop the national community: education, economic improvement, and civic responsibility. This so-called organic work became
for Warsaw positivists like Aleksander Swiętochowski a new patriotism

in which reason, work, progress, modernity, and wealth replaced the traditional calls to faith and freedom.

The new attitude advanced unevenly throughout the partitioned land. In Russian Poland, the bitterness of defeat and the impossibility of any open politics made the new notions of apolitical work and progress particularly apt after the failed 1863 rising. In German Poland, economic opportunities, high educational levels, and rule of law, contributed to the rapid emergence of a progressive middle class a generation earlier. In Galicia, the Polish landowning nobility interpreted the new age as a justification for collaboration with the Habsburgs, and then cultivated a powerful position at the Habsburg court.

Thus, by the last quarter of the nineteenth century, a new "Poland" was emerging, though it was still without a mark on the map. Industrial developments in Russian Poland, parts of Galicia, and German Poland created a rapidly expanding proletariat in mushrooming cities fed by a steady stream of peasants, now freed from serfdom. Those who remained on the land had to create a new life with the collapse of serfdom. In the late nineteenth century, a general population boom, which could not be absorbed by the urban job market, resulted in a torrent of emigrants. At first, temporary workers migrated to the mines and mills of Western Europe, but by the 1890s more Poles were traveling farther and returning rarely, if at all. This was the beginning of a mass Polish emigration to North and South America, which accounted for several million emigrants by the start of World War I.

Previously, Poland had been a land of peasants and landowners with a handful of artisans, laborers, and traders. The rapid rise of urban manufacturing transformed Poland, and a middle class and an intelligentsia emerged. Drawn from ruined *szlachta* or former peasants, both classes also had strong Jewish components. The large Jewish population of historic Poland, disproportionately urban, played a major role in the social and economic modernization of the country. However, as an increasing number of Christian Poles flocked to the cities, competition arose between the well-established Jewish commercial class and the newcomers. Whereas traditional Poland had been noted for its toleration of Jews and other minorities, the social organization of modernizing Poland was accompanied by anti-Semitism.

These profound social and economic changes gave rise to three distinct trends in politics. The peasants, the bulk of the nation, found themselves squeezed by overpopulation, and the famous "price scissors" of falling prices (due to imports of foreign grain) and rising commodity prices. Their plight was acute and worsening. The political movement of populism arose to speak for the peasants and promote a pragmatic response to immediate practical problems. Largely devoid of ideological basis or goals, populism advanced no specific solutions to the Polish question and was not interested in international issues. Paradoxically, the peasants, the largest class of Poles, became so absorbed in the day-to-day class and economic issues that they left the formulation of political grand strategies to other parties, which represented far smaller segments of the population. Accustomed for centuries to follow the leadership of the landowners, the liberated Polish peasants now followed the political leadership of the intelligentsia.

Further crippling the potential of populist politics was its almost bewildering fragmentation. From its inception in late nineteenth-century Galicia, populism has been rent by faction, personality clashes, and corruption, as indicated by the appalling motto of one of the early populist leaders, "If they're giving you have to take." Populism developed a reputation in Poland, long before 1914, as a squabbling mass of petty interests. Whereas all three parts of the partitioned country eventually developed populist parties, it was Galicia that became the capital of Polish populism. Here the movement first began and, owing to little competition from urban parties, here that populism retained the largest following.

Alongside the populism of the peasants, the era saw the emergence of socialism based on the expanding proletariat. The equation of factory production with economic progress especially in comparison to the traditional torpor of the countryside, gave socialism an intellectual appeal as the engine of economic progress. Urban growth made the proletariat appear to be the harbinger of a new world—organized, efficient, and better educated than the peasant.

Early in its development, Polish socialism split into two camps. One wing, the Marxists, stressed the international character of socialism and rejected Polish patriotism as an anachronism, in favor of class loyalty. This faction eventually made common cause with the Russian Marxists within the tsarist empire and was the seedbed for Polish communism. Its rival, the Polish Socialist Party (Polska Partia Socjalistyczna or PPS) adopted national liberation as a coequal goal with socialism. Profoundly patriotic, passionately anti-Russian, the PPS appeared to be a version of the traditional Romantic notion of the struggles of enlightened, democratic Poland against the barbarity of the eastern enemy.

Just as populism found its center in Galicia, Polish socialism's stronghold was Russian Poland with its large proletariat and brutally oppressive tsarist rule. The most devotedly revolutionary of all the modern Polish political movements, socialism had from its inception a fascination with direct action, terrorism, and close organization. In all these aspects, socialism differed from the amorphous and often inert political temper of the populists.

Nationalism is the final major movement in modern Polish politics. Nationalism was essentially a modernizing strategy based on both an analysis of the past and a vision of the future. Elements of the social Darwinism of the era, which stressed struggle and "survival of the fittest" as basic to the human condition, are apparent. We can see, as well, echoes of the Kraków school's "pessimistic" interpretation of Polish history. Enormously influenced by the impact of Germany's rapid rise to continental predominance on the basis of military strength, economic efficiency, and a ruthless campaign against traditional German localism, the Polish nationalists adapted a similar strategy for Poland. The modern Pole, to borrow the phrase of the movement's chief figure, Roman Dmowski (1864–1939), had to be a rational, hardworking, secular man of business or industry. Since national unity required the creation of a homogeneous national community, toleration of minorities was to be replaced by competition. The result would hone the Poles' aggressive instincts and make them more worthy for the continuing struggle of modern life. Especially noxious to the nationalists were the Jews whose large role in commerce and the professions were seen as obstacles to Polish domination of these key avenues of economic and social advancement.

The nationalists, called the *endecja* after their Polish name,[3] were equally ruthless in their condemnation of the Polish past. The old Poland of manor and *szlachta* had failed and had to be rejected as outmoded. Traditional Polish patriotism with its nostalgic evocations of the multinational Commonwealth was not only misdirected, but it dulled the Poles to the need for pitiless struggle. Thus the movement was nationalistic, not patriotic, and anticonservative, rejecting what the nationalists saw as the szlachta's pointless dedication to a failed past.

All three movements were committed to modernization and national integration, but with striking differences. The nationalists saw Poland as a nation of ethnic and linguistic Poles and wanted to exclude all others from membership, leaving assimilation or hostility the only choices for minorities. To the nationalists, the socialists' focus on the proletariat, and the populists' focus on the peasants, threatened to divide the Poles along class lines, and hence both were dangerous and divisive. The populists, by contrast, began with the simple conclusion that, since the peasantry made up the vast majority of the population of Poland, their good would be the nation's. The socialists, by stressing the centrality of the proletariat to the emergence of a modern Polish economy, saw the worker as the future of Poland and believed that socialism would serve Polish interests best, though indirectly, by serving the proletariat.

Liberalism and conservatism, powerful movements elsewhere in Europe, were marginal in Poland. The small bourgeoisie furnished a weak base for liberalism, and tumultuous circumstances were not conducive to its growth.[4] The conservatives were a curious presence on the Polish political scene. Very influential in Galicia because of their close association with court politics, and still an economic and social force in the other two partition zones, the conservatives were officers without an army. Composed almost exclusively of landowners and a few intellectuals, the conservatives were crippled by two burdens. First, they faced the daunting problem of determining what should be "conserved" from a humiliating and depressing century of foreign occupation. Second, the conservatives were not in a position to champion, and hence gain the support, of any of the three powerful components of the Polish population: the peasants were represented by the populists; the workers, by the socialists; and the rising bourgeoisie, which often regarded the gentry elite with resentment, by the nationalists. Hence, conservatism was powerful from 1867 to 1918 in Galicia where it enjoyed the patronage of the Habsburg state, but once Poland became independent, after 1918, it virtually disappeared as a political force.

Paradoxically, however, in a larger sense, Polish politics was conservative by definition. All of the movements consciously served some Polish goal and indirectly endorsed the notion of the existence of some definable Polish characteristics and traditions that had survived the partitions. It was this acceptance of a national continuity that made all Polish politics essentially traditionalist and hence conservative.

Indeed, the emergence of the three major camps in Polish politics reflected a larger trend in Polish history. At the close of the nineteenth century, the Poles were placed in a peculiar position. So much time had passed since the extinction of their Commonwealth that much of the world had ceased to regard it as having any relevance. Since it was the ultimate lost cause, the Poles would have to decide whether patriotism was a sensible, let alone attractive, disposition. There were, after all, a number of powerful arguments in favor of accepting the verdict of the partitions as final. First, the long separation of Polish lands had resulted in their absorption into the economic worlds of the partitioners. In a very real sense, Russian Poland was more linked to Russia than it was to Galicia or Poznania, which were parts of the Austrian and German states, respectively. Warsaw was far more distant from Poznań or Kraków in 1914 than it had been before the partitions.[5] Second, the efforts at reviving Poland had been a disastrous failure, including crushing defeats in 1794–1795, 1812–1815, 1831, 1846, 1848, and 1863. Each had been followed by persecution, economic ruin, and demographic trauma. In the case of the east, it had meant the virtual obliteration of five centuries of Polish civilization over a vast area. Finally, the Poles had frequently deluded themselves into thinking Europe supported them in their efforts. After a century, however, this illusion had finally died. The Polish question had disappeared completely from the agenda of international diplomacy.

Nonetheless, in the last years of the nineteenth century, an obvious resurgence of Polish sentiment was visible and growing as a result of several factors. The last generation to know defeat firsthand, the veterans of 1863, were disappearing; leadership was passing to a new cadre of leaders who grew up in a world of Polish neo-Romanticism, a second wave of the exalted martial patriotism which first had dominated Polish thought almost a century before. These leaders once again dared to raise a political agenda and speak about Polish independence, not just economic or educational progress. Whether the force behind this revival of the old assertiveness was ultimately hope—that circumstances were again ripe for action—or desperation—that time was running out for any possibility of national rebirth—is unclear.

The rebirth of the national movement was strikingly illustrated in the arts, which stimulated as well as reflected the change in national temperament. The gigantic historical panoramas of painter Jan Matejko (1838–1893) celebrated the great victories of Polish arms; uncompromising nationalism surged through Maria Konopnicka's (1842–1910) poetry; and perhaps most strikingly, the huge literary project of Henryk Sienkiewicz (1846–1916)—a vast trilogy, over three thousand pages—celebrates the grandeur and tragedy of the Commonwealth in its last decades of glory. Although artistically flawed and historically inaccurate, the *Trilogy* is a national epic which creates an entrancing image of a great and powerful Poland, in sharp contrast to the division and weakness of the present. The effect of this work on Polish readers cannot be exaggerated.

By century's end, the Polish community was scarcely recognizable from that of only a few decades before. Polish peasants were emancipated everywhere. They had built up a network of economic cooperatives and educational societies, and a vigorous press and uncountable political parties competed for their favor, especially in relatively free Galicia. Expanding cities throughout the partitioned country witnessed the rapid growth of the bourgeoisie, proletariat, and intelligentsia. The old Poland of serf labor and *szlachta* was gone.

Galicia was not alone as a source of new promise. The combination of German economic dynamism and national discrimination had galvanized the Polish national movement there; a movement which had recently spread to Silesia and Prussia. Constitutional reforms in Russia after the Russian Revolution of 1905 allowed the creation of Polish political parties and a vigorous press. Now all three partitions boasted Poles serving in imperial parliaments, the most significant Polish political activity since 1795. By the turn of the century, a new voice had emerged—transatlantic Polonia[6]—the growing community of Poles in North America who were fast emerging as an important influence in Polish politics. Numerous, relatively affluent and free to proclaim their patriotism unhindered, Polonia helped revive its homeland.

By 1914, however, no living person could remember a free Poland; it existed only in the imagination. The partitioning powers had not been disturbed in their possession of the former Commonwealth since Napoleon's time generations earlier. Poland, as an entity, had not had a nineteenth century, and the unity of its territories and peoples had been disintegrated. Polish civilization, once the integrating force from Poznań and Kraków in the west to well beyond the Dnieper in the east, had been virtually exterminated from much of the borderlands where it was now a minority faith, resented by the new nationalisms of the minorities of the old Commonwealth. As the east receded, the western border seemed to grow, incorporating large stretches of Silesia and Prussia to the west and north where Polish nationalism now rose to challenge German domination. The frontiers of Poland were being reshaped by demographic changes and national stirrings long before diplomats and soldiers studied maps. Just as a geographically new Poland was emerging, so too was a new Pole. Formerly the *szlachta* had been the exclusive bearer of national consciousness; by 1914, the bourgeoisie, and much of the proletariat and peasantry were definitely "Polish" in consciousness, though the definition of that consciousness was far different from the traditional version characteristic of the squires of the Commonwealth. In the absence of a Polish state, the intelligentsia assumed a huge role in defining and shaping the national agenda.[7] Hence, invisible movements were redefining the limits of Polish civilization in Europe. Even if, by some miracle, Poland could again appear on the map, would it be a reborn state or a new creation, after such a long discontinuity?

NOTES

1. This line is from the song of the Polish legions who fought in Italy. It later became the Polish national anthem.

2. The Austro-Prussian War of 1866 was the second of Bismarck's three wars that resulted in the unification of Germany. The first was the defeat of Denmark, which brought the provinces of Schleswig-Holstein into Prussian hands, and the third was the defeat of France in 1870–1871, which created the basis for the inauguration of the Germany Empire in 1871.

3. The nationalists created the National Democratic party whose name in Polish, Narodowa Demokracja, is abbreviated as ND, which creates the noun *endecja*, the nationalists.

4. Brian A. Porter, "The Construction and Deconstruction of Nineteenth-Century Polish Liberalism," in *Historical Reflections on Central Europe*, ed. Stanislav J. Kirschbaum. (New York, 1999), 37.

5. Rosa Luxemburg (1871–1919), born in Poland and a major figure in the international socialist movement, argued that economic developments had made the rebirth of an independent Poland impossible.

6. Polonia is the name given to Poles, or those of Polish descent, living outside the homeland. Hence, there are, for example, a German, French, and American Polonia, among others.

7. Daria Nałęcz has argued that the intelligentsia became the "spiritual government of Poland and played a role unique in Europe"; Daria Nałęcz, *Sen o władzy: Inteligencja wobec niepodległości* [*The dream of power: The intelligentsia and independence*] (Warsaw, 1994), 5–6.

4

War and Independence, 1914–1918

Poland is the only major state in European history to have disappeared from the map and later reappeared, and then after the lapse of more than a century. The essential dilemma of Poland's reappearance is that it reentered Europe less consequentially than it had left. In other words, for complex reasons to be discussed in this chapter, Poland was not restored, but reinvented, and, as a result, fit ill into the role it had previously played in the European structure. The results for Poland, and for Europe, were considerable, and they are still plainly in evidence.

Poland was not supposed to be an issue in World War I, and it became one only by necessity and to the annoyance and distraction of the war's chief actors. As a result they addressed Poland, about which they knew virtually nothing, only when it intruded itself into more important matters or could be used as a convenient example for vast schemes of international reconstruction. None of the powers ever really had a Polish policy, although, as the war progressed, Poland often featured prominently in various peace programs. The key here is to realize that Poland was always a derivative concern, never an important feature of any of the great powers' vision of the future. The result was compromise and confusion.

Poland reemerged as a result of two factors. The first was the development of the war itself, unfolding quite beyond the anticipations and control of its participants. The war essentially made Poland, or, more accurately, the war unmade the partitioning empires, and their dissolution allowed Poland to resurface. Of even greater importance was the existence of a large concentration of Poles who exhibited a high degree of national consciousness. The powers could not have re-created Poland—even if it had suited them—had the Poles not been available for that project.

There had been no serious developments in the Polish question in international politics for generations because the three partitioning states shared a common interest in avoiding the issue. As for the other powers, Poland was insufficiently important to risk complications in the east of Europe for returns problematical at best. As long as that proposition held, Poland would never resurface as an international issue. However, in 1914, the partitioning powers were ranged in opposite camps, and the western states, over the course of the war, determined that Poland was a question worth raising.

The war began when Austria-Hungary invaded Serbia, with the encouragement of Berlin. To forestall Russian action in defense of Serbia, the Germans threatened Saint Petersburg and thus indirectly Russia's ally, France. This provoked hostilities between Germany and Russia, which Berlin sought to win by first disposing of France in a rapid offensive, which, by necessity, violated the neutrality of Belgium. After some hesitation, stung by the action against pathetic Belgium, and fearing a destabilizing German victory over the Franco-Russian allies, Great Britain entered the war against Germany. Hence, the initial battle lines of the war pitted Germany and Austria against Russia in the east, where hostilities would necessarily be joined on the lands of the Commonwealth. In the west, Germany would face France and Great Britain, later joined by Italy and, in 1917, the United States to name the major actors.

The creation of two hostile camps in the years preceding hostilities and the rising frictions between them had raised the specter of war long before its actual outbreak. The Poles in all three partitions, plus the numerous emigré community—Polonia—exhibited enormous and expanding activity in anticipation of a war which, for the first time, would place the partitioners on opposite sides. Logically, at least one of them had to lose; extraordinarily, all of them did.

The Poles were divided between those who wished the entente—France, England, and Russia—to be victorious, and those favoring a victory for the Central Powers, or Germany and Austria-Hungary. The pro-entente alignment favored the defeat of Germany, which they regarded as Poland's principal antagonist. There was considerable sympathy for the French and English, and not inconsiderable hope that both could be won to favor the cause of Polish restoration. Russia was, however, a problem. Even the most devoted Polish champion of the entente realized that Russia enjoyed an odious reputation among the Poles. Only a handful of Poles entertained vague pan-Slavic hopes about collaboration with the ancient eastern antagonist, rather more hoped that an enlightened Russian perception of the danger of German expansion would create the grounds for a Polish-Russian reconciliation. Neither anticipation lasted past 1915. Thereafter, the pro-entente Poles were held together by fear of German victory and hope of western support. The most influential representatives of this orientation were the flamboyant pianist, composer, and politician Ignacy Jan Paderewski, and the acerbic and domineering Roman Dmowski, considered the father of modern Polish nationalism.

Similarly, the pro–Central Powers camp among the Poles was motivated by hostility toward Russia. These Poles were so convinced that Russia was the central nightmare of Polish history that cooperation even with the Germans was acceptable to exorcise it. Austria played a special role here. Whereas virtually no Poles had any positive feelings toward Berlin, many were well inclined toward Vienna. Indeed, the pro–Central Powers camp actually contained two quite distinct strains: a sincere "Austrophile" element, which hoped for Austrian victory, and the so-called independence faction. The Austrophiles envisioned a triumphant Habsburg state enlarged and transformed by acquiring the historic Polish lands then under Russian control. Thus two-thirds reunited, the Poles would become, at the very least, equal partners in a new state with Austria. The Achilles heel was the relative weakness of Austria within the Central Powers. As Germany rapidly came to dominate the alliance, Austria's ability to pursue a Polish policy to the liking of her Polish allies faded, leaving them linked to Germany, a fate distasteful to virtually all Poles.

The other strain among the pro–Central Powers Polish camp, the independence faction, was dominated by the charismatic Józef Piłsudski, who regarded cooperation with Vienna as a temporary tactical necessity rather than a strategic alignment. Austria was useful "as a sword against Russia; a shield against Berlin," he said—a temporary expedient to be jettisoned should the unpredictable fortunes of war allow the Poles an opportunity to pursue a truly independent course. The independence devotees stressed preparation of a separate Polish military component, to be ready for action should a propitious moment arrive. At the beginning of the war, this policy appeared quixotic, a reckless reappearance of the Romantic fascination with bold military fancies.

The first weeks of the war confounded the anticipations of all the countries involved. The German offensive against France in the west, designed to win the war there in several weeks, crested and stalled at the Marne and settled into a virtual stalemate. Meanwhile, in the east, the commander in chief of the Russian army, the tsar's uncle, Grand Duke Nikolai Nikolaievitch, issued a proclamation on August 14, 1914, promising the Poles unity and broad autonomy. Russia had decided to beat the other partitioning powers to the punch and consolidate Polish support at the very outset. However, the bold Russian gambit proved stillborn: the Germans won smashing victories over Russia at Tannenberg and Masurian Lakes, and the tsarist military position was damaged, never to recover fully.

With the Russian bid to capture the initiative regarding Poland misfiring, the field was left open to the Central Powers. Here the chief actor was Austria. As early as 1908, Piłsudski's political allies began preparing the cadres for a future Polish army in close cooperation with Vienna. In exchange for promises of Polish support in the case of war with Russia, Vienna turned a blind eye to extensive Polish efforts at drilling and performing large-scale maneuvers and even supplied the Poles with surplus equipment. When hostilities actually commenced, a minuscule Polish force, under Piłsudski's personal command, took the field at once. Elements of these legions crossed the Russian border and tried to raise a revolution in the Congress Kingdom. Though the precocious effort proved a fiasco, it demonstrated both the audacity of Piłsudski and the possibilities of Austrian-Polish cooperation. The legions, which grew to a considerable force by 1916, served under Austrian operational orders, but wore distinctive uniforms, and used Polish as the language of command. Although small, the legions constituted the first identifiably Polish army since the collapse of the November Rising in 1831. Their military exploits and reckless courage captured the imagination of Poles everywhere, making Piłsudski a national hero early in the war.

Piłsudski's legion reflected a rapidly developing consolidation of Polish political activity in Galicia. By 1914 a large number of factions had combined to form a loose Supreme National Committee (Naczelny Komitet Narodowy, or NKN) which provided political leadership, though riven by factional disputes. The NKN established a feeble but ambitious network of propaganda agencies abroad, collected money for the legions, and tried to consolidate Polish opinion, including the considerable immigrant population in North America, behind a pro-Austrian, or at least anti-Russian, position in the war.

Though Austria seemed well poised to control or at least exploit the Polish issue to maximum advantage, Vienna's role in Polish affairs proved relatively insignificant. Pro-Austria Poles were unable to convince the imperial government to take bold initiatives regarding Poland, for example an equivalent to the manifesto of the Russian grand duke Nikolai. Internal opposition from the powerful Hungarian and German factions in the empire blocked any action that might have led to a three-part–Austrian-Hungarian-Polish empire with the Poles holding a dominant position. Even more important, any fundamental rearrangement of the partitions to consolidate Polish territory under the Habsburgs would require the active cooperation of Berlin. However, from early in the war, it became obvious that Germany, not Austria, would be the senior military partner. As Vienna's military position deteriorated steadily, Berlin effectively prevented any major Austrian initiative regarding Polish matters, an arena which the Germans gradually came to dominate. By 1916 only the true Habsburg loyalists among the Poles remained adherents. For the independence faction of Piłsudski, Austria had rapidly worn out its usefulness.

In the other Polish camp, by 1915, Dmowski had concluded that Russia could not be a vehicle for Polish hopes. The grand duke's manifesto had briefly encouraged many Poles in Russia that Slavic reconciliation was possible and that, by cooperating with the tsar, Polish lands could be reunited after being wrested from German and Austrian control. Although this would have been a partial victory, Dmowski was content to think in stages.

By 1915 it was obvious that those hopes were false. Despite the manifesto, no active policy regarding the Poles was adopted by Russia. The Russians resented Polish efforts to form military units alongside their forces and the project collapsed, leaving the Polish Legions of Piłsudski without rivals. More important than the recalcitrance of tsarist officials to work with the Poles was the continuing decline of Russian military fortunes. By late 1915 the Central Powers had broken the eastern front and had thrown the Russians back hundreds of kilometers. By year's end most of historic Poland was in the hands of Germany and Austria. Moreover, the Russians adopted a ruthless "scorched earth" policy, of wholesale destruction in the face of the enemy advance, causing massive dislocation and suffering for the Polish population: villages were burned, livestock slaughtered, food destroyed. As a result, starvation, disease, and economic ruin were the last Russian "contributions" to the territory.

Dmowski concluded that the basis for his program had disintegrated, and he left Russia for Western Europe where he strove to build an anti-German Polish faction in exile. He hoped to convince the Europeans that a restored Poland was in their strategic interests, now that Russia's ability to determine entente policy regarding Poland had visibly been weakened by defeat and withdrawal. The West, however, was scarcely disposed to attach any significance to Polish issues. Dmowski and his colleagues realized that their first efforts would have to be devoted to reacquainting the world with the existence of Poland and the aspirations of its people.

Russia's military eclipse, the lack of Western interest in things Polish, and the rapid decline of Austria left the stage open for new forces to assume the initiative regarding the Polish question. For a brief time Polish emigration became the chief focus of national activity.

Early in the war, Paderewski and novelist Henryk Sienkiewicz decided to create a relief agency in neutral Switzerland to collect funds to aid Poles devastated by the war. Ostensibly nonpartisan and dedicated to alleviating Polish suffering regardless of the cause and location, the agency, the Polish Victims Relief Fund (known as the Vevey Committee from the site of its headquarters), reflected the pro-entente, anti-German orientation of its founders. By 1915 the Russian scorched-earth withdrawal had turned Poland into the largest humanitarian problem of the war. Paderewski left Switzerland for London and Paris to organize branches of the Vevey Committee to expand the committee's resources. In April he traveled to America, where a large Polish community in a huge neutral country promised a major expansion of the committee's efforts. Paderewski, however, had more than relief in mind. He wanted to organize the perhaps four million American Poles into a powerful political lobby and win both American public opinion and the administration of President Woodrow Wilson in support of his vision of the Polish cause.

Paderewski was uniquely situated for his task. Already world famous as a pianist and composer, he had also embarked on a career as a national sage, delivering himself of patriotic orations at auspicious occasions. The maestro knew everyone useful to know, and he was the favorite celebrity of the exalted. Vain, haughty, and erratic, Paderewski's bizarre appearance, midway between leonine and Chaplinesque, made him a unique public personality. His belief in Poland, an exalted Poland of his imagination, was so consuming that it made his patriotism an ennobling creed which charmed foreigners and inspired his countryman. For many in Western Europe and in the United States at the time of World War I, Paderewski was Poland, which was advantageous for both.

Under Paderewski's autocratic and capricious direction, the large Polish community in the United States became a significant lobby for the national cause. Meanwhile the maestro cultivated the rich and powerful, winning by 1916 the devotion of President Wilson's most intimate advisor, Colonel Edward M. House, and, through him, Paderewski gained access to the White House.

Paderewski's arrival in the United States coincided with the American "discovery" of Poland. The reason for this is quite simple, though most indirect. Poland had become a battlefield from the very start of the war, but the Russian collapse of 1915 and the precipitate withdrawal had led to massive civilian suffering which was beyond the capacity of the Central Powers to alleviate. Hence they encouraged outside agencies, like the Rockefeller Foundation and the American Red Cross, to investigate. This served a double purpose, and German cynicism is rather apparent. First, Polish suffering was largely the fault of Russian ruthlessness and ineptitude, and publicizing it would embarrass the entente in the eyes of world opinion. This was a peculiarly useful development because London and Paris had been branding Germany since 1914 as barbaric in its occupation of Belgium. Poland was thus the Central Powers' Belgium. The Germans were quite sincere in wishing to cooperate in any effort to feed starving Poles because they knew that relief could only come by abridging the British blockade of Europe, the principal Allied means for the strategic strangulation of Germany. Feeding the Poles would thus weaken the blockade. Hence London opposed the Polish relief effort with a passion, and the Germans supported it with convenient humanitarianism.

The chief battleground for Polish relief became the United States. Polish efforts gained much publicity. Moreover, the context was sympathetic: an innocent people made wretched by a war not their own. British opposition and German maneuvering dragged on for months while the Poles starved and Americans became exasperated. Gradually a clamor to intervene led to Congressional resolutions, and even presidential action, when Wilson offered his services as a mediator in 1916. The result was victory masquerading as defeat. The contradictory strategic goals of the belligerents prevented any serious relief for Poland. However, the arduous and frustrating campaign eventually brought Poland before the eyes of the public, gave Paderewski an emotional platform upon which to appeal to the American public, and made Poland a serious cause in America. Relief issues ultimately caused public figures, including Nevada's Senator Francis Newlands to inquire, rhetorically, why the Poles, who were suffering so egregiously, should not thereby earn the independence so long denied them? Relief was the bridge that connected the ignorance and apathy that had so long characterized the West's attitudes toward Poland with the sympathy characteristic of the war's final stages.

Sympathy is immensely useful, but only if the political forces of the world allow it to be brought to bear. By 1916 this was happening. The Central Powers had decided to seize the initiative regarding Poland and gamble on a new departure regarding the east. On November 5, 1916, Berlin and Vienna jointly proclaimed, in the Two Emperors' Manifesto, the recreation of the Polish kingdom. Motivated by everything except concern for the Poles, the manifesto designated no specific territory as constituting the state and made clear its political dependence on the Germanic powers. The initiative regarding the Poles was more prompted by the battles of Verdun[1] and the Somme[2], where Germany had sustained gigantic casualties, than by any specific developments in Poland.

By late 1916 the Central Powers were beginning to reach the limits of their manpower potential. Russia, whose military performance had been poor in 1914 and disastrous in 1915, had found new lows in 1916. The east beckoned with strategic opportunity while the west devoured the dwindling reserves. Poland might be the means of winning the war for the Central Powers if Polish manpower—estimated by the Germans at 1.5 million possible soldiers—could be tapped and the active support of the country could be inspired. These would require major concessions. Only the promise of independence would have the galvanic effect necessary to rally active Polish support. Suddenly, in 1916, the demands of the war had given Poland a leverage it had not had since the partitions. The Central Powers were willing to reverse a century of policy and resurrect the very country they had done so much to destroy. To be sure, they attempted to win the Poles without conceding anything of real significance by ringing the November 5th declaration with vagaries and conditions which, it was hoped, would keep a restored Poland as a small and manageable client state (its borders were not defined and it was to be closely associated with the Central Powers). After November 5, 1916, the Polish Question in international affairs was fundamentally altered. By proclaiming the restoration of Polish independence, howsoever circumscribed, the Central Powers had loosed a process beyond their ability to control.

The Central Powers' initiative was quickly echoed. Within a few weeks, the Russians announced that Poland would be autonomous after the war and endorsed the notion of a "free Poland composed of all three now divided parts." For Paris and London, the Russian announcement, grudging and tardy though they knew it to be, freed them to pursue a more active Polish policy. Their fear was that the Germans, who already controlled the bulk of Polish territory, would, by their November 5th act, capture Polish support as well and in so doing win the military balance in the west. With the Russians finally crowded into concessions, the west could now attempt to enter a bidding war for Polish support, if only to neutralize the Central Powers. Suddenly, everyone was interested in the "Polish Question."

Polish and German views of the November 5th manifesto, however, were diametrically different. For Berlin, the principal goal was to create a mechanism to recruit Polish manpower while ensuring German strategic domination of the east. Serious work to establish a functioning Polish administration was ignored after initial ceremonial flourishes, but Berlin eagerly strove for recruits. Germany made elaborate plans to attach eastern Poland to Prussia and to subordinate Poland to Germany economically.

Piłsudski entered the new kingdom's Provisional State Council—supposedly the nucleus of a Polish government, it was essentially a powerless agency under German control—in charge of military affairs, but he was anything but a loyal ally of the Central Powers. Regarded contemptuously by the Germans as a "military dilettante and demagogue,"[3] Piłsudski strove for maximum concessions for Polish autonomy, arguing that a "real" Polish army would require the prior establishment of a "real" Polish government, which the Germans would not grant. Convinced that possibilities for collaboration with the Central Powers were limited, Piłsudski bided his time and increasingly relied on his recently formed Polish Military Organization (Polska Organizacja Wojskowa, or POW), a secret network composed of his most devoted followers. To a close collaborator, he predicted an imminent revolution in Russia and mused: "Now let Roman Dmowski play his hand. I gave him an ace to use [i.e., the Legions]; let him make a play; let him demand more from the other side."[4]

Piłsudski did not have long to wait; 1917 was crowded with events crucial to the reemergence of Poland. On January 22, in a speech to the

U.S. Senate, President Wilson cited "a united, independent, and autonomous Poland" as exemplifying the better world to emerge from a just conclusion to the war. This was a significant development because the United States was the first major power to adopt a Polish policy *before* belligerency, and it was one not obviously calculated for any military advantage.

Several months of complicated maneuvering followed to determine the center of gravity of Polish politics. Essentially there were three foci, each with distinctive advantages and disadvantages. In Western Europe was Dmowski and his pro-entente nationalists. Having abandoned Russia in 1915, Dmowski had concentrated his attentions on London and Paris, but he was frustrated by the Western powers' willingness to concede to the Russians all initiative regarding Polish matters. However, by 1917, Russia's collapse and the prospect of the Poles being railed behind the Central Powers finally opened up possibilities for movement. After many preparatory steps, Dmowski created the Polish National Committee (Komitet Narodowy Polski, or KNP) in Paris to coordinate action in the west in August 1917. The KNP, composed exclusively of Dmowski's political allies on the right, was little more than an extension of his will, despite its impressive membership list. The KNP's access to Paris and London was an emigré organization, a political general staff without an army hoping to be taken seriously by the Western governments. Ultimately the KNP's success would depend on matters beyond its control: the Western countries had to regard Poland as sufficiently weighty in the war to need someone, indeed anyone plausible, to represent Poland. Since the West would need the KNP almost as much as the KNP needed the West, both could overlook the fact that the KNP was a self-appointed factional group quite out of touch with Poland. Second, the KNP would be as influential as Paris and London were decisive in determining allied Polish policy. Dmowski had staked everything on the wager that the Polish question would be decided in Western Europe. He had guessed wrong earlier when he lingered in Russia, and almost guessed wrong again.

For a while it looked as though the decisive locus in Polish affairs would move across the Atlantic to the United States with Paderewski as the chief spokesperson. Various Polish organizations in the United States gave him the right to do virtually anything at any time in their name. Moreover, Paderewski had consolidated his status as the unofficial ambassador of Poland in Washington, D.C. The Wilson administration regarded the maestro as the preemptive authority regarding Polish affairs.

But in fact the maestro had little influence on American policy toward Poland. Washington's sympathy for the cause of Polish independence was rather circumscribed. It did not envision a large role for Poland in postwar Europe.

As America moved toward entering the war in 1917, Paderewski planned to stage a virtual coup in international Polish politics. He would try to convince Washington to let him create an army of 100,000 or more from among the Poles living in North America. An intimate of Wilson, the leader of millions of American Poles, with a military force to throw into the war, Paderewski would be transformed from the spiritual inspiration of his countrymen to their political leader.

The final locus in the determination of Polish affairs was the occupied homeland. Here, both the advantages and the problems were considerable. Obviously, Polish politics in the homeland would be significant to all Poles. If the Poles of Warsaw spoke freely, those in Chicago or Paris would fall silent. However, Warsaw was under German domination, and Polish efforts there seemed crushed by the sheer weight of German military power. Piłsudski, as was so often the case, was prescient when he anticipated that for much of 1917 the tempo in Polish matters would be set outside the country.

In March 1917 the Russian revolution overthrew the tsarist government, and power passed to a fragile dual authority of radical socialists in the so-called Soviet and moderate parliamentarians of the provisional government—which shared power unevenly and jealously in Russia. One of the first acts of each of the authorities was to announce the freedom of Poland. The provisional government called for an independent Polish state, reuniting its three historic parts, and denounced tsarist policy regarding the Poles as "hypocritical." This reborn Poland, however, was to be "united with Russia by a free military alliance," a condition wisely not defined. The Soviets outbid their rivals in magnanimity by calling for Poland's "complete independence." Polish political activity exploded in Russia after the revolution; particular emphasis was placed on the creation of a separate Polish army. Previous efforts along these lines had produced virtually nothing, but with 600,000 Poles serving in Russian ranks, the possibility of a major, distinctly Polish, force on the eastern front was a tremendous attraction to Polish leaders in Russia and abroad. Not only the Poles were aware of this military potential. Buoyed by the change in Russian policy, Paris and London now hoped to engage the Central Powers in competition for Polish military and political support.

On April 2, 1917, the United States entered the war against Germany. Two days later, Paderewski addressed a huge Polish throng in Pittsburgh and called for the immediate creation of a Polish military force in America, before general mobilization caused Polonia's manpower to be "lost imperceptibly in an enormous American sea."[5] Kościuszko's Army, of at least 100,000, was to be offered to the Americans as a distinct unit of its national forces.

Rather than embrace Kościuszko's Army, Washington dithered and delayed. The Wilson administration viewed a separate Polish force as, at least a distraction, and at worst a contradiction to the unity of its armed forces. Paderewski watched helplessly as his dreams of leading Polish affairs from America aborted, dispersed in a sea of bureaucratic confusion.

The KNP suffered almost the same fate. In June 1917 the French government suddenly announced the creation of an autonomous Polish army to be recruited from Poles worldwide. The KNP, though headquartered in Paris, was stunned by a development not of its own design, but they quickly maneuvered to endorse it. Paderewski and the American Poles tried desperately to oppose the effort.

This struggle between European and American Polonia for leadership in emigré politics was coupled with a larger struggle over which great power would be the principal patron of the Polish national movement. Ultimately France, and hence the KNP, won, because the Americans showed themselves to be too unconcerned and the British decided to support the French in face of American procrastination.

By the end of summer, a Polish army was being recruited—the fitful and clumsy product of Allied compromise and confusion—mostly in the United States. Paderewski reluctantly endorsed the project which had supplanted his own and accepted membership in Dmowski's KNP as well as functional subordination. Dmowski made efforts to salve the maestro's gargantuan vanity by giving him limitless authority in America, which he would have exercised anyway. The army was raised largely by the Polish Falcons organization in America, trained in Canada, financed by the French on loans largely from Americans. The KNP became the "political directing authority" for the army and began pressing for recognition as a virtual Polish government in exile. It never reached its goal, but by late 1917 all the Allies, including the United States, had agreed on some formulation that designated the KNP as the representative of Polish interests.

The KNP also gained the right to name the commander of its growing army, more than 100,000 by war's end, and chose Colonel Józef Haller. Haller, an Austrian Pole, who had served in the Habsburg army and commanded a brigade in the Polish legions, was brave, patriotic, and melodramatic. Politically unlettered and already promoted beyond his military competence, Haller was no threat to the political leadership of the KNP.

At the same time Dmowski's KNP also effectively consolidated the Poles of Russia, thus rendering the KNP, and really Dmowski, the principal Polish leader outside the occupied homeland. The task of the KNP was to crowd the Allied governments into clear declarations of support for the restoration of Poland at war's end. This proved a formidable task as the belligerent governments were reluctant to tie their hands regarding European reconstruction while the war still raged. After much lobbying by the Poles, the Allies issued a series of pronouncements which included an independent Poland as a component of a worthy peace. None, however, included specifics or elevated Poland to a fundamental war aim.

In January 1918 Wilson included Poland as the thirteenth of his famous "Fourteen Points":

> An independent Polish state should be erected which should include the territories inhabited by indisputably Polish populations, which should be assured a free and secure access to the sea, and whose political and economic independence and territorial integrity should be guaranteed by international covenant.

Despite elation over the fact of Wilson's pronouncement, most Poles were disquieted after a careful reading of the text. In reality the thirteenth point was a compromise between Wilson's sincere but uninformed championing of the cause of Polish independence and the extremely cautious recommendations of his principal advisory body, the so-called Inquiry. Fundamentally, Wilson's Poland ignored Poland's historic borders. It was to be designed within problematical so-called "ethnographic" boundaries. Without a specific coastline, it was to have, somehow, "access to the sea." Its national security was so tenuous that its survival would depend on the workings of some "international covenant." Moreover, the whole project was only a good idea—something that "should" eventuate—not a necessity. Thus Wilson's Poland was far from that envisaged by the Poles.

Piłsudski appeared to be in political eclipse as Polish events accelerated in the west. Continued frustration in working with the Germans helped convince him that cooperation with the Central Powers was rapidly drawing to a close. After the Bolshevik Revolution which overthrew the short-lived Provisional government and brought communism to power in November 1917 plunged Russia into chaos and civil war, the Polish question shifted dramatically. The eastern front was ending. When the new Communist authorities of Russia began conducting armistice negotiations with the Central Powers in December, Piłsudski had to reorient himself to a new reality in which, as noted by historian P. S. Wandycz, the Central Powers, resurgent after Russia's collapse, had become "the main obstacle to the realization of Poland's independence."[6]

Piłsudski and his associates resigned from the German-created Provisional Council of State. Most of the legionnaires refused to take an oath of loyalty to the Central Powers and were arrested, as were Piłsudski and his chief of staff, Kazimierz Sosnkowski, both of whom were sent to Germany and imprisoned at the fortress of Magdeburg in late July 1917. The legions were effectively dead, and Polish relations with the Central Powers had been reversed from careful cooperation to hostility. The POW began to plan a coup d'état. The German hopes of using the November 5th proclamation as a means to create a major Polish army had proven a fiasco; only a handful had been recruited. However, with the war victoriously concluded in the east, the Germans no longer needed the Poles.

In fact, the Polish position in the east deteriorated rapidly after late 1917. At the peace negotiations between the new Bolshevik government of Russia and the Central Powers which opened at Brest-Litovsk in December 1917, Polish interests were dealt with complete cynicism. The supposed government in Warsaw[7]—little more than a puppet administration—was not allowed to attend the negotiations. A separate treaty with the Ukrainians gave them a slice of eastern Poland[8] and Austria made a secret promise to divide Galicia into Polish and Ukrainian administrations, destroying the historic unity of Austrian Poland. The Central Powers had decided at the Treaty of Brest-Litovsk, concluded in March 1918, to jettison the Poles for new clients in the east. Berlin was busily fostering Lithuanian, Ukrainian, and even Belarussian schemes of independence to hem in the Poles geographically and render them politically docile. Outraging the Poles was a minor inconvenience if the war could be won rapidly in the west, and new, weaker, and more pliable clients could be found in the east. The Austrians had long toyed with the idea of playing the Poles off against the Ukrainians in another chapter of traditional Habsburg divide and conquer tactics. Vienna was virtually a spent force, and its capacity to influence Polish affairs was minimal. Berlin had assumed the dominant voice here as well.

Polish reaction to the Brest-Litovsk Treaty was massive and immediate. The pro-Austria camp disintegrated, the Council of State resigned, Polish units in Austrian service mutinied, Piłsudski's POW redoubled its activities, and armed clashes with the German occupation authorities broke out. The pro–Central Powers orientation in Polish politics had collapsed in the last months of the war.

Fortunately for the Poles, the brief German window of opportunity, created by victory in the east, did not stay open long enough for them to reposition in the west in sufficient time and force to achieve victory there as well. By November 11, 1918, the Germans had been defeated and signed the armistice. The Habsburgs had not lasted that long. In the capital of their zone of occupation, Lublin, a prominent Polish socialist, Ignacy Daszyński, declared a People's Government. In Galicia itself the Austrian administration collapsed and the Poles simply took over; from the ruins Austria sued for peace. Similarly German authority had collapsed in Warsaw where, on November 10, 1918, Piłsudski arrived by train after his release from German imprisonment. He had only one uniform and had worn it in confinement for sixteen months; he was exhausted, sick, and ragged. He was also the chief of state of reborn Poland.

Poland's reemergence in November 1918 occurred under conditions of almost indescribable confusion. Piłsudski, regarded as a national hero, quickly dominated the scene in Warsaw, but how far his writ ran was problematical at best. To the western powers he was either an unknown with a revolutionary past, or worse, a German hireling who had fallen out with his masters. In the west the KNP represented Poland, albeit with ambiguous authority. Paderewski was in many ways an independent contractor, officially merely the KNP's Washington representative, but still harboring huge ambitions to play, with American support, the dominant role in Polish affairs. By war's end, Dmowski did not trust the maestro, whom he suspected, quite correctly, of poor judgment. Reciprocally, Paderewski resented Dmowski's ruthless insistence on maintaining all real power in his own hands, trying to be both philosopher and architect of Poland's future.

In Poland the situation was chaotic and threatening. The only uniformity was ruination. The majority of economic assets in Poland had been destroyed; more than three-fourths of the factories were idle; less than half, and in many areas only a quarter, of the arable land was under cultivation; much of the livestock of the country had been lost. German (and to a lesser extent Austrian) requisitioning had carried off stocks of raw materials, industrial equipment, and spare parts; their systematic deforestation had caused incalculable harm. Human losses were staggering: there were more than 1.5 million military casualties of soldiers in foreign uniforms and uncountable numbers of civilian casualties.

> The Poland that reemerged in 1918 was a ruined county with an impoverished and hungry population. Currency confusion and inflation led to black markets, speculation, and disorder. That such a country avoided revolution, became integrated, and survived large scale struggles which lasted until 1920 was [little] short of miraculous.[9]

But what Poland had emerged? Had the events of 1914–1918 overturned the partitions and returned Europe to 1795, or was this to be a new state, part of the architecture of a new continent? If so, what principles would be used to reconstruct Poland, and what would be the result for the Poles and for the world?

NOTES

1. The longest battle of Word War I, Verdun, lasted from February 21, 1916, until year's end. Two million men were engaged, and France and Germany each suffered about 350,000 casualties.

2. Essentially a British effort to relieve the French position at Verdun, the Somme began in July 1916 with British attacks soon supplemented by French efforts. The battle ended, inconclusively, in mid-November with over 400,000 British, almost 200,000 French, and 650,000 German casualties, an irreplaceable loss that prompted a manpower crisis.

3. The words are those of Hans von Beseler, the German Governor General of occupied Poland, as quoted in Piotr S. Wandycz, *The Lands of Partitioned Poland, 1795–1918* (Seattle, WA, 1974), 353.

4. Wacław Jedrzejewicz, *Kronika życia Józefa Piłsudskiego, tom pierwszy, 1867–1920 [The chronicle of the life of Józef Piłsudski, vol. 1, 1867–1920]* (London, 1977), 346–347.

5. This is from Paderewski's speech of April 4, 1517, in *Archiwm Polityczne Ignacego Paderewskiego [The Political Archives of Ignacy Paderewski]* (Warsaw, 1973), vol. 1, 117–120.

6. Wandycz, *Lands of Partitioned Poland*, 356.

7. The so-called Regency Council was formed in October 1917 to replace the Provisional State Council which had become defunct.

8. This was a portion of the eastern Congress Kingdom, the district of Chełm.

9. Wandycz, *Lands of Partitioned Poland*, 369.

5

Wars, Experiments, and Frontiers, 1918–1921

It was axiomatic in Polish political thought after 1795 that reconstituted Poland would be, in territory and population, a great state. This notion, so fundamental as to remain unspoken, derived from two sources. The first is the matter of historic continuity. Polish patriotism was ultimately nothing more than a pledge in favor of history; that what had existed was sufficiently worthy as to be paradigmatic. That this would extend to the dimensions of the state was merely a component part of this conviction. Essentially, any place cannot be Poland, only Poland can be Poland and Poland was where Poland had been. There is, thus, at the base of the Polish territorial project in 1918, a simple inclination towards restoration, in this case of the pre-partition Commonwealth.

Second, there was the prompt of geopolitical realism. Poland was certainly flawed in the eighteenth century, but it fell because it could not withstand the pressures of its neighbors. From this episode a very simple lesson could be drawn: in the open plain of the east of Europe, between large communities of Russians and Germans, both traditionally hostile to Poland, positing a small Poland as viable was nonsense.

That there should be a large Poland seemed, at least to the Poles, to be beyond question. However, a simple restitution of the status quo ante was daunting. During its 123 years of nonexistence, Poland had seen a

drastic evolution of its historic territories. Russia's forcible depoloniza-
tion of the east had been accelerated in the late nineteenth century by
the appearance of nationalism among the ethnic minorities of the
borderlands. A Lithuanian and Ukrainian nationalist movement had
considerable support, and even the primitive White Ruthenians (now
better known as Belarussians) had a modest stirring of ethnic self-
consciousness. Traditionally, loyalty to the Commonwealth had been a
supranational creed based on historic attachment to a common tradition
and common institutions. As such it had been almost the exclusive property of the numerous *szlachta*. Though Polish patriotism diffused from
its original class basis, its origins were unmistakable. By contrast, the
aggressive new nationalisms of the nineteenth century were populist,
based on the peasantry as the undefiled bearers of language and culture.
Hence, in the borderlands "Polish" meant more in class than in ethnic
terms by the close of the century. To be sure, Polish patriotism had been
largely replaced by the *endecja's* exclusivist nationalism as well. The borderlands had become the battleground of several competing modern
creeds, including a Polish version.

Just as nationalism threatened to shrink Poland in the east to ethnographic dimensions, it promised to increase it in the west by the same
process, as the new nationalism spread among the previously inert Polish
masses under German control in Silesia, Prussia, and Pomerania. Thus
the Poles were aware that Poland would probably be re-configured as a
result of the developments of the long nineteenth century, but few anticipated the radical diminution which awaited them. The Poland which
eventually emerged was the smallest state to bear that name since the
Piasts, undoing half a millennium of Polish history and culture in the
east. It was a product of neither history nor ethnography but an attempt,
variously, to accommodate both, conformed to neither, and created a
state peculiarly well-designed for domestic conflict and international
weakness.

Poland in 1918 was the focus of two different territorial programs.
The first, led by Roman Dmowski, the brilliant, dispassionate, and logical
leader of the nationalist political movement, or *endecja*, represented the
integrationist conception. This program argued that the historic link to
Lithuania had caused Poland to reorient itself radically to the east with
catastrophic results. First, Poland was inevitably drawn into a contest for
predominance in Eastern Europe against Turks, Tatars, and eventually
Russians, which proved ruinously exhausting. It had also meant aban-

doning the Baltic and the west, the historic territory of Piast Poland, which had been gradually lost to the Germans while the Poles were off in eastern adventures. Not only was this a ruinous misdirection of Poland's obvious geographic and historic role, but it was yet more pernicious because it caused the internal reorganization of the state into a multinational melange in which the Polish element declined, becoming hopelessly dispersed in the endless east. Weakened in the east by overextension, abandoning the precious economic and strategic assets in the west to the Germans—who used them to consolidate themselves into power—Poland was the inevitable victim of the partitions which were history's verdict on the great national mistake.

The great enemy of Poland, according to Dmowski, was Germany, which had played a chief role in the partitions, and had striven mightily to crush Poland since. Hence, Polish reconstruction had to undo the aberrational path begun in 1386 (the Polish-Lithuanian union) which ended in the extinction of 1795. Dmowski's goal was a Poland that had regained its western provinces and thus returned to a Piast (i.e., pre–1386) geopolitical orientation. By abandoning the *kresy* Poland would end the quarrel with the Russians over the east which had injured both countries but Poland more. Pan-Slavism,[1] Dmowski hoped, would strengthen both Poland and Russia against the threat of Germany, the common enemy. Poland would end the disastrous position of having an enemy on two fronts by attaining reconciliation in the east. Though this meant the loss of territory, it would, in reality, be a gain, because the lands thus lost were not inhabited by ethnic Poles but a crazy-quilt of many nationalities whose continued association with Poland would weaken it. Those non-Poles who remained in the new state—and some would as a result of the complex settlement patterns, particularly in the east—would be integrated as rapidly as possible into the national community. This, in turn, presumed the existence of a national model: Polish in language, Roman Catholic in religion, and conscientious and loyal to the state. The continued existence of minorities would therefore weaken the social fabric. Dmowski passionately disliked the Jews, whose language, religion, and customs were different from the Poles'. Because of their traditional prominence in business and the professions, Dmowski believed that they blocked the formation of an expanding Polish middle class and sapped the strength of the nation. Whereas Dmowski regarded Jews who converted to Catholicism and assimilated to Polish culture as fellow Poles—shunning racial anti-Semitism—he doubted the country's capacity to absorb and "polonize" huge minorities, including a strikingly large and concentrated Jewish population. Because the Jews were heavily concentrated in the eastern borderlands, Dmowski regarded the loss of these lands to Russia as in many ways a blessing in disguise.

To Dmowski, the new Poland should be as homogeneous as possible, reshaped in the east and west, a strong state on the German model, the enemy who, ironically, was also the guide to the future. A progressive state, based on business and industry, Poland would be led by people who, like Dmowski, were rational, modern, and pragmatic, and who had abandoned the disastrous Polish penchant for nostalgic reminiscence and Romantic reveries. Dmowski's geopolitical program and his nationalism formed a seamless whole.

Although Dmowski presented elements of his program in different contexts decades before the war, his full territorial program was not unveiled until 1917 and fully elaborated only in 1919 at the Paris Peace Conference. Poland would begin from 1772 as a link to historic continuity, but its new borders would relinquish much of the east, approximating the line of the second partition, while adding Silesia and other territories in the west. Even this Poland would have a minority population of almost 40 percent which Dmowski regarded as being within the capacity of the Poles to assimilate with reasonable speed. The minorities would be granted no local autonomy or special status. Dmowski's aggressive brand of nationalism and his geopolitical views were inextricably joined. His vision of Poland has aptly been called "integral nationalism."

Quite apart from his cavalier disregard for minorities—or, in the case of the Jews, open hostility—Dmowski's program suffered from several essential flaws. First, it assumed that Poland would be able to compete successfully with Germany and enjoy cordial relations with Russia. Neither assumption was explained, merely posited. Second, the new state would be the worst possible division of the borderlands. Neither relinquishing nor encompassing the ethnically mixed lands, the Dmowski frontier would split them, leading to unavoidable problems of border revision—a kind of repetition of the partitions.

This sort of Poland was in stark contrast to the so-called *federal* solution which was associated prominently with Józef Piłsudski, although he never elaborated the scheme, requiring us to reconstruct it from his comments and actions.[2] The federalists also began with a historical critique but one diametrically opposed in its reading of the meaning of the Polish historical experience. For Piłsudski, it was the Polish-Lithuanian union that first opened up the possibility for Poland to play a major role in Europe.

Federalism was to be oriented eastward. A compromise could be found with the Germans in the west—the functional equivalent of Dmowski's Polish-Russian reconciliation—so that Poland could concentrate on its historical nemesis: Moscow. Here the central role was played by the eastern borderlands which became a historic barometer of Polish security. Piłsudski saw for Poland a vast mission in the east, as much moral as strategic, by which the Poles would free the borderland nationalities—primarily Lithuanians, Belarussians, and Ukrainians—from Russian rule and create some sort of association that would guarantee to them, and to the Poles, security by pushing Moscow back to the early eighteenth-century borders of the Russian czar of Peter I. The result would be a geopolitical revolution in Europe that would marginalize Russia and render Poland a point of coalescence for a considerable population and area. This would, in turn, counter the threat from Germany by giving Poland the intrinsic strength to compete with Berlin, and it would make Warsaw an attractive partner for a European combination designed to balance German power.

The central issue for both federalists and nationalists was the population of the minorities in the former Commonwealth's east. For Dmowski, they were at best a negotiable asset to be forfeit to the Russians in return for reconciliation; at worst, a source of weakness and disunion for Poland which would have to absorb its minority populations with ruthless efficiency to be able to compete in the modern world. For Piłsudski, the minorities were, paradoxically, the source of Polish greatness. At its height, the Commonwealth had created an extraordinary, perhaps unique state, integrating a vast and diverse population through a unifying state culture, Polonism, while leaving the population to preserve their ethnic, linguistic, and religious diversity. This was accomplished peaceably, a great achievement, which showed that even ethnic minorities like, Lithuanians and Ukrainians could be Polish patriots. It is thus not surprising that Piłsudski, from ethnically diverse Wilno (today's Vilmius),[3] had the reputation of being philosemitic and some of his closest collaborators were Jews and other minorities.

It is from his territorial program that Piłsudski clearly emerged as a patriot, as opposed to Dmowski the nationalist. Piłsudski tried, in all of his political efforts, to resuscitate and revive the severed continuity of Polish history; the moving passion of his politics was traditionalism.

Dmowski, by contrast, was a modernist who attempted to solve the problems bequeathed by the Polish past by finding guideposts from modern ideas and examples.

The federalist conception was flawed, perhaps even more than the nationalist philosophy. First, it assumed that the developing nationalism of the borderlands could somehow be accommodated under a recreated multiethnic commonwealth. This assumption did not take into account the force of national movements—principally Lithuanian and Ukrainian—which had grown significantly in the decades before the war and had been stimulated by the hostilities and the cynical ethnic politics played by all parties to the conflict. Second, it overestimated the Polish capacity to work a geopolitical revolution in the east of Europe, creating a new power capable of withstanding both Germany and Russia. Without the active support of the victorious allies, such an overhaul as the European balance was impossible. Here Piłsudski may be faulted for his inability to perceive the vital necessity of winning the West to his vision. It is not that he failed in this effort, that was damnable—after all it probably was an impossible mission—but the fact that he did not try.

The Poles were far from being the sole architects of their reborn state. The victorious allies, meeting at Paris in 1919, played the principal role in setting the borders in the west and south; the vital eastern frontier was largely the result of armed conflict between Poland and Bolshevik Russia. The Paris Peace Conference did not create Poland; Poland was a fait accompli before the delegations ever arrived in the French capital to remake Europe after the war. The disintegration of the Austrian, Russian, and German empires, plus efforts made by the various nationalities of Central Europe, were largely responsible for the emergence of new or reborn states on the map. The Peace Conference nonetheless superintended the process of the birth of a new Europe and played a decisive role in a number of specific territorial issues.

It is important to understand the general strategic stances the powers brought with them to Paris. Only France, Great Britain, and the United States, the so-called Big Three, are important here. Italy played virtually no role in regard to Polish affairs, and Japan, the last of the five major powers represented, played even less. Of the three major actors, the French were generally most supportive of Polish claims. Twice in living memory, the Germans had invaded France. Once defeated, once barely surviving,[4] France was unhesitatingly in favor of any claims made against former German territory, and they regarded a powerful Poland as an inevitable ally against Germany in the future, an important consideration because Russia, the traditional French eastern balance to Germany, was in the midst of a revolution and chaos and could not be depended upon to resume its previous role soon. Poland, however, was not the only French ally in the east, and Paris was often more attentive to the claims of Prague than it was to those of Warsaw.[5] Poland was for France an important, though by no means irreplaceable ally, a provisional status which the Poles did not always understand.

Even more problematical was the French attitude toward Russia. Simply put, Paris would have preferred the reemergence of a powerful non-Communist Russian empire to the reappearance of Poland because Russia was a proven ally against Germany. However, as the hope for the defeat of the Communist "Reds" in the civil war in Russia gradually vanished, Paris had to accept Poland as a strategic stand-in for its former tsarist ally. There was, nonetheless, a residual French concern for the protection of the strategic interests of Russia—if only in the hope that, one day, some version of Russia would prove to be a useful check against a German effort to regain lost territory. The result was that France was a Polish champion against Germany but was less dependable elsewhere.

Great Britain was Poland's nemesis at the Peace Conference, and in the British prime minister, David Lloyd George, the Poles found a formidable and indefatigable opponent. London's opposition to Polish claims was not, however, based on personality differences, although Lloyd George detested Poland's chief delegate, the arrogant and abrasive Dmowski, and patronized Ignacy Jan Paderewski, the other Polish representative. Essentially, British opposition derived from a view of Europe utterly incompatible with Warsaw's. Germany had been England's principal trading partner in the decades before the war, and the British were convinced, with good reason, that the rapid restoration of Germany was essential to the revival of the European economy, including their own. Massive territorial losses by Germany would slow and perhaps cripple that country's recovery with continental implications. Since French claims against Germany would have to be indulged to a considerable extent, including the restoration of Alsace-Lorraine, if only to preserve amity among the victors at Paris; Belgium had a preemptive moral claim acknowledged since 1914—Eupen and Malmedy; and the British had covetous eyes on German colonial assets for themselves, London had reached the limits of its willingness to exact German concessions almost before the Poles had begun their list. The outlook for a Polish-British understanding in regard to the east was even poorer. In so far as the

British had ever considered the question of Polish restoration, it was usually imagined as constituting a very minor state; the Congress Kingdom of 1815–1830 was often cited by the British as a model. Anything larger, with its concomitant major restructuring of the continent, was utterly distasteful to London, which did not wish to become involved in vast eastern schemes. Indeed, London preferred the large empires of the pre-1914 era to the many small states of the postwar period. Polish strategies were, from London's perspective, little more than the irresponsible fancies of a minor and distant actor.

The views of the United States, as represented by President Woodrow Wilson, occupy a place apart in regard to the Polish question. In many ways the most outspoken champion of Polish interests, Wilson was thought by many, especially Lloyd George, to be a devoted advocate of Poland. This was, and is, a fundamental misunderstanding. Actually, Wilson combined a sincere sympathy for Polish aspirations to independence with a set of very clear preferences regarding European construction which, if taken in concert, would restrict Poland to a small, weak state completely dependent on the successful functioning of larger mechanisms, particularly the proposed League of Nations Wilson's preoccupation.

The president, like his British and French colleagues, did not seriously entertain the possibility of supporting, let alone sponsoring, the construction of independent states in Lithuania, White Ruthenia (Belarus), Ukraine. This is a fundamental point as it means that Polish claims in the east were considered in a context in which the counterclaimant was always Russia, not one of the borderland nationalities.

Wilson had early fixed on the notion that European borders, including Poland's, should be determined ethnographical. He caused his special advisory committee, the "Inquiry," to prepare elaborate studies to find Polish majorities on the map around which to draw state frontiers. This was a gargantuan problem. First, the nationality structure in the east was very complicated—with Ukrainian, Belarussian, Lithuanian, and other populations scattered throughout—and ethnographic frontiers, to be completely accurate, would trace impossible lines. Second, the only statistics the "Inquiry" relied upon for the area were the 1897 Russian census, which even they admitted was "utterly unreliable" regarding the Poles. Third, the Poles were required to prove majority status to be awarded a territory, even when the area in question was so heterogeneous that only a plurality was possible. Fourth, The non-Polish population of the *kresy*, or eastern borderlands, was allowed to play an extremely odd role. They were to be counted against Polish claims in calculating the future attribution of a territory, but they were not to be counted as an argument against Russian claims to the same territory. Hence, an area with a large Polish minority in a mixed area of Ukrainians, Jews, and Belarussians would not be assigned to Poland but would, by default, go to Russia which might have no ethnographic presence there at all. Finally, the "Inquiry" was given the astonishing requirement that it posit, as an alternative to Polish control of a territory, the existence of a "democratic and federal" Russia. Of course, such a Russia had not, did not, and was not likely to exist; therefore, the Poles were forced to compete against an idealized counterclaimant to which no realistic objections could attach.

Perhaps even more significantly, the very basis of the Polish territorial case rested on a combination of historic rights and strategic necessities, both of which Wilson rejected out of hand, leaving the two sides with no common ground regarding territorial issues. Polish arguments about defensible borders were meaningless to Wilson, and his ethnographic guideline, epitomized in his references to "free self-determination," effectively made Poland a new state rather than a reconstituted one, a blow to Polish claims to being "an historic people."

The interplay of great power preferences, marginally affected by Polish claims—presented with great force and detail by Dmowski—resulted in a series of decisions regarding the Polish borders which were individually problematical and cumulatively unfortunate. In sum, the powers were attempting to ease Poland back onto the map with as little alteration in the traditional balance of power as possible; whereas the Poles were assuming that Poland's rebirth would bring about a revolution in the geopolitics of Europe. The two notions were contradictory, and the Peace Conference satisfied neither.

The Polish border with Germany was enormously controversial because the Germans were passionately opposed to any territorial losses to the Poles whom they regarded with ill-disguised contempt. There were three particularly difficult issues: the Baltic coastline, the associated but quite separate problem of the port city of Danzig (now known as Gdańsk), and the disposition of the mineral-rich territory of Upper Silesia in the south.

Dmowski's presentation of territorial claims on January 29, 1919, was extraordinary. His specific and cogent performance, presented first in French and then in English, was regarded by Allied diplomats as "wonderful" and "masterly." He claimed Poznania, all of Upper Silesia, and much of East Prussia, leaving only a small portion of East Prussia, sparsely populated but heavily German, outside the Polish frontier. The conference then referred the matter to the Commission on Polish Affairs, a body of "experts" appointed by the powers to make specific recommendations. Here the Polish claims were somewhat reduced and qualified but essentially sustained.

However, when the commission reported its views to the Supreme Council, Lloyd George responded with vehement objections, which Wilson gradually endorsed. The French were isolated and the commission's efforts were overruled. The results, after much wrangling over an extended time, were devastating to the Poles: East Prussia and Upper Silesia would be decided by a plebiscite, and the vital port of Danzig would become a free city outside Polish borders. The Poles were livid. Lloyd George's chief motivation was to appease Germany as much as possible—but only after the Great Powers, particularly Great Britain, had gotten what they wanted. The legend that the Welshman was concerned about strategic problems in the east if Poland were to be enlarged too greatly at German expense is fatuous. Lloyd George knew almost as little as Wilson of the history and geography of Eastern Europe and his solicitude for Polish security was insincere.

Working out in practice the theoretical determinations of the conference was a series of disappointments for the Poles. The East Prussian plebiscite was a farce: the conference did nothing to police the vote, leaving the German administration intact. As if that were not enough, the vote actually took place during the Russian invasion of Poland in August 1920, when the very existence of the country was in doubt. As a consequence, the total for Poland was abysmal and resulted in much of the territory being awarded to Germany.

The Upper Silesian settlement was even more complex. There were three Polish military risings (led by Wojciech Korfanty who had been the Silesian Polish leader in the German parliament) in the province and vicious fighting on both sides which did much to inflame Polish-German hatreds for a generation. Ultimately, the League of Nations divided the province after a plebiscite gave Germany a clear majority.[6] The border was torturous and further contributed to frictions between the two countries.

The most famous aspect of the border was, of course, the creation of the free city of Danzig. This port, the only major maritime outlet for all of Poland, was made into a quasi-independent state, under the administration of the League of Nations, but with considerable local autonomy.

Poland had the use of the port facilities, the right to regard the city as within its customs frontier, and the responsibility of representing it in foreign affairs. Polish rights could be enforced by a military presence, but only a token force was allowed. With Danzig a free city, and the East Prussian plebiscite a German victory, Poland regained only a small portion of Pomerania, the so-called corridor which separated the bulk of Germany from East Prussia by a fragile band of territory on the Baltic.

From the perspective of eighty years, it would be difficult to devise a solution more designed to inflame Polish-German antagonism, and provide the possibilities for perpetual friction, than the western borders devised at the Paris Peace Conference. Although a million Germans were left on the Polish side of the new borders, two million Poles remained in Germany. Moreover, Poland, along with several other states, was required to sign the Minorities Treaty, which obliged it to provide certain protections for ethnic and religious minorities, who were subsequently allowed to present purported breaches of these guarantees to the League of Nations. Originally designed to protect the large Jewish population of Poland from any state-sanctioned discrimination, the treaty was, on balance, ethnically and politically unfortunate. First, not all countries were required to sign, and the Great Powers refused to include themselves, thus assuming a dubious moral superiority. Hence the treaty was a preemptive negative judgment against the capacity of Poland to govern itself justly. Second, since even the defeated powers were not required to sign, a situation was created whereby Germans in Poland could bring Poland before an international tribunal on charges of minority abuse, but Poles in Germany, traditionally the objects of discrimination, had no such right. The result was, predictably, that the Poles resented the Minorities Treaty as an infringement on their national sovereignty and an aspersion on their honor.

The Conference of Ambassadors, the temporary successor of the peace conference, was responsible for determining Poland's southern border with the newly created state of Czechoslovakia. Bitter controversy swirled around the area known as Teschen Silesia, which had been part of the defunct Habsburg Empire.[7] A small province with important mineral deposits and strategic communication centers, Teschen had a diverse population of Poles, Germans, and Czechs. When the Austrian Empire collapsed, the local population established a committee which devised a settlement of Polish and Czech claims leaving most of the area to the Poles, reflecting their numerical preponderance. However, the Czechs seized the province by force in January 1919, and the whole issue was unceremoniously dumped into the laps of the Great Powers. After much dithering, the powers, meeting at the Belgian town of Spa in August 1920, presented the Czechs with the bulk of Teschen to the Poles' outrage. The decision, which made little ethnographic sense, was a result of inept Polish diplomacy and the powers' increasing desire to have done with territorial embroilments and leave a fait accompli, however unjust, alone. Moreover, with the United States already absent, the Spa Conference was dominated by Lloyd George, no friend of the Poles, and here the usual support from France did not help Warsaw's case because the French were even more inclined to support the Czechs than the Poles. As a result, the Poles were convinced that they had been wronged and that the Czechs had committed robbery. The Teschen issue contributed to Polish-Czech estrangement in the interwar years, which was injurious to them both.

It is crucial to realize that the conference's decisions regarding Poland—the complex and militarily indefensible "corridor," the fragile free city, and the legal supervision of the Minorities Treaty—constituted, in sum, a solution to the Polish question by which the country was reconstituted as a kind of experiment, whose very existence was dependent upon the successful establishment of Wilson's League of Nations. Without the League to create a new order in Europe, in which traditional rivalries and threats were neutralized, Poland would be vulnerable to the point of helplessness. This was not an oversight on the part of the Great Powers, particularly Wilson, who saw in reestablishing Poland a means of a dramatic demonstration of a new world order, rooted in the League and sustained by a new structure of international relations. Unfortunately for Poland, Wilson's new order never took place, the League proved ineffective, and the Poland that rested on these constructs did not survive a generation.

If the western borders were determined largely by the Paris Peace Conference, Poland's eastern frontier was ultimately the result of a military struggle with Soviet Russia. In the east, Piłsudski harbored a grand vision of pushing the Russians back to their ethnographic frontiers while championing the cause of the Lithuanians, Belarussians, and Ukrainians. In the place of Russian imperialism would be erected some federal system, inspired by, if not modeled on, the old Jagiellonian Commonwealth. By reasserting its Jagiellonian role as a point of coalescence for the east, Poland would serve its own strategic interests while aiding the national causes of others. Piłsudski was remarkably flexible in his tactics and never provided any detailed plan of how he envisaged a restructured east. Though he was ultimately motivated by a deep concern for the strategic needs of Poland, his support for the borderlands peoples was sincere. It was a great misfortune for Poland that Piłsudski failed so utterly in presenting the idealistic and generous motives of his eastern policy.

Piłsudski's vision was doomed because it rested on a number of hopeless assumptions. The first was that the ethnic non-Poles of the borderlands would cooperate willingly. As a matter of fact, with few exceptions, most regarded the federalist scheme as tantamount to absorption by Poland and preferred a vulnerable independence to the security of collaboration with Warsaw. Second, Piłsudski exaggerated Poland's military capacity to work so huge a project in the face of certain Russian opposition. Only the Western powers' active support could have been sufficient for the task, but they were not interested in radically restructuring the European balance. Piłsudski's third error was in assuming that his own countrymen would prefer some loose federal links in the east to a more integrated, Dmowskiite Poland. Although Piłsudski was a national hero in 1919, it was Dmowski's nationalism, not Piłsudski's traditionalism, which more closely reflected the country's political preferences.

Piłsudski's efforts to create a federal system in the east, and the war between Poland and Russia fought in the borderlands, are inextricably linked events. The opening shots of that war were fired in the Belarussian village of Bereza Kartuska, in February 1919, when Polish troops clashed with Russian Bolsheviks in the amorphous borderlands between the two countries. Soon after, on April 19, the Poles reached Wilno, Piłsudski's hometown, where they were welcomed with great enthusiasm. Piłsudski announced that "the Polish army has come bringing you all freedom and independence. I want to give you the possibility to decide internal, nationality, and economic matters as you deem proper."[8] In many ways, Wilno was the key to Piłsudski's entire eastern dream. The historic capital of Lithuania, it was regarded by Lithuanian nationalists as the center of their national life. However, its population was overwhelmingly and passionately Polish; the ethnic Lithuanian element formed an insignificant 2 percent of the city's population. The surrounding area was a mosaic of nationalities: Poles, Belarussians, Lithuanians, and a sizable Jewish population. Piłsudski hoped to use the city as a lure to gain Lithuanian cooperation to reestablish some federal link with the Poles as the first step in his restructuring of the east. Unfortunately for his plans, the

Lithuanians were more afraid of the reality of a close relationship with a far larger Poland than they were of the possible danger of Soviet Russia. All of Piłsudski's efforts regarding the Lithuanians came to nothing. Overtures to the leaders of the feeble Belarussian national movement were without result.

The southern counterpart of Wilno was the great city of Lwów (now Lvov in Ukraine), where a large Polish majority existed in a province (Eastern Galicia) whose population was Ukrainian in majority. After fierce fighting, by July 1919, the Poles wrested all of Eastern Galicia from the Ukrainians, who fell back to the east where they were, in turn, pressed by the Soviet Russians. The Ukrainian nationalists, still a weak force, were wedged between two powerful claimants to their ethnic homeland. Thus the Poles were in conflict with the very people they had hoped to win over as allies against the Russians. Much would depend on which enemy the Ukrainians feared the most.

Direct clashes with the Russians were absent throughout most of 1919 because the Bolshevik government was preoccupied with winning a civil war with the anti-Communist "Whites." By the summer of 1919, the government of V. I. Lenin, the Communist leader of Russia, began negotiations with the Poles and offered to divide the borderlands between them. Piłsudski, however, was convinced that any division of the territory would provide only temporary security, and the negotiations proved fruitless. Both sides prepared for a decisive showdown and began massing troops.

The Western powers adopted a curious and contradictory attitude toward the Polish-Russian border dispute. Their real interest was in promoting a victory for the anti-Communists, the Whites, in the Russian civil war, although they were unwilling to intervene to the degree necessary to achieve this. The Whites fought for the territorial restoration of the former tsarist empire, which would have resulted in a tiny Poland, probably a recreation of the Congress Kingdom. As a consequence, the powers encouraged the Poles to fight the Bolsheviks, seize the borderlands, and turn them over to the Whites—obviously not a program that appealed to the Poles. As for the nationalities of the *kresy*, the Western powers disregarded them and assumed they would be reabsorbed by Moscow.

Given the uncertainty over the Russian civil war, the powers did not wish to determine boundaries in the east. Their preferences were clearly indicated, however, when, in December 1919, they proposed an eastern frontier for Poland that approximately traced the frontier of the Congress

Kingdom of 1815–1830. Although suggested as a minimal and provisional border, this notion, which has passed into history by the inaccurate designation of the Curzon Line, was a great blow to the Poles. It was in essence the extreme limit of Russian territorial claims against the Poles, and it reflected no effort by the powers to make ethnographic sense of the borderlands. As a matter of fact, when Warsaw responded by saying that the area should be allowed a plebiscite under League supervision, the powers simply ignored the Polish proposal.[9]

In the military showdown between Poland and the Bolsheviks, Piłsudski acted first. He concluded an alliance with his erstwhile opponent, the Ukrainian leader Semyon Petlura. A Polish-Ukrainian army was to throw the Bolsheviks out of Ukraine, which was to become an independent state. Then the Poles would withdraw. In return for this military assistance, the Ukrainians would drop their claims to Eastern Galicia (in whose chief city, Lwów, the Poles and Ukrainians had been fighting bitterly) and join Poland in an alliance. This would, in effect, restore much of the pre-1667 balance of power in the southeast. Petlura had opted for Poland over Russia, but would his decision influence the minds of his countrymen?

The allied army struck in late April intending to defeat the Russians in a lightning campaign to win the war in one bold stroke. Unfortunately, the effort was misdirected and the bulk of the Russian forces avoided defeat. Though the Polish-Ukrainian army took Kiev, it could hold its position only a few weeks. The Ukrainians, exhausted by warfare and bewildering changes of rule,[10] feebly supported Petlura. In the summer of 1920, the Bolsheviks countered in the north and threatened to outflank the Poles who retreated precipitately from the Ukraine, causing the collapse of Petlura's plans for an independent Ukraine. When the Polish position in the north buckled, the Russians launched a second major drive, based on the massed cavalry of General Semyon Budyonny in the south. Poland was faced with military disaster.

In this catastrophic circumstance, the Poles turned to the Allies who were meeting to discuss postwar reparations at the Spa Conference. The results were humiliating. The Western powers were absolutely opposed to Piłsudski's eastern campaign. In both Great Britain and the United States (which was not represented at the conference), it was regarded as naked Polish imperialism, an invasion of "Russian territory." The fact that virtually no "Russians" inhabited the area and that Poland and Ukraine were allies went virtually unmentioned. The French were sympathetic to the Polish position but lacked the ability to send serious aid, and the British promised aid only if the Poles agreed to accept the Curzon Line (now suddenly no longer a minimal, but a maximal frontier for Poland) and leave millions of Poles to the Russians. Even the Bolsheviks rejected the line as unfair to the Poles and continued their westward march unabated; the Allied effort at mediation was abortive.[11] A Franco-British military and political mission, featuring French General Maxime Weygand (and including a young officer named Charles de Gaulle), arrived in Warsaw, but no significant aid was ever sent. The mission, described by a senior diplomat at the Spa Conference as a "palliative," accomplished nothing and symbolized the bankruptcy of Western policy regarding the Polish-Russian conflict.[12]

In the meanwhile, the Bolsheviks prepared the nucleus for a Communist government for Poland which traveled with the Red Army. In mid-August 1920 their advance columns, under a former tsarist lieutenant and now the Bolshevik commander, Mikhail Tukhachevsky, bore down on Warsaw anticipating its fall. Lenin assumed the rapid collapse of all Polish resistance as the first step in the overthrow of the capitalist system in Europe and thus viewed the campaign against the Poles in a broad ideological and strategic framework.

However, the Russian plans were overturned when Piłsudski engineered a brilliant counterstroke before Warsaw on August 16. In a little heralded but crucial encounter, General Władysław Sikorski held the Bolsheviks to the north of the city while a Polish force, daringly concentrated by Piłsudski by means of forced marches, struck the Russians in the flank to the south. The Poles won the Battle of Warsaw. The Russians reeled back, their northern wing isolated and beaten as well. Now the Poles were in full pursuit and caught the Russians in the decisive Battle of the Niemen in late September in Lithuania and trounced them again, convincingly. The Poles also regained the initiative in the southern theater and forced Budyonny to flee in the last great cavalry action in the history of warfare.

It was a tremendous victory for the Poles, the first over a major opponent with decisive consequences since Jan Sobieski's action at Vienna in 1683. These battles saved Poland from a defeat that would have had incalculable results. Piłsudski's victory secured Poland its independence and saved Europe from serious consequences. It was perhaps the greatest Polish military triumph of all time. Ironically, it was also completely insufficient.

Victory over the Russians was dearly bought by the Poles, who were utterly spent by the end of 1920. The peace negotiations between Warsaw and Moscow were concluded at the Treaty of Riga in March 1921. The frontier split the borderlands. Although it was a military setback for the Bolsheviks, the Treaty of Riga did not injure any vital Russian interest and left them in control of the vast majority of the territory they had acquired in the partitions. By contrast, the treaty was a disaster for Piłsudski's federal dream. Belarussian territory was split: the dream of an independent Ukraine, allied with Poland, was doomed. As a final gesture, Piłsudski again tried to resuscitate the relationship with Lithuania in the fall of 1920, but Wilno became a bone of contention rather than a bridge for reconciliation. Nationalists on both sides wanted it, and Piłsudski's efforts failed, resulting in a dramatic turn of events in which the supposedly independent Polish forces occupied the city on October 9, 1920, and established an ostensibly independent state. This pathetic attempt, called the Żeligowski coup after the commander of the troops (General Lucjan Żeligowski) who seized Wilno, failed, and the subsequent plebiscite resulted in an overwhelming vote for incorporation into Poland. Wilno, the symbol of the Polish-Lithuanian Commonwealth, became an eastern provincial city in a Polish state. Relations between tiny Lithuania and Poland were deplorable for the interwar era, and the bitterness lingers even today.

Ironically, Piłsudski's dream of reviving the Jagiellonian federal system in the east, for decades condemned by critics as Romantic blindness to the realities of history, now appears in a different light. With the collapse of the Soviet Union, the Russian domination of the borderlands is over, a domination which resulted in incalculable suffering for the local population. At the end of the twentieth century, Poland, Ukraine, and Lithuania seem to be realizing their profound interdependence and groping, slowly, toward regional cooperation and an end to mutually destructive territorial disputes. Piłsudski, who may well have been ahead of, rather than behind, the times, has perhaps been vindicated.

Poland's victory in the conflict with Soviet Russia was completely misunderstood in the West which followed the war with a mixture of indifference and annoyance. In the West, the notion of Poland as an anti-Communist crusader attempting to destroy the Bolshevik experiment was widely criticized, especially on the political left, which never forgave the Poles for having warred against socialism.[13] Poland which, in its nineteenth-century struggle for independence from the monarchical powers had become the darling of progressive opinion in the West, was now seen as the epitome of reaction. Ironically, the political right in the

West also resented the Poles' attempts to revolutionize traditional power relationships in the east and saw the war as impudent Polish imperialism causing chaos in presumptively Russian territory. Given Piłsudski's proud unwillingness to follow Western counsel, and the fact that Warsaw launched its campaign without any consultation, the Western powers were convinced that the Poles were reckless and disobedient to their efforts to rearrange the world.

This estrangement from the West was a dreadful burden for the new state which was often its own worst enemy. In the midst of the fighting in the east, reports filtered back of anti-Semitic outrages committed by Polish troops and civilians, principally at Wilno, Pińsk, and Lwów. Though the Poles denied the charges and noted extenuating circumstances, verified reports made clear that the Jewish population had been the victim of periodic violence, though its magnitude remains very unclear.[14] Poland's image as an anti-Semitic state, already well established thanks to Dmowski's public and intemperate remarks made in Paris at the peace conference in 1919, was reinforced with doleful consequences. It was part of a very difficult start for the reborn state.

NOTES

1. Pan-Slavism, the idea of cultural, and hence possibly political, union of all Slavs, became fashionable by the mid-nineteenth century. Although it enjoyed strong support from Russians, Czechs, and some South Slavs, it has rarely found favor among the Poles.

2. As a matter of fact, other prominent Poles, for example, Paderewski, are probably better exemplars of federalism; the maestro even prepared a lengthy memorandum detailing a federal solution to the Polish question. However, because of his peculiarly significant ability to implement his ideas, Piłsudski should be regarded as the principal exponent of the notion.

3. Wilno, historic capital of the Grand Duchy of Lithuania, had few ethnic Lithuanians among its population in 1914. The city was Polish and Jewish, the surrounding area heavily Polish.

4. France was defeated in the Franco-Prussian war of 1870–1871 and barely survived thanks to the narrow Marne victory of 1914, in World War I. Of course, after the era under discussion, Germany defeated France in a third invasion in 1940.

5. Competition between Poland and the new state of Czechoslovakia for France's favor was one, though only one, of the reasons the two neighbors did not cooperate closely in the interwar period—a practice that proved disastrous for both.

6. The plebiscite resulted in 707,605 for Germany and 479,359 for Poland. The Poles later complained that almost 200,000 of the German votes came from so-called out-voters, those born in Upper Silesia, but no longer resident who had to return to vote. The fact that centuries of German control left the economic resources of the area in German hands also made the vote for Poland smaller than the real numbers would have suggested.

7. Teschen is the German spelling; in Polish, the area is known as Cieszyn.

8. Wacław Jędrzejewicz, ed., *Kronika życia Józefa Piłsudskiego, 1867–1935: Tom Pierwszy: 1867–1920* (New York, 1977), 438.

9. Piłsudski first raised the issue of a plebiscite in the *kresy* with the British scholar Halford Mackinder on December 15, 1919.

10. Since 1917 the Ukrainians had been ruled by the tsar; the Russian Provisional Government; the nationalist "Rada"; Hetman Skoropadsky, who ran a regime in collaboration with the German occupation forces; the Rada redux; the Bolsheviks; and Petlura and the Poles. The major Ukrainian political inclination by 1920 was to be left alone.

11. The response by Moscow is explained by the fact that Lenin already assumed that the war was won and did not wish to halt the westward march of the Red Army.

12. Nonetheless, many historians have subsequently ascribed serious deeds to the mission and frequently made Weygand the victor in the war. Both are untrue.

13. The fact that Poland also had strained relations with post-war Germany further antagonized the left. After World War I the German government was dominated by socialists and, as a result enjoyed great sympathy in left-wing circles. Thus Poland's problems with Germany and Russia were both a strategic nightmare, and also provoked the hostility of the international left.

14. An investigation of the charges of systematic anti-Semitism in the reborn state, led by the prominent American Jewish political figure Henry Morgenthau, largely exonerated the Poles.

6

The Second Republic, 1918–1939

For more than a generation the Communist regime in Poland taught that the Second Republic (1918–1939) was a failure, and the argument was quite persuasive. Poor, backward, and beset by problems, the second Republic's collapse in 1939, in the opening stages of World War II, seemed to confirm the negative evaluation of its critics. However, the establishment of the new Third Republic in 1989 has prompted a radical reconsideration of the earlier era within a transformed context. The Second Republic is no longer regarded as a dismal prelude to the advent of the Communist regime, but as the logical precursor to contemporary Polish democracy.

Fundamentally, the Second Republic was bedeviled by a series of structural problems: economic backwardness, minority unrest, and political instability. Although none of these were fatal defects, Poland's difficult geographical situation exacerbated their consequences and sapped the country's security resulting in a vicious circle of weakness and frustration. The result was a very flawed effort at creating a safe and democratic state. Each of these structural defects deserves separate analysis.

THE POLITICAL SYSTEM

An initial compromise made between Józef Piłsudski and Ignacy Jan Paderewski, in January 1919, resulted in Piłsudski's being designated head of state and the maestro's being named prime minister and head of government. Roman Dmowski, who was at the Peace Conference in Paris, became the country's chief representative abroad. This sharing of power did not last long but it averted what would have otherwise been a disastrous conflict among three most powerful and ambitious men who had served as national patriarchs during the war. Elections were held in late January 1919 in the central areas of Poland already under secure control. Former Austrian and German Poland were represented by their delegates who had formerly been elected to the Reichsrat and Reichstag, the Parliaments of those empires.

The 1919 elections resulted in a badly splintered vote among a myriad of small parties. In general, the right—dominated by the *endecja*, or the nationalist political movement—held about 30 percent of the vote in the first years of the Second Republic; the left claimed about a fifth of the electorate; and the center parties, more than 40 percent. A small grouping representing the national minorities gained between 3 and 4 percent. Thus neither the left nor the right could govern without the center, itself a rather loose aggregation. This prompted oscillating lurches of coalition rule, with occasional islands of non-party administration, less controversial but essentially unpopular. Politics were very fluid, with factions crystallizing and evaporating rapidly. Until the wars for the frontiers were over, however, Piłsudski retained extraordinary powers.

The Communist movement deserves special mention here because of its later prominence. Its significance in the interwar period was trifling. Founded in 1918, the Communist party of Poland was a political disaster. A feeble organization which peaked at barely 10,000 members (few of them workers), and most of them not ethnic Poles, the party rejected the very idea of Polish independence and worked against the sovereignty of its own country. This politically suicidal disposition resulted in the party's being declared illegal in 1919. It existed precariously underground until Stalin dissolved it in 1938. World War II gave it opportunities it could not have earned on the basis of its appeal.

In 1921 peace reigned, and a constitution was belatedly adopted. Interwar Poland was a parliamentary regime, modeled after the French Third Republic. This system, which made the lower house (the *sejm*) enormously powerful, also made the president little more than a figurehead, without a veto over legislation, and even constitutionally debarred from acting as commander in chief in time of war. This structure reflected the *endecja*'s chief political aim of neutralizing Piłsudski through the constitution.

The result was a pyrrhic victory for the right and the destabilization of Polish politics. Essentially, the *endecja* was almost powerful enough to govern the country, but not quite, whereas Piłsudski, although the dominant political figure, did not have an organized political base. The result was that—to paraphrase journalist Stanisław Mackiewicz—Polish politics was essentially a struggle between Dmowski and Piłsudski, although it was often acted out through proxies. This came to a head in 1922 when the first presidential election—according to the constitution to be decided by parliamentary vote—resulted in a ferocious struggle ending in a defeat for the *endecja*'s choice. The victorious candidate, moderate leftist Gabriel Narutowicz, was then assassinated by a fanatical proponent of the nationalist cause. For several months, Polish politics were dominated by polarizing rancor and vengeance which gradually faded but never disappeared.

After 1918 Piłsudski tried to maintain an anomalous position by insisting that the army be virtually beyond civilian control, a kind of separate world with vague but enormous significance, with himself, of course, at its head. This setup, which he justified on the basis of Poland's perilous international position, had a good deal of practical force, but it was utterly incompatible with a democratic polity and reflected his own career as a revolutionary and soldier. In 1923 he retired from government, bitter and convinced that Poland's unstable government was undermining its already fragile security.

The 1920s were not a good time for parliamentary democracy in Poland. Persistent economic problems, including periods of galloping inflation, led to periodic strikes, some of mammoth proportions involving bloodshed. A tariff war with Germany in 1925 only made matters worse. Several of the transitory governments in office were accused of corruption, almost certainly with good cause. Elections returned a bewildering galaxy of parties, more than one hundred in the early 1920s, which further disintegrated political unity. News from abroad also suggested to many that Poland's international position was deteriorating, which made the domestic chaos the more intolerable.

Finally, in May 1926, Piłsudski staged a coup d'état and seized power. For years he had denounced the political system in increasingly shrill and uncompromising terms, insisting that its instability and factionalism were virtually treasonous given the European situation. He organized a military demonstration and assumed that the government would simply hand power over to him. However, even many of his old comrades could not equate personal loyalty to Piłsudski with a willingness to ignore the constitution. His devoted lieutenant Kazimierz Sosnkowski was so distraught that he attempted suicide, bungled the job, and spent the rest of his life nursing his injuries. Ultimately, the result was a brief but bloody clash, which nearly became a civil war and left many hundreds dead and more wounded. Piłsudski was securely ensconced in Warsaw, but Poland's new democracy was in shambles.

Piłsudski had no plans. He merely wished to assert strong leadership, bring foreign affairs under control, and ensure that the army was free from parliamentary caprice. This incomplete agenda was to characterize Piłsudski's renewed tenure in Warsaw, which lasted until his death in 1935. Marshall Piłsudski insisted that military and foreign policies be under his command, through a variety of parliamentary contrivances, but left the rest of political affairs to others. Piłsudski wished, somehow, to preserve a democratic system, but remove security concerns from partisan politics, an impossibility which rendered post-1926 Poland an almost indefinable amalgam of democratic practice and authoritarian rule.

Piłsudski's great days were clearly behind him by 1926, and the next years did much to diminish the significant place in Polish history his earlier services had won him. Because he was convinced that parliamentarianism must be maintained in Poland, even though he had acted against it, he refused to create a dictatorship, and even his brief tenure as prime minister (1926–1928) was largely symbolic and characterized by a lack of involvement in most issues. Until 1935 the post was often filled by the scholar Kazimierz Bartel, a colorless, though not inefficient, executor of Piłsudski's will. The post-coup president, Ignacy Mościcki, was an obscure academic, whose stately appearance made him look well cast for a largely ceremonial role. Piłsudski ran the army himself as he did foreign policy, although here he surrendered its everyday tasks to others, especially after 1932 when Colonel Józef Beck became Piłsudski's virtual second self as the architect of Warsaw's foreign policy. The other governmental posts were held by Piłsudski's devoted "boys" from the legions, now, like Beck, mostly senior officers and thus called collectively "the Colonels," along with a small number of apolitical technical specialists. Piłsudski's rule was referred to as the *sanacja*, an almost untranslatable term suggesting both moral regeneration and efficient administration. It was little more than a series of clichés rather than a consistent ideology. Its basic components were patriotism, civic virtue, and dedication to Poland's raison d'état—the whole glued together by ferocious loyalty to Piłsudski as the personification of the nation's struggle for independence.

Piłsudski did not disband parliament, but he tried to create, or more precisely had others attempt to fashion, a base of support for the *sanacja* through a series of rather ill-conceived stratagems. In 1927 the Nonpartisan Bloc for Cooperation with the Government (Bezpartyjny Blok Wspołpracy z Rządem, or BBWR) was created. Its hopelessly amorphous twin goals were to combat the *endecja* and to support Piłsudski without creating any separate political entity.[1] Although BBWR supporters did well in the election, Piłsudski's relations with the *sejm* deteriorated steadily, the inevitable consequence of trying to combine democracy with authoritarianism. In 1930 Poland was in a crisis when economic difficulties, as well as increasing clashes with the extremists among the Ukrainian minority, produced widespread national tension. This brought about a confrontation in parliament in which a coalition of left and center, the so-called Centrolew, challenged the *sanacja*. Piłsudski's reaction was direct and brutal. A host of opposition leaders were arrested and held incommunicado. Persecutions continued, and the ensuing election of 1930 was a sorry spectacle with the BBWR having virtually arrested its way to a comfortable victory. Although most detainees were soon released, it was a shocking episode. The establishment of a concentration camp at remote Bereza Kartuska, filled with terrorists, Communists, and Ukrainian nationalists, was a blot on Poland's image as a civilized state.

The government made little use of its tainted 1930 electoral success, and its helplessness in face of the Great Depression further discredited it. Piłsudski, increasingly weakened by deteriorating health, reclusive, and bitter, presided over a steadily more authoritarian regime. He died in 1935, leaving the country truly bereft. For all of his recent failings, he was a giant presence on the Polish scene, and the country felt his loss keenly. Consciously Piłsudski had made himself the symbol of Poland restored, and his death automatically posed the question of whether Poland could endure without him.

For the last years of independence, Polish politics was a rather lamentable struggle of Piłsudski's disciples to hold onto power by transforming Piłsudski's personal legacy into a coherent political ideology, an impossible task. Piłsudski was no ideologue and he led by example, not through the power of argument. One did not agree with Piłsudski; one loved him—not for what he did, though it was considerable, but for what he represented: he was the personification of old Polish greatness.

The principal, players in the struggle for power after 1935 were president Mościcki, who quickly emerged as a more ambitious and adroit politician than had been anticipated, and the superficially impressive but rather pathetic general Edward Śmigły-Rydz, who assumed the role of Poland's first soldier after Piłsudski's death. A collection of prominent legionnaires coalesced in various combinations round one or another. Despite the unseemly, rapid promotion of Śmigły-Rydz to the rank of marshall—a controversial effort to boost the general and reassure the public—his military obligations clearly overwhelmed him. Poland's dire international position required Śmigły-Rydz to be a great soldier. Tragically, for both Poland and himself, he was not. Incomparably brave, ferocious in appearance, though in reality a gentle man, he had had a brilliant career during World War I and later showed himself to be an exceptional battlefield general in the frontier wars of 1918 to 1921. However, the highest reaches of command were utterly beyond him, and he lacked Piłsudski's strategic imagination and extraordinarily flexible mind. The regime tried to present him as a great captain, but he was a hopelessly inept generalissimo.

The major attempt of the Piłsudskiites to consolidate the country under their guidance was the creation of the Camp of National Unity (Obóz Zjednoczenia Narodowego, or OZON), a strange collection of various pro-Piłsudski political factions and other groups designed to unite the nation around the ideals of patriotism, strong government, and civic virtue. The ideology of OZON, cobbled together from various and contradictory sources, was a rather motley assemblage. By the late 1930s, it was clear that Polish politics had been successfully captured by the *endecja*, whose integrated program had developed a broad national following, despite the fact that its founder, Roman Dmowski, had had only a brief political career after 1919, was largely incapacitated by 1930, and died in January 1939. Ironically, even the Piłsudskiites of OZON had to pilfer elements from the *endecja* to provide a context for their diffuse notions. Seemingly, Piłsudski's vision had died with him. The Poland he had tried to build—decentralized, multinational, and evocative of the old Commonwealth—had never appeared. The Poland that emerged on the map after 1918 was essentially the Dmowskiite version, and it is no wonder that the *endecja* program ultimately prevailed. Piłsudski had kept alive the alternative version of Poland by his own powerful presence;

his death left Poland ironically in the formal control of his devotees but dominated by the ideology of the *endecja*.

THE ECONOMY

For many years the economic performance of the Second Republic was condemned according to the simple criterion that, by 1939, the major economic indicators had failed to reach the prewar levels, making the whole era of independence an economic failure. Performance in absolute terms was indeed dismal, but in relative terms, it was even worse because the same era witnessed the virtual transformation of Russia and, after 1933, the reemergence of a German powerhouse. Poland's feeble economy made Warsaw's claims to being a serious power appear pathetic if not laughable.

Innumerable problems beset the economy. The country was reknit from three quite dissimilar parts with the attendant problems of communication and transportation. Previously severed markets were reintegrated, and currency, banking, and investment patterns were scrambled. World War I had caused immense destruction, and subsequent hostilities with the Germans, Russians, Lithuanians, Ukrainians, and Czechs resulted in further damage. By an odd logic the Peace Conference declared Poland ineligible to receive reparations, thus no help could be expected from that source. Foreign loans, on which Paderewski was particularly keen, were few and direct investment was insubstantial.

The vast majority of Poles (over 65 percent) were involved in agriculture, primarily on unproductive dwarf holdings. Industry was generally underdeveloped and poorly distributed. Only former Russian Poland had a substantial manufacturing sector. Austrian Poland's industry was scanty and obsolete. Formerly German Upper Silesia, with its mining and manufacturing, was a rare exception. Private capital for investment in either agricultural or industry was small, and a vigorous state role did not begin until late in the 1930s and its effects were difficult to gauge.

The level of literacy was low, and the rapidly expanding population could neither be absorbed by the small industrial base nor find productive employment in the overcrowded rural economy. With immigration restrictions in the United States, the prewar safety valve for excess population was closed, dooming the Polish countryside to deepening poverty.

Despite this gloomy overview, the situation was actually more positive than it appears. First, the traditional method for judging the Second Republic's economic performance is to set 1913, the last prewar year, as a base line. However, newer appraisals consider 1913 an artificial standard—which ignores the huge effects of both the war and the reunion of a long trifurcated country—and begin instead with 1919 when, for example, industrial production was only 30 percent of the 1913 level.[2] In this more realistic light, the Second Republic can be seen to have made considerable progress overall. Especially rapid growth was noted in the late 1920s when several years of industrial expansion were recorded, and the Baltic city of Gdynia began a meteoric rise as a major port. Built from scratch by the Poles, Gdynia caught and surpassed long-established Gdańsk (the former Danzig) as a commercial center; its trade volume increased almost 3,000 percent in the 1920s. Although this progress was cruelly interrupted by the world depression, by the late 1930s Poland was clearly emerging: industrial production was almost 20 percent higher than the pre-depression level, and very significant new areas were being developed. The Central Industrial Region, a bold initiative of 1937, developed a new modern industrial base involving roughly a fifth of Poland's area and population. Components of modern industry, including armaments, were built from scratch, which laid the basis for modern manufacturing in many key areas. Simultaneously, Warsaw became the center of new high-technology production. The architect of this new policy, Vice Premier Eugeniusz Kwiatkowski, elaborated an impressive strategic plan for modernizing Poland over the next fifteen years which was, tragically, still in its infancy when World War II began. Agriculture lagged behind, but even here considerable strides had been made in land redistribution. The long-range hope for rural poverty, however, was industrial modernization and a resultant new employment and settlement pattern. Considering the ruination the country had inherited, and the little amount of time that elapsed before the Great Depression stifled its recovery, the fact that Poland, by 1939, had far surpassed its 1919 base year was a commendable achievement.

THE MINORITIES

Poland's ethnic and religious composition affected both its domestic stability and national security. The composition of interwar Poland was in many ways the worst possible solution to the ethnographic aspect of the Polish question. Essentially, Poland had neither the national homogeneity envisioned by Dmowski, nor the multinational expanse dreamed of by Piłsudski, but something in between which invalidated both programs. Arguably, a far larger Poland might well have had fewer, rather than more, minority problems. The Poland that emerged in 1918–1921 was close enough to being homogeneous—ethnic Poles accounted for more than two-thirds of the population, and no other group had more than 14 percent of the total—that the nationalist temptation to run Poland as a unitary rather than multinational state proved unavoidable, with regrettable consequences. Poland had sizable minority populations in the east, all of whom were but fragments of larger ethnic communities, split by international frontiers. In the west and north there was a substantial German element, and a very considerable Jewish population.

In the Polish census of 1921, an ethnic breakdown showed the Poles formed about 70 percent of the population; Ukrainians, slightly more than 14 percent; Jews, 7.8 percent, and about 4 percent each for Germans and Belarussians. A decade later saw a slight increase in the relative weight of the Belarussians and Jews and a drastic decline in the number of Germans due to out-migration and low birthrates. In religious composition, Roman Catholics accounted for about 65 percent; Uniates, Orthodox, and Jews each formed about 10 percent; and a small, rapidly dwindling Protestant minority accounted for the rest. In comparison to the whole of the region between Germany and Russia, this placed Poland roughly in the middle in terms of national homogeneity.[3]

The Ukrainians, the largest minority group in Poland, were heavily concentrated in the southeastern portions of the country where they constituted the absolute majority in three large provinces (Wołyń, Tarnopol, and Stanisławów). Of all the Ukrainians, those in Poland had the highest level of national consciousness; southeastern Poland had been for a generation the heartland of Ukrainian nationalism. Relations between the Poles and Ukrainians were strained throughout the interwar period and reached critical levels in 1930 when the Poles launched massive repressive measures designed to crush the militant nationalist movement among the Ukrainians.

In general, the Polish Ukrainian policy in the interwar years deserves low marks. The Polish state did very little to accomplish a compromise with the Ukrainians. Warsaw made it clear that it regarded them as unwanted guests in a Polish state and expected their assimilation. Warsaw's policy of encouraging ethnic Poles to settle in the east to alter the demographic pattern was clumsy and much resented. Fanatical Ukrainian nationalists resorted to terrorism and assassination to demonstrate their opposition to the Polish state, and the links between them and the German government were well known to Warsaw. On the other hand, a sizable percentage of the Ukrainians were willing to accept Polish rule as inevitable. After all, the areas of heaviest Ukrainian population had always contained a large Polish population, and marriages between Poles and Ukrainians were common. The vast majority of Ukrainians could probably have been won over by a more generous policy. Given the fact that interwar Poland was Dmowskiite in content despite Piłsudski's role in shaping it meant that Warsaw was unwilling to regard its minorities as anything other than potential enemies. Polish-Ukrainian reconciliation was a tragic lost opportunity for both peoples, but since the Poles controlled the machinery of the state, their burden of guilt is heavier. At this time, it should be recalled, the Soviet Union was treating its own Ukrainian minority with genocidal brutality—a massive "artificial famine" in the Soviet Ukraine which resulted in perhaps millions of deaths. In Poland, ultimately the conflict was between an embittered Ukrainian nationalism, which had failed to win its own state, and a frustrated Polish nationalism, which had failed to create the state of which it had dreamt.

The Belarussian minority was, by comparison, a far simpler problem for Warsaw. Desperately poor, with the lowest literacy rate in Poland, the Belarussians were nowhere a majority in Poland, though a large minority in the east and northeast. The Belarussians exhibited a very low level of national consciousness and only a feeble national movement. Among Roman Catholic Belarussians, educational advancement or even movement to a city often resulted in rather rapid Polonization.[4] Many Poles were convinced that the Belarussians were but a transitory ethnic problem, though a serious economic difficulty because of the intractable poverty of the eastern provinces.[5] In other words, the economic backwardness of eastern Poland produced circumstances that heightened ethnic and religious frictions, including Polish-Belarussian tensions. However, given peace, it is likely that the Belarussians would have been assimilated into Poland in a few decades. The fact that, at the end of the twentieth century, a strong Belarussian national movement has still not emerged suggests that the Polish tendency to regard the Belarussian problem as essentially soluble had considerable justification.

The German minority represents an unusual problem. In absolute numbers a relatively insignificant component of the second Republic's population, even in their areas of highest concentration (in Upper Silesia), the Germans constituted only about one-fourth of the total. More important, the Polish Germans were destined gradually to fade. Their birthrate was much lower than that of the Poles, and a gigantic out-migration to Germany steadily reduced their numbers as well. Given time, the German element in Poland would have declined to numerical insignificance. In fact, an American scholar has argued that the German population had halved by 1939, when they probably constituted not much over 2 percent of the population of the entire country.[6] However, the Germans were disproportionately vexatious for interwar Poland for two very important reasons. First, they were a powerful economic force in the western part of the country and consequently were very influential. In large areas in western Poland, the Germans predominated among major landowners and held a powerful position in industry. Second, they were actively patronized by Berlin, especially after the advent of Adolf Hitler in 1933, as a prop to German policy in the east which sought to weaken Poland and revise the Versailles Treaty which had given former German territories to Poland. The result was that the Germans repeatedly complained of discrimination by Warsaw and sought redress under the controversial Minorities Treaty at the League of Nations. Polish reaction was understandably hostile.

The Germans of Poland were really the victims of larger Polish-German geopolitical antagonism and were unlikely to be won to peaceful collaboration with the majority population. For many Germans, however, cohabitation with the Poles was a pattern of centuries and many families were of mixed lineage. Given a better climate of Polish-German relations, there is no reason to assume that Poland's Germans could not have become a contented, and shrinking, community. The international situation simply prevented so happy an evolution.

Perhaps the most insoluble, and doubtless the most tragic, minority problem of interwar Poland was that of the Jews. The Jews of the Second Republic were the remnant of the huge Jewish community of the Commonwealth, who constituted at one time as much as 80 percent of all the world's Jewry. In the reborn state, the Jews accounted for between 8 and 10 percent of the population.[7] Although there had been a considerable wave of adoption of Polish culture since the late nineteenth century, the vast majority of Polish Jews were not culturally assimilated. They had a highly characteristic distribution pattern: overwhelmingly urban, they were heavily concentrated in commerce and industry as well as the liberal professions, and virtually invisible in agriculture, thus the inverse of the majority population. In addition, the Jews were disproportionately concentrated in the cities of central and eastern Poland; in the centers of the eastern borderlands, such as Pińsk, Grodno, and Brześć, they were the majority of the population.

Polish-Jewish relations began to show signs of serious deterioration in the late nineteenth century when nationalism began to spread among the Poles along with a new socioeconomic profile. This placed the Jews in an impossible position. For four generations there had been no Poland, and the Jews had had to accommodate themselves to new masters, the partitioning powers. Throughout the long nineteenth century there was no Poland for the Jews to assimilate to, just a persecuted and dangerous patriotic movement which was of dubious attraction. Hence, over the decades, some Jews retained their loyalty to a lost Poland, but the majority Russified or Germanized or tried to be left alone. To the Jews, this was a matter of survival, especially in ferociously anti-Semitic Russia; to the Poles, it was a failure to be patriotic. Most Jews combined a profound sentimental attachment to their ancestral Polish homeland, without the patriotic loyalty to a Polish state. When Poland was reborn, the Poles could exult in the re-creation of their country, but what did it mean for the Jews? Many Jews had joined Polish political movements, especially Piłsudski's Polish Socialist Party, but none were members of Dmowski's *endecja*, which was more powerful among ethnic Poles. Far more were part of the Russian Marxist movement which, being without Polish or Russian patriotism, was a safe haven for Jews. Although there was a sentimental basis of support for Poland among the Jews, inevitable after more than six centuries of residence in the country, to most Poles, the failure of the Jews to react like Poles to independence rendered them suspect. During the Polish-Russian War, much of which was fought over the most heavily Jewish areas of Poland, the fact that the Jews usually adopted a neutral position between Polish and Bolshevik armies enraged the Poles who reacted with outbursts of violence and began to regard all Jews as secret Communists. Anti-Semitic outbursts at Wilno, Lwów and Pińsk made many Jews associate Polish rule with brutal anti-Semitism.

In the Second Republic, increasingly under *endecja* influence, the Jews were triply targeted: a distinct minority and therefore an element of weakness to the Dmowskiite worldview, competitors for control of the modern portions of the economy (i.e., commerce and industry), and assumed sympathizers with the hated enemy to the east, the Soviet Union. The fact that perhaps half of the membership of the Polish Communist party, and even more of the leadership, was contributed by a Jewish minority of 10 percent unfortunately only enforced this suspicion.

It appears that many Polish Jews saw in Communism an ideology of universal brotherhood, and looked upon the Communist party

as an instrument of transplanting to their country the highly idealized Soviet pattern. In a country as anti-Russian and anti-
Communist as prewar Poland, the pro-Communist sentiments of
many Jews were eagerly exploited by the native anti-Semites, who
tended to identify Jewishness with Communism.[8]

As the Polish economy deteriorated during the Great Depression and
the rise of Hitler and the collapse of the League of Nations in the 1930s
underscored the fragility of Polish security, Polish society became increasingly concerned about unity and safety. Thus the Jewish situation
deteriorated, especially after Piłsudski's death in 1935. Although Poland
never passed anti-Semitic legislation, discrimination against Jews was
widespread in administrative practice, including restriction to institutions of higher learning. Public outbursts of anti-Semitism, including economic boycotts and occasional street violence, were quite frequent in the
late 1930s. It was a sad last chapter in the ancient tradition of Polish-
Jewish cohabitation in the lands of the old Commonwealth.

Piłsudski's famous dictum that Poland will be a great power or it will
not exist seems like an epitaph for the Second Republic's vain search for
security in the interwar era. Two elements of the geopolitical situation
were baleful realities: In the west, Germany was unreconciled to the loss
of its territory to reborn Poland and was hostilely disposed toward Warsaw; in the east, the Soviet Union regarded Poland as a barrier to the
spread of communism to Europe. The threat of Russo-German cooperation at Poland's expense, the deadly combination that had produced the
partitions, hung heavily on Warsaw's consciousness after 1918. After the
borders were set and Poland reemerged as a middle-sized state of limited
resources and large problems, its ability to solve this security problem
was restricted.

Theoretically, three solutions existed to achieve security in the era.
First, Poland could repose its trust in the larger forces structuring the
postwar world. Here we may consider both the League of Nations as a
putative replacement for traditional Great Power alignments, as well as
the actions by those powers to maintain the world they had created in
1914–1919. If Europe remained secure, Poland would remain secure.
However in 1933 Hitler came to power in Germany and at once began
to re-assert that country's claims to continental preeminence. His efforts
to rebuild German military might, though in clear violation of the Versailles Treaty, went unchallenged by the Western Powers. By 1935 the
collapse of the structure of European security, built around the League

of Nations, became evident. In that year Italy brutally invaded Ethiopia while the League watched helplessly, demonstrating its ineffectiveness. In 1936 Germany remilitarized the Rhineland along its western border—another violation of the Versailles Treaty—and thereby undermined the security of France and Belgium and, indirectly, France's allies Poland and Czechoslovakia as well. The same year civil war broke out in Spain in which Italy and Germany—now allies—intervened, as did the Soviet Union on the opposite side, an imbroglio which made the disintegration of European order obvious. By 1938 Hitler's Germany was sufficiently rearmed to make aggressive strides. In March he annexed Austria (the so-called Anschluss), and in October he convinced England, France, and Italy to cooperate in the dismemberment of Czechoslovakia at the Munich conference. By 1938 German sights became trained on Poland and Europe was in disarray.

Traditionally, the powers had taken it upon themselves to preserve the continent's order. Given the League's failure, they would have had to assume that role again. This offered little comfort to the Poles. Of the principal architects of the postwar world, the United States, Great Britain, and France, the first decided to absent itself from an active role in European affairs although it retained a vigorous economic involvement. Great Britain made it very clear that it regarded the east of Europe as far beyond its conception of Britain's role on the continent. As a matter of fact, very soon after the Paris Peace Conference the British openly favored indulging German desires for a fundamental revision of the Versailles Treaty, inevitably at Polish expense, in an effort to appease the Germans and thus render them, it was assumed, or at least hoped, a more constructive member of the European community. However, this assumes that German demands for treaty revision could have been accommodated while still maintaining Polish security, a dubious proposition. Bismarck's sage remark that no one is rich enough to buy security through concessions immediately comes to mind.

Of the major powers, this left only France with an active interest in preserving the Eastern European status quo. Given the weakness of France both politically and economically, this disposition was bound to be transitory, especially after Paris alienated itself from its British and American allies. Inevitably, French resolve began to crumble; its ability to force the Germans to abide by the treaties was already badly eroded as early as 1925.[9] In 1929 the French began to construct a line of defensive fortifications, known as the Maginot Line, along its eastern border. Among other things, it convinced Poland and Czechoslovakia, France's eastern allies, that the French had adopted an essentially defensive military posture in regard to Germany, which was hardly reassuring for the eastern states. With France relinquishing the crushing burden of preserving the European status quo, the post-1918 world was essentially in flux.

If neither the League of Nations nor the Great Powers could preserve continental security, other options still existed for the Poles. The most obvious was to build up a system of regional alliances which would present a potential aggressor with daunting military power. Warsaw embarked on a series of these projects after 1919, but all ended in failure. Attempts at a so-called Baltic Bloc, which would have linked Poland with series of small states to the north, foundered on the rock of Polish-Lithuanian discord. Certainly Polish-Lithuanian bitterness was deep-seated after 1918: both sides implacably demanded Wilno; Poland won, but Lithuania refused to accept it.

Even a greater loss, and another area in which Polish foreign policy deserves low marks, is the sorry state of Polish-Czechoslovakian relations throughout the entire interwar period. The effective cause of the alienation was a territorial dispute, the nasty affair of Teschen. But this was so minor an issue that it could have been overcome by an exercise of enlightened statesmanship. Prague deserves at least as much blame for this sad state of affairs as does Warsaw. The Czechs regarded close relations with the Poles as inevitably dragging them into difficulties with the Soviets with whom Prague had no quarrels. Moreover, Prague was jealous of its status as the more significant player in East Central Europe and tried to keep the far larger Poland from challenging it. The Czechs had an exaggerated sense of their own invulnerability. The Poles never appreciated how interconnected was the security of Czechoslovakia with their own. Warsaw tended to regard the Czechs with disdain, and thus Poland and Czechoslovakia, working at cross-purposes, helped divide rather than consolidate the smaller states of Central Europe in some sort of security arrangement. Although Poland had neither many nor important cards to play in this area, it did far less than it could have and the cost was considerable.

The one real achievement of the whole era in this area was the creation of a common Polish-Hungarian border, the first step in an effort to build what Colonel Beck envisioned in 1938 as a "Third Europe,"[10] balancing both German and Russia. Unfortunately this project was realized only months before the outbreak of World War II. It was far too little and far too late.

In light of these circumstances, Polish security would require one of the two remaining options: Either Poland would have to remove the threats to its security by appeasing its potential enemies, or, failing this, it would need to have the intrinsic strength to dissuade an aggressor or endure an attack. In other words, Poland would be required to be what it pretended to be—a major power. This, in turn, required dexterous diplomacy and considerable resources, and Poland was seriously deficient in both categories.

Initially after independence, Poland's failure to rearrange the map of the east and create a federal bloc able to oppose either Germany or the Soviet Union left it to improvise a foreign policy. According to Piotr Wandycz, the distinguished student of Polish foreign policy, "Poland became a middle-size state too large to be anyone's satellite, but too small and too weak to be a great power. Many of the subsequent problems of Polish diplomacy stemmed from this half-way house position."[11] Indeed, this is probably an understatement. Reciprocal hostility between Warsaw and both Berlin and Moscow posed a security dilemma Poland never mastered. Initial efforts to build regional links produced feeble results, and Polish foreign policy was left with only two fundamental alliances both concluded in 1921: one with powerful France and the other with relatively weak Romania.

Neither was, in itself, a guaranty of Polish security. Whereas Poland regarded the French alliance as the cornerstone of its foreign policy, the far more powerful French considered it merely a possible option, thus building a dangerous asymmetry into the relationship. Moreover, whereas France considered Poland a useful ally against Germany, France's reaction to a possible Polish-Soviet clash was unpredictable. Finally, as France's weight in European affairs faded rapidly in the 1920s, the value of the alliance declined. The Romanian alliance was a useful step in the direction of a central European bloc, but it had significance only within this larger context. By itself, poor Romania, militarily insignificant, was of little value to Poland.

By 1926, when Piłsudski returned to power, the international situation was already ominous for Poland. France was pursuing an illusory détente with Germany, Great Britain continued to be aloof from Central European affairs and sympathetic to revisionist noises from Germany, and the Soviet Union, though quiescent, was about to embark on a major industrial and military buildup. Piłsudski decided to pursue a policy of "balance" between the threats from Germany and the Soviet Union by attempting to retain working relations with both and avoid falling under the tutelage of either. This resulted in many tortuous twists and turns in Polish diplomacy, but the main outlines were to retain independence with relatively few assets to expend. The greatest threat to Polish security was the possibility of Russo-German collaboration which would almost certainly be realized at Polish expense. This prospect, which existed throughout the entire interwar period, was Poland's particular night-mare. By 1932 Polish-German relations remained frozen in hostility, and Poland felt constrained to sign a nonaggression treaty with the Soviet Union, which, it hoped, might begin to prise apart the jaws of Russo-German collaboration, which Piłsudski saw as threatening Poland. With Hitler's coming to power in 1933, Piłsudski may well have suggested to France the possibility of a bold move—a preventive war against Germany[12]—but settled for a 1934 Polish-German nonaggression declaration. Thus Poland had virtually identical relations with both its neighbors; the balance was positioned precisely. However, as Piłsudski well knew this could only be a temporary status. He predicted only four years of peace, and he did not solve Poland's security dilemma.

In reality, Poland's security was beyond its capacity to ensure. After Piłsudski's' death in 1935, Beck who had been his lieutenant and now became the architect of Poland's foreign policy, pursued an active, in-deed aggressive, policy in Europe, often overplaying Poland's rather weak hand. His brusque methods won him few friends, and he was widely suspected of harboring pro-German sentiments, which was un-true. Essentially however, the threat to European security was not from Beck's occasional lapses in diplomatic gentility, but from Hitler's desire to pursue an aggressive policy and the Soviet hope of strategic profit in case of a war between Germany and the Western powers. England and France, who did little to restrain German aggression, were far more re-sponsible for the war than relatively insignificant Poland.

By 1938 Germany had absorbed Austria and was about to consume part of Czechoslovakia at Munich with British and French concurrence. Beck decided to force beleaguered Czechoslovakia to cede the contested Teschen area. This certainly was an act of ungenerous diplomacy, given the Czechs' travails, but would it have been better to allow the Germans to gain the territory which was strategically significant and contained a large Polish population? Certainly Beck, who disliked President Edvard Beneš of Czechoslovakia quite thoroughly, never appreciated the mili-tary value of the Czech state for Poland's own security and can be rightly criticized. Support for Czechoslovakia was in short supply in the Europe of 1938, and Poland was not the only country to fail in this regard. In

September 1938, England and France agreed, in the infamous Munich Pact, to the German annexation of the border regions of Czechoslovakia. The Czechs were not invited to the negotiations that determined the fate of their country. Hungary and Poland both presented territorial demands which the beleaguered Prague was unable to resist. It was German aggression and allied complicity that doomed Czechoslovakia; Poland's recapture of Teschen was a marginal issue at best. Had Poland not claimed the area and its Polish population, it would have fallen to Germany. Thus, Poland's recapture of Teschen from the collapsing Czechoslovakia in 1938 was certainly tasteless, but, given the circumstances, strategically correct.

Over the following months, German attentions turned to Poland, and Germany made various demands for border changes, began inciting the German minority in Poland as it had so effectively done to the Sudeten Germans in Czechoslovakia, and occasionally changed the tenor by proposing German-Polish cooperation against the Soviets. Poland stoutly rejected all German threats and blandishments.

In March 1939, Germany broke its promise at Munich about having no further territorial demands in Europe and occupied the remnant of the Czech lands. Hungary seized the extreme eastern part of the state giving her a border with Poland. Earlier in the era this might have been a useful link because Hungary was well-inclined toward Poland, and Beck briefly was fascinated by the chimera of constructing his Third Europe of Poland, Hungary, and Italy. But the hour was far too late and the impetus far too feeble for any such realignment. Indeed, the major significance of the fall of Czechoslovakia was that the Germans now surrounded Poland on three sides, undermining her strategic situation.

The German action was followed quickly by a dramatic British public "guaranty" of Polish sovereignty and independence on March 31, 1939, followed by a mutual aid agreement a few days later. The British seemingly had finally been roused to action and were drawing the line at Poland after the Czech barrier had fallen. In reality, the British did little or nothing to improve Poland's military position and did not even hold talks on mutual defense measures. Furthermore, the British made a number of overtures to Hitler making it clear that their commitment to Poland was halfhearted at best and would be abandoned if Germany were willing to negotiate a "second Munich" as it were. Britain had never been committed to the preservation of Poland's territorial integrity, and the April accord did not change things as wartime diplomacy would confirm. Once the war began, the British made it clear that they would fight it according to their own strategic plan, whether this meant sacrificing Poland to Hitler or no. A vigorous British commitment to the security of Eastern Europe, begun early in the interwar era, could well have re-written the history of the century. As it was, the tardy, ambiguous, and grudging British guaranty to Poland did little to protect or preserve Polish sovereignty.

In the last months of peace, the Germans and the Western powers both pursued some understanding with the Soviets in anticipation of imminent hostilities: the Germans to avoid a major conflict in the east and to isolate Poland, assuming Western inaction; the allies to present Hitler with so daunting a prospect of a two-front war that he would quail, or, if the worst came, have a major eastern foe in the form of the Soviet Union. For their part, the Soviets hoped for a mutually destructive struggle among the capitalist states and had little interest in rescuing Britain and France from the German threat, certainly none in aiding the despised Poland. Soviet negotiations with the West were pointless from the start and were conducted in bad faith. The Soviet insistence that their troops be allowed complete discretion to enter Polish territory should they join against the Germans, which the Poles rejected as compromising their sovereignty, was never a serious issue despite the attention later given to it by many historians. The Soviets raised the issue merely to draw the Western powers, isolate Poland, and up the ante in their simultaneous negotiations with Germany.

Hence, the so-called Hitler-Stalin Pact of August 23, 1939, stunned the world. This fact indicated the degree to which the cynicism and aggressiveness of Soviet policy were unappreciated. The secret protocol of this treaty, whose existence was denied by the Soviet government almost to the end of its existence, detailed a new, fourth, partition of Poland and a description of spheres of influence in the east for the new allies, closely following the "Curzon line." This division gave Germany and Soviet Russia each roughly half of Poland's territory, though more than 60 percent of the population lived in the western and central areas accorded to Germany. The attack on Poland which began World War II was now made possible.

In retrospect, the foreign policy of interwar Poland is difficult to appraise. Certainly the failure of the Second Republic to preserve the state's independence was a catastrophe. Polish policy was often ungenerous and short-sighted, for example in regard to the Czechs and the Lithuanians. Beck's arrogance was inappropriate, and his overestimation of Poland's ability to compete with Germany was delusional. Whereas various schemes of Baltic or Danubian blocs showed imagination, they overestimated Poland's ability to craft solutions to its security problems.

However, this list of failures and errors, which could easily be extended, is ultimately beside the point. It was the Great Powers which had the responsibility, and more important the capacity, to construct and maintain continental security. They failed as both architects and guardians. Weak Poland could not counteract the effect of this dereliction. It is tempting to regard the Second Republic as geopolitically doomed from birth. However, this is a temptation to be avoided. A belief in historical inevitability is little more than lack of imagination masquerading as analytical sophistication. What happened will always seem predetermined. For the collapse of Europe in 1939 Poland deserves little blame; not because its actions were so wise but because its capacities were so small. Its punishment exceeded its culpability.

NOTES

1. BBWR supporters were to remain members of whatever political party with which they had been affiliated.

2. Here we depend upon the arguments of the contemporary economic historian Wojciech Roszkowski.

3. Poland was far more ethnically Polish than Czechoslovakia was Czech, or Yugoslavia Serbian, but it was more diverse than Bulgaria or Hungary, and roughly on par with Romania.

4. Roman Catholic Belarussians were often simply considered Poles, a practice that incensed nationalist Belarussians.

5. Underpopulated, with low agricultural productivity, scanty natural resources, a primitive communications and transportation infrastructure, few urban areas, and little industry, Belarus had been largely neglected by the tsarist administration rendering it one of the poorest areas of Europe.

6. Edward D. Wynot, Jr., "The Polish Germans, 1919–1939: National Minority in a Multinational State," *Polish Review* 17, no. 1 (Winter 1972): 1035–1058.

7. The larger figure if the Jews are counted by religion: the smaller, if by ethnicity—two distinct categories of the Polish census.

8. M. K. Dziewanowski, *Poland in the 20th Century* (New York, 1977), 198.

9. In 1923 France had attempted to force the Germans to abide by the Versailles Treaty's clauses regarding reparations payments by occu-

pying the Ruhr. London and Washington were unsympathetic to the French move and, isolated, Paris was forced to step down—an enormous symbolic defeat. In 1924 France accepted a redefinition of German reparations obligations which effectively prevented it from forcing Berlin's compliance. In 1925 Paris signed the Locarno Treaty by which Germany recognized the inviolability of the French border, but the price was Paris's abandonment of the protection of the borders of Poland and Czechoslovakia, its eastern allies, which Paris did not insist be given similar guarantees. Whereas the Locarno Treaty seemed to bring an era of comity between Berlin and Paris, it was an illusion which, in reality, began the dismantling of French security arrangements.

10. Polish efforts to create some sort of north-south bloc of states, stretching from the Baltic to the Black Sea or even the Adriatic Sea, date from the birth of the Second Republic. Polish-Czech hostilities usually precluded any serious result. However, in 1938, Beck's "Third Europe" assumed the disappearance of Czechoslovakia as a prelude.

11. Piotr Wandycz, *Polish Diplomacy, 1914–1945: Aims and Achievements* (London, 1988), 16.

12. The evidence regarding Polish advocacy of "preventive" war against Germany is not conclusive and has been variously interpreted.

7

World War II, 1939–1945

The effects of World War II were more catastrophic for Poland than for any other country. During the war, over seven million Poles were killed, including more than three million Jews, thus virtually ending the history of Polish Jewry.[1] Even the huge human losses of Soviet Russia, Yugoslavia, and Germany were proportionately much smaller; Western European casualties were insignificant in comparison. The damage done to Poland was almost incalculable. Any monetary amount becomes a meaningless figure alongside the reality of the destruction of Poland's cities: Warsaw, the national capital, 84 percent destroyed; Gdańsk, 55 percent devastated; Wrocław, Szczecin (then Stettin), Poznań, and other cities seriously damaged. Systematic looting by the Germans, as well as wholesale pillage by the Russians, stripped the country of historic treasures of inestimable value.

Of all the members of the victorious coalition over the Axis, only Poland was diminished in size. All of the historic eastern borderlands, the *kresy*, were seized by the Soviets while they were Hitler's confederates and retained by them when they became the allies of the Western powers with their approval. Territorial compensation in the west was less than half the loss in the east, and it was, moreover, among the most devastated areas of Germany, including virtually leveled Wrocław, the former

German city of Breslau. In the east, Wilno and Lwów, the second and third most important cities in independent Poland, were gone, as was Grodno, the historic seat of the Polish parliament, and much more besides. Poland was territorially mutilated, its new borders set almost capriciously. In the southeast, a pencil line drawn arbitrarily on the map resulted in a nightmare of severed roads, railways, and rivers. In the north, the Soviet desire for a Baltic port was responsible for a frontier across historic East Prussia, creating a Russian enclave along the southern Baltic (today's Kaliningrad oblast). Russia gained its most extreme ethnographic claims, and Poland was reduced to its smallest dimensions in history.

This ruined and reduced territory was consigned to the Soviet orbit, and for more than half a century, Poland was a Communist land, a political fate particularly inappropriate for the country given its traditionalism and religiosity. Poland, probably the greatest loser of World War II, had made the greatest sacrifices for victory.

World War II began at 4:45 in the morning of September 1, 1939, when German units attacked the tiny Polish garrison at Danzig (now Gdańsk). On October 6, the September campaign ended with Poland utterly defeated and occupied by German and Russian troops.

Poland's rapid defeat was a combination of a disastrous strategic disposition of forces exacerbated by crushing numerical and qualitative inferiority. The basis of this situation was the determination by Poland that, given the enormous German superiority, it could prevail in war only as a part of a coalition of powers. In other words, Poland had to conceive its struggle against Germany as part of a larger effort because a Polish-German contest in isolation would mean certain defeat. France and more recently England had pledged by treaty to support Poland.[2] If Poland could hold the Germans, even though being beaten, for fifteen days, France was obliged to launch an all-out offensive on the western front. This, coupled with expected action from the British, if only the engagement of the Royal Air Force, would require the Germans to slacken their pressure on the Poles and divide their forces in the face of a two-front war. Poland would, therefore, fight alone for a fortnight, but if it could hold out, it would be part of a powerful combination that would face Germany in a repetition of the scenario that had defeated it in 1918.

But how could Poland endure the first agonizing fifteen days while fighting Germany alone? Military analysts have repeatedly emphasized that Warsaw chose the worst possible disposition of forces: attempting to defend the very long frontier with thinly stretched units, easy to penetrate and turn with powerful armored thrusts and thus painfully vulnerable to segmentation and encirclement by the more potent, mobile German army. Poland did not regard itself as free to adopt a strategy of abandoning the border and falling back to more easily defensible positions in the interior with shorter, denser lines. First, such a strategy would immediately surrender to the Germans the most valuable economic assets of the country in western and central Poland. In a long war—and only a long war would allow Poland to emerge as one of the victors—this loss would prove disastrous. Second, if Poland did not resist along the entire frontier, what would happen if Germany offered peace after having seized the western provinces? Warsaw, having watched Czechoslovakia betrayed by its allies in 1938, was not sure it would not be similarly abandoned and have to face, as had Czechoslovakia, a delayed destruction after the West had lost interest in its fate. Poland chose to resist, to the utmost, along the entire national frontier, a political decision that compromised the country's ability to defend itself militarily.

In March 1939, Germany had seized the remainder of Czechoslovakia. This put the Poles in a weak strategic position regardless of what dispositions they adopted. German units thrusting north from Slovakia or south from Prussia would already be far behind Polish lines holding the western border; indeed, all of western and central Poland could be rather easily severed. The narrow Polish corridor was militarily indefensible, and the Polish units assigned to it, Army Pomerania, in Polish terminology, all but doomed to destruction. Any sustained defense of the frontiers would thus automatically threaten the Polish army with strategic encirclement; withdrawal would collapse the front and prevent prolonged resistance. Because the border was so long, fortifying all of it was financially impossible, and isolated strong points would have been pointless. Hence, the border was without defenses. The Polish position was strategically hopeless.

The disparity of forces further darkened Polish prospects. In simple numerical terms, the relationship of armies did not appear to be extraordinarily disproportionate. Poland's fully mobilized strength of perhaps a million was certainly inferior to the German army's 1.5 million, but not overwhelmingly so, and all of German's forces certainly would not be engaged. However, Polish mobilization, begun in late August 1939, was rescinded under pressure from France and Britain "not to provoke the Germans" and to allow a last chance for diplomatic initiatives to succeed. When these failed, Poland had to resume mobilization under chaotic circumstances. Fully one fourth of the army never reached its units. The German invasion force thus enjoyed a crushing numerical advantage. Moreover, unit firepower of the German army, the *Wehrmacht*, was reckoned to be four times greater than the Polish equivalent, drastically worsening a serious tactical inferiority.

However, in modern warfare, the principal determining element in victory has been not weight of numbers, but relative strength in two principal arms: aircraft and tanks. Here the Polish position was catastrophic. The Luftwaffe, or German air force, with 3,652 aircraft, 90 percent of which were less than three years old, faced a Polish air force comprising 397 planes. Sixty French bombers, promised in May 1939 to augment the Polish force, never arrived. Poor liaison between air and ground units, as well as serious problems with supply and communications, further reduced the Polish air force's ability to contribute to the war.

Even more striking was the disparity in armor. Only one Polish tank brigade was operational in September; another was just days short of readiness. Tanks were not concentrated in powerful units as they were in the *Wehrmacht*, and even if this had been done, with only a few tanks available, and virtually all lightly armed and armored, they would not have been able to withstand the more than 3,000 German tanks or panzers.

Far less dramatic than tanks and planes, but equally significant in explaining the course of the campaign, was the enormous German superiority in mobility. With thousands of trucks, the Germans could ride; the Poles had to walk. The Germans could attack a Polish position with overwhelming firepower and then outrace the defenders while they tried to regroup. The Polish ability to break off and withdraw in order to reform and offer coherent resistance was rendered virtually impossible by the simple fact that the Germans could move faster. Hence, coordinated resistance quickly disintegrated into scattered opposition.

Finally, perhaps more important than any count of planes, tanks, or trucks, is the simple monetary comparison of the two armies: since 1933, the Germans had spent an amount on their military more than thirty times greater than the Poles—this despite the fact that Warsaw devoted more than 50 percent of the national budget, a crushing amount, to defense needs. The Poles faced an army infinitely better provisioned in every necessity of war.

The initial bombardment of Polish positions in Danzig was accompanied by a massive assault along a broad front. Essentially, the Germans attacked in two powerful blows from north and south. The German Third and Fourth Armies, operating from East Prussia, thrust south toward Warsaw, scarcely one hundred miles distant, and southwest to sever the Polish corridor. The more powerful German southern front, whose combined strength was almost 900,000, comprised three armies: the Eighth, Tenth, and Fourteenth, which crossed the Polish border in a series of spearheads from the territory of occupied Czechoslovakia. Simultaneously, the Luftwaffe attacked across the entire expanse of Poland, purposely bombing and strafing civilian targets. A German scholar, Wolfgang Jacobmeyer, who deemed the German war on Poland "singular" for its viciousness, quoted Hitler's war directive as providing its context:

> I have given orders . . . that the aim of the war is not to reach a certain line, but the physical destruction of the enemy. Thus I have ordered—for the time being only in the East—my Death's Head Units to kill mercilessly and pitilessly man, woman, and child of Polish descent and speech. . . . Poland will be depopulated and settled by Germans. . . . Be hard, be pitiless, act faster and more brutally than others. The people of Western Europe must be horrified. This is the most humane way of conducting the war.[3]

Within a week the struggle for the frontiers was over. The long complex Polish border could not be held; German armor was impossible for the Poles to stop; and the Polish air force was overwhelmed in the skies, leaving the army without air support. The front was broken in many places within seventy-two hours despite desperate resistance; reserves had been thrown in and were already virtually exhausted; maneuvering was difficult and, in daylight, suicidal because German aerial superiority prevented movement. The commander in chief, Marshal Edward Śmigły-Rydz, rapidly lost overall control of the battle, which devolved into each of the seven Polish armies fighting a separate, often uncoordinated action.[4]

On September 8, the Poles launched their only major counteroffensive of the war when General Tadeusz Kutrzeba, a bespectacled scholar of military history who had never commanded troops in battle, boldly ordered his Army Poznań to attack the German Eighth Army in flank as it passed incautiously south of him on its way to Warsaw in the east. In the resulting Battle of the Bzura, the Poles held the initiative for two days, but when the Germans diverted powerful forces and the bulk of their airpower to the problem, they regained the initiative and gradually reduced Kutrzeba to a increasingly small pocket where the fighting became ferocious. After huge losses, including the deaths of three Polish generals in the field, Kutrzeba's battered forces had to surrender or try to break out and get to Warsaw. These meager reinforcements were no help, however, as the capital was virtually encircled and subjected to ceaseless aerial and artillery bombardment. When its supplies were exhausted and the fires could no longer be extinguished, Warsaw capitulated on September 27, 1939.

Meanwhile the government as well as Śmigły-Rydz had fled, tracing a tortuous course toward the southeast corner of the country and the Romanian border, enduring elaborate detours and delays. The Poles were frantically attempting to form a new defensive line to the east and rally the army to await anticipated help from the western allies. If all else failed, they would cross the border into Romania as previously arranged with Bucharest.

The preoccupation of the Polish authorities was with their allies who had pledged to come to Poland's defense. France had promised a major offensive fifteen days after mobilization, but for the first two agonizing days of the war, neither Britain nor France had even declared war, though the French had ordered mobilization. As the Polish front collapsed and the army tried to extemporize some means of continuing the defense, the inaction on the western front became increasingly harrowing to the Poles. September 17, 1939, was one of the blackest days in Polish history. Fifteen days after mobilization had gone by and there was no French offensive; the British had done nothing. The western front had not materialized and Poland was doomed, its prewar strategy of survival as part of a coalition utterly ruined. But worse was yet to come. On that same day, the Soviet Union launched a massive offensive along the entire Polish eastern border, breaking the 1932 nonaggression declaration and falling upon a country virtually defenseless.

The initial response by the Polish High Command was to order an all-out resistance to the Soviets, but, after a few hours, Śmigły-Rydz concluded that this would lead to a massacre, and he issued a general directive that ordered immediate withdrawal to Romania or Hungary and opposition to the Soviets only if attacked. The struggle against the Germans was, however, to go on. This order, virtually impossible to fulfill, indicated the commander in chief's hope to preserve as much of the Polish army as possible for later use and avoid pointless bloodshed. The situation for the Polish forces in the east was desperate. With most of the army fully engaged against the Germans, only the lightly armed Frontier Defense troops were able to resist the Soviet onslaught, which numbered almost one million troops supported by more than 1,000 planes and perhaps as many as 4,000 tanks. The resistance was, nonetheless, ferocious. Volunteers, firemen, and teenage scouts joined to defend the Polish east. Long repeated accounts of only several hundred Soviet casualties have been recently revised by new research which places the Soviet losses at from 8,000 to 10,000. Polish casualties, with units often fighting both Germans and Russians alternately, were very heavy and tragic. The defense of Grodno, for example, was followed by a Soviet massacre of the prisoners, a pattern repeated at Wilno, Oszmiana, and elsewhere. Officers were often murdered after their surrender, and atrocities committed against the civilian population were widespread.

Although isolated resistance to the Germans and Soviets lasted through the first week of October, the Soviet invasion was the finishing blow for Poland. The government representatives crossed into Romania, anticipating an unhindered passage to the West. Instead the Romanians, under German pressure, interned them. Exercising a clause in the Polish constitution, president Ignacy Mościcki transferred his office to Władysław Raczkiewicz in Paris. An exile government, under the premiership of General Władysław Sikorski, a prominent soldier and politician, was quickly formed there as well. Thus began the history of the Polish government in exile which was to last until the fall of communism in 1991.

The trapped leaders of the Polish government had a pathetic fate. Virtually imprisoned under appalling conditions, they were censured by their political opponents for failing to prepare the country for war. Śmigły-Rydz, beset by doubt as to whether to stay with his men and share their defeat or to cross into Romania and act as the center for a new army in exile, chose exile. He was immediately castigated as a coward by his political enemies and fell into a deep depression. In 1941 he escaped Romanian internment, returned surreptitiously to Warsaw, and joined the underground as a simple soldier under a pseudonym. He died of heart failure a few months later. A man of limited military gifts, he failed to do what no soldier could have done.

The balance sheet on the September campaign is worth contemplating. Polish casualties were high: 70,000 Poles fell on the battlefield; 133,000 were wounded. Over 500,000 were captured, about two-thirds by the Germans. Both German and Polish figures place the *Wehrmacht*'s losses at about 45,000. Material damage to the Germans was considerable: 300 aircraft were shot down; 1,000 tanks and armored cars were destroyed; and 11,000 other vehicles were lost. The Wehrmacht used 80 percent of its ammunition. It took the Germans many months to replace these losses. Whether this time was well utilized by Poland's Western allies is doubtful. If we compare the Polish military performance against the German and Soviets with the later efforts made by the Western allies to defend France, in which the Belgian, Dutch, British, and French forces actually enjoyed a numerical advantage over the Germans, the Polish effort deserves high marks indeed.

Three issues deserve separate treatment. The first is the famous false report, repeated by even highly regarded specialists, that the Polish military depended on cavalry to stop the German assault and, in a combination of reckless bravado and military incompetence, launched charges against the panzers. This is not true. The Polish cavalry had strict orders to use their mounts only to bring them into the vicinity of battle and attack on foot. Moreover, the horse allowed Polish cavalry units a mobility that the infantry could not match, and the cavalry demonstrated considerable combat effectiveness in September 1939. In fact, when the cavalry did charge German positions they did so with considerable success, demonstrating the fanatical courage for which they were famous. Finally, the Poles were not alone in maintaining cavalry units. The Germans had almost 200,000 horses in the campaign, and the horse was widely utilized in all the world's armies at that time and later.

Second, the Polish air force was not destroyed on the ground in the first hours of the war but, in fact, was cleverly and secretly relocated to secondary fields on the eve of the attack. The Germans bombed empty bases in their initial attacks, and the Polish air force contested the skies with the Germans until the Soviet invasion and collapse of supplies grounded them. The performance of the Polish air force, flying obsolete aircraft under the worst possible conditions, was astonishing, and their reputation for aerial combat was later demonstrated in the Battle of Britain when Polish air units outperformed both the Germans and the British by a wide margin.

Finally, in the late 1920s, Polish counterintelligence managed to obtain the secret German coding device known as "Enigma" and a few years later Polish cryptographers broke the code. In the summer of 1939, the Poles passed this secret to Britain and France along with several reconstructed German coding devices. This access to German secret communications, later called the "Ultra Secret," was a significant Polish contribution to the war, although the ultimate importance of Allied knowledge of the German codes is still subject to debate among specialists.

Occupied Poland fell into three zones. In conformity with their prewar agreements with the Nazis, the Soviets seized more than half of the territory of Poland. After a few weeks of random violence, arrests, and repression, eastern Poland was absorbed when rigged elections—in contravention to established international law—supposedly demonstrated that the population wished to join the Belarussian and Ukrainian Soviet Socialist Republics. Thus 13 million Polish citizens, including a plurality of 5 million ethnic Poles, passed to Soviet administration, populating an area half again as large as England.[5]

In the winter of 1940, the Soviets began a massive deportation effort. In just twenty months, as many as 1.7 million were shipped to Siberia, the Soviet far north, and Kazakhstan. Among those deported were government employees, religious figures, landowners, and members of sporting clubs; in short, anyone in any way distinguished by wealth, education, or attainments that might be associated with Polish culture. Approximately half of the deportees were women and children. Transported under barbaric conditions that often lasted a month, half of the deportees perished. The Soviets worked a demographic revolution in the historic Polish east by conducting a systematic de-Polonization and social restructuring of their newly acquired territories. It is estimated that perhaps as many as 1.5 million Poles died at Soviet hands between 1939 and 1945.[6] In the long, historic view it was the most brutal step in the process begun under the tsars to remove the Poles from the *kresy*.

The Germans divided their portion of Poland into two quite separate regions. Incorporated directly and immediately into the Reich were those portions of Poland formerly bordering on Germany, an area of almost 100,000 square kilometers, 90 percent of whose 10 million citizens were ethnic Poles. In order to prepare the area for annexation, special units accompanied the invasion force equipped with extensive lists of locally prominent citizens who were seized and shot—more than 15,000 in a few weeks. The whole of this territory was to be immediately and forcibly Germanized. Two million Poles were forced out and dumped to the east, and their homes, businesses, and properties were seized by the Germans.[7] The remaining Poles were to be completely denationalized.

Their newspapers, libraries, schools, and museums were closed, and their language was declared illegal. Ominously, the Polish Jews were singled out for special treatment; they were to be concentrated in cities and then transported to central Poland. Both operations were exceptionally brutal.

Central Poland was a territory apart. Officially called the General Gouvernement (GG), this was the portion of Poland not annexed to Germany but became a dumping ground for Poles and Jews cast out of their homes in the western provinces. Here, in the remaining quarter of the former Second Republic, the 12 million inhabitants were to be allowed to live as Poles, though under strict German control presided over by Hans Frank from Kraków where the seat of this government was located.

> All the universities and secondary schools were shut, as well as the museums, archives, libraries, book and newspaper publishers; radio receivers were confiscated; a list was drawn up of Polish books to be destroyed, and the playing of musical works by Polish composers was prohibited. The battle against Polish culture, and the attempt to stifle and obliterate it from history extended to such lengths that monuments were destroyed, works of art were removed, and every expression of Polish national identity was hunted down. . . . The Germans decided that Poland was to become a country consisting solely of slaves, and treated as a colony where Polish culture, the intelligentsia, and anyone with an apparent sense of national belonging would be wiped out. The conquerors wanted to carry out their plan quickly, and therefore reached for an instrument which they considered infallible, namely terror.[8]

Jews were required to wear distinguishing armbands bearing yellow Stars of David. Soon they were deprived of their property, restricted in their movements, and forced to leave their jobs. By late October 1939, Jewish males were required to perform manual labor. Soon thereafter the camps were established. Worse was yet to come.

The German occupation of Poland is one of the most atrocious stories of the twentieth century. Many have argued that the long-range goal of German occupation was the biological extermination of the Poles, to follow in the wake of the obliteration of the Jews. Certainly the Germans made huge progress toward that end between 1939 and 1945. In the spring of 1941, Berlin decided that the GG was to endure from fifteen to twenty years. The Poles who survived the war would then be deported to Siberia, somehow Germanized, or liquidated thus ending the historical existence of the Polish nation. Toward this end the Germans took a number of concrete steps. Their effort at wholesale resettlement was the most ambitious but the largest failure. Certainly the deportation of Poles from the annexed territories was drastic:

> The deportations, which reached a high point in 1940, were conducted under appalling conditions; people were forced into cattle cars and in the freezing weather of 1939–40 transferred to the General Gouvernement where they were unceremoniously dumped. Many died, especially children.[9]

The second stage of this plan foundered when only a few hundred thousand Germans were imported, many of whom never left their temporary resettlement housing. Thus the demographic structure of western Poland was not seriously altered. Undeterred, the Germans decided on vaster schemes in 1942 and 1943 when they undertook a massive effort to deport the population of the Zamość area, in the eastern GG, to prepare it for an influx of Germans. The operation resulted in the complete emptying of 293 villages over the next several months. In all, 31 percent of the entire population of the district, more than 150,000 people, were removed under ghastly conditions. A peculiar feature of this program was the organized kidnapping of blond, blue-eyed Polish children to be shipped to the Reich to be raised as Germans. As many as 50,000 children met this fate. Similar efforts at systematic depopulation were undertaken in the Białystok region of northern Poland and elsewhere.[10] Although the German plans undoubtedly caused demographic injury to Poland, the resettlement of the area by imported Germans was never accomplished.

Despite these failures, German occupation was a demographic catastrophe for Poland. Hans Frank gave orders, under instructions from Berlin, to exterminate the Polish elite—a term very broadly understood. Thus in late 1939, the faculty members of Jagiellonian University in Kraków were arrested and sent to a concentration camp where most died. In the spring of 1940, the A-B (*Ausserordentliche-Befriedungsaktion*) program was launched which was responsible for the murder of 6,000 educated Poles, including distinguished members of the Polish *sejm*, artists, writers, Olympic champions, politicians, and many others. In the ensuing years, the Germans systematically annihilated 45 percent of Poland's physicians and dentists, 57 percent of her attorneys, 40 percent of her professors, 30 percent of her technicians, nearly 20 percent of the clergy, and the majority of the journalists, to name only a few categories. A vast network of more than 200 concentration camps was erected throughout Poland and quickly became filled. All in all, the Germans killed 5,384,000 Polish citizens under occupation in addition to 644,000 victims of military action. This total includes virtually the entire Jewish population of the country.

THE FATE OF POLISH JEWRY

The fate of Poland's Jews is a heart-rending tragedy enfolded within another tragedy. Though the Poles suffered egregiously, only the Jews of Poland were singled out by the Germans for total annihilation. In this pursuit, the Germans were remarkably successful. The Polish Jews were concentrated in ghettos in many of the larger Polish cities; the largest, in Warsaw, Kraków, and Łodź, were established during 1940 and 1941. The penalty for leaving the ghetto, or for aiding someone else to do so, was death.

Subjected to unspeakable brutalities, starved—the daily food ration for Jews in Warsaw was 184 calories—and tormented, they were then shipped, starting in 1942, to several huge death camps, of which Auschwitz, conveniently located near main rail lines, was the largest and most infamous. Other major extermination centers were Chełmno near Łodź, Majdanek and Bełżec near Lublin, Sobibór, and Treblinka. In all an estimated 6 million European Jews were killed in the Holocaust, including virtually all of Poland's historic Jewish community of 3 million people.

The relationship between the Poles, who suffered under German rule, and the Jews, who suffered far worse, is sensitive and controversial. Many Polish Jews have been critical of their Christian fellow citizens for failing to help them in their extremity. Here, however, we must remember that, unlike the situation in German-occupied Western Europe, the penalty for aiding Jews in Poland was death. Some Poles, however, assisted the Nazis in discovering Jews in hiding and blackmailed Jews who were trying to "pass," and profited from Nazi seizures of Jewish property. How large a percentage of the Polish population behaved so abominably is difficult to estimate. The Polish underground executed those found guilty of such actions. The Government in exile established a Council of Assistance to the Jews (Rada Pomocy Żydom, or Żegota) in 1942. Żegota was charged with assisting the Jews living in hiding outside the ghettos by providing them with living quarters, documents, food, medical care, and financial help, and by facilitating communication be-

tween members of the same families living in different localities." Żegota
maintained 4,000 Jews in Warsaw alone and had branches in many other
places.[11] "The Polish underground army (Armia Krajowa, or AK) maintained a military liaison with Jewish fighting organizations within the
ghetto and supplied it with arms, instruction, and advice. When the Jews
of Warsaw launched a heroic and suicidal uprising in April 1943, the
AK provided weapons and ammunition, though far short of what was
needed, and launched a number of attacks to break through to the ghetto
to deliver arms. Some Polish soldiers fought in the ghetto alongside the
Jews and helped a pathetic few to escape. At the high point of the fighting, the Star of David flag flew alongside the red and white banner of
Poland. The Warsaw ghetto rising was crushed; the help given by the
Poles had been ineffective.

It is impossible to determine the degree of culpability of an entire
nation, especially under circumstances so extraordinary. Only a handful
of the 3 million Polish Jews survived German occupation; the number of
survivors has been estimated at between 50,000 and 200,000. Ever since
World War II, the fact that so much of the Holocaust occurred in Poland,
and that the Poles were witness to the greatest tragedy in Jewish history,
has affected the relationship between these two peoples. World War II
brought an end to the seven-century history of the Jews in Poland and
retroactively charged that entire history with an emotional significance
that both communities are still attempting to understand.

In occupied Poland, an elaborate underground authority, with both
civil and military functions, had been created almost at once after hostilities had ended at the direction of Śmigły-Rydz. Sikorski, however,
whose partisan distaste for the Piłsudskiites was one of his most unfortunate attributes, insisted that all underground activities be directly sub-
ordinated to his government in exile. He ordered dissolved the incipient
organization in Poland and created the ZWC (Związek Walki Czynnej,
or Union of Armed Struggle) which would be commanded by General
Kazimierz Sosnkowski from exile. Civilian affairs were under a separate
administration which eventually became an astonishingly elaborate system of everything from a judicial to an educational system which allowed the Poles to run, under German noses, the semblance of a Polish
state, though at great danger.

By 1942 the ZWC had been renamed the AK and had grown rapidly
to considerable proportions. At its peak strength the AK numbered almost 400,000 men and women. During the course of the occupation it

suffered over 60,000 casualties fighting the Germans, not counting the 1944 Warsaw rising. In 1940 the impracticality of running so large an underground army, with multiple divisions and responsibilities, from exile was realized, and effective command of the AK was entrusted to the dashing and energetic Colonel Stefan Rowecki in Warsaw. In the summer of 1943, Rowecki was captured by the Germans and the far less able General Tadeusz Bór-Komorowski took his place.

Despite its considerable numbers, the AK was utterly incapable of engaging in any direct military struggle with the Germans and had to restrict its activities to diversion, intelligence operations, and preparation for major action only when circumstances were drastically altered. The underground military network technically embraced the Soviet zone of occupation as well, but coordination between the two areas was intermittent, and the Soviet secret police, the NKVD, proved far more effective than the Gestapo in controlling the Polish underground.

Although the vast majority of the underground military forces in Poland were under AK auspices, there also existed two additional armed groups. On the far political right stood the NSZ (Narodowe Siły Zbrojne, or National Armed Forces). Fanatically anti-Communist and often rabidly anti-Semitic, the NSZ numbered perhaps 25,000 men. The AK tried repeatedly to subordinate the NSZ, but no lasting accord was ever achieved. Although units of the NSZ often fought devotedly against both the Germans and Soviets, its adherents also murdered leftists and Jews and turned some over to the Nazis. On the whole, the NSZ was an embarrassment to the government in exile. On the far left the Polish Communists had created an armed force, the AL (Armia Ludowa, or People's Army). Organized in 1943, and a fraction of the size of the AK, the AL was not particularly active in fighting the Germans. It devoted most of its efforts to penetrating units loyal to the government in exile.

In addition to the large but militarily insignificant forces in Poland, the Polish government in exile rapidly reassembled units abroad. At first composed of troops who had managed to reach the West after the fall of Poland, it was supplemented by volunteers from Polish communities abroad and eventually Polish prisoners of war (POWs) in Russia. The Polish navy, much of which had escaped destruction in September, a small merchant marine, and remnants of the Polish air force were also rebuilt with French and, later, British aid. Growing throughout the war, the Polish forces in the West eventually reached approximately 200,000 men.

General Władysław Sikorski was a capable leader with considerable military talent, boldness, and imagination. However, in the international

arena the position of the Polish government after the September campaign was most unenviable. Poland was the enemy of both Germany
and the Soviet Union, but its Western allies had declared war only
against the Nazis. Moreover, Western analysts tended to discount the
Polish performance of September, and whereas the French were most
supportive of Sikorski personally, both Britain and France had been critical of his predecessors in the prewar Polish government. It was obvious
from the treatment given to Sikorski and his armed forces that neither
Britain nor France regarded Poland as a significant ally.

The course of the war continued to undermine the already marginal
status of Poland aboard. The Poles played a major role in the Anglo-
French expedition to Narvik (Norway) in the spring of 1940, but this
proved a vain and rather ill-considered British effort to prevent the stunning German victory in Denmark and Norway. Far more significant was
the German campaign of the summer which conquered Belgium, Holland, and France and sent a defeated British army scurrying for home at
Dunkirk. The fall of France was a catastrophe for the Poles: "Forty thousand Poles had fought in the battle of France and all were lost."[12] The
painfully reconstructed Polish army was forced to begin again from
nothing. Moreover, with the occupation of France, Poland would have
to rely exclusively on Great Britain, a country which had traditionally
shown very little interest in or sympathy for Poland.

In the last half of 1940, the spectacular Polish contribution to the Battle
of Britain, in which Polish squadrons outperformed the RAF and played
a disproportionate role in defeating the Germans, briefly raised Polish
prestige in England and provided a sorely needed morale boost for the
Poles. The virtually simultaneous distinguished service by the Polish
Carpathian Brigade in the North African Campaign added further luster
to Poland's combat renown. However, in June 1941, Germany invaded
the Soviet Union, and the inevitable and ironic result was that Poland
was doomed to lose World War II no matter its outcome.

When World War II was transformed from a German effort to dominate the world, with vital assistance provided by the Soviets, to a mammoth struggle between the two erstwhile allies, Poland's position became
complicated beyond measure. To the Western allies, joined in December
1941 by the United States, keeping the Soviet Union in the war was
essential to defeat the Germans. Poland was, by comparison, a minor
ally whose wartime contributions, though certainly noteworthy, could
not be decisive for victory. Hence, the Allies inevitably sacrificed Polish
interests to the Soviet Union. Poland's hopes to emerge from the war

independent and whole were completely dependent on Soviet preferences. From the Polish point of view, the remainder of the war was a
gradual demonstration of their own insignificance in the geopolitics of
the war.

Sikorski, to his credit, realized at once that the outbreak of hostilities
between the Soviet Union and Germany had reduced Polish leverage.
With the Germans rolling relentlessly eastward in the last half of 1941,
he tried to conclude a working relationship with Moscow that would
allow the Poles the maximum advantages at a time when the Soviets
were at their weakest. By demonstrating to the British that Polish-Soviet
differences were not insuperable, Sikorski hoped to avoid forcing Britain
to make a choice between Poland and the Soviet Union that would inevitably result in the Poles being abandoned. However, the Sikorski-
Maisky Pact, signed at the end of July 1941, which reestablished relations
between Poland and the Soviet Union, was of dubious value to the Poles.
The Soviets, despite their military difficulties, demanded enormous concessions that virtually would acknowledge the loss of all eastern Poland.
It did, however, provide for the establishment of a Polish army in the
Soviet Union. Though Sikorski had no real alternatives, this pact shat-
tered Polish unity and morale. Several cabinet ministers, including the
respected Sosnkowski, resigned in protest, and many Poles believed that
Sikorski had failed to protect vital Polish interests.

Sikorski's hope of using the pact to achieve a working relationship
with the Russians was answered with a series of frustrations. He was
eventually able to locate and secure the release of Polish POWs in Soviet
hands since 1939, but his hopes of creating a major Polish military force
on the eastern front, fighting in conjunction with the Soviets and thus
elevating the weight of Poland in Allied military councils, proved impossible owing to Soviet obstinacy and deceit. Sikorski had estimated
that as many as 250,000 Poles, held captive since the Soviet invasion in
September 1939, might be available for military service in the Soviet Union. Dreadful Soviet treatment, complex Anglo-Soviet machinations behind Sikorski's back, and the personal agenda of the Polish commander
in the Soviet Union—the militarily competent but controversial General
Władysław Anders—eventually led to the collapse of Sikorski's dream
of a major Polish military force in the Soviet Union, and the Polish troops
were withdrawn to the Middle East and British operational command
by the end of 1942. The vital cadre of officers Sikorski needed to expand
the Polish forces did not accompany them: they had been murdered by
the Soviets in 1940.

If efforts to work with the Soviets proved unavailing, equally frustrated were the Polish attempts to convince the Western allies to adopt a cautious approach in their wartime strategy lest it leave the Soviets in control of Eastern and Central Europe at the moment of Germany's defeat. Sikorski's well-argued strategic memoranda in this regard were ignored by London and Washington. Indeed, one of the principal criticisms of Sikorski is his inability to realize the degree to which the British and Americans were wedded to the Russian alliance—not only as a combination to defeat Hitler, but as the cornerstone of postwar reconstruction. His attempts to alert the west to a Soviet menace did little more than convince Britain and the United States that the Poles were troublemakers who were disrupting Allied harmony.

By early 1943, Hitler sustained a devastating double setback. Anglo-American forces landing in North Africa had defeated Germany and its Italian ally in the Mediterranean. At almost the same time the German 6th Army in the east surrendered before Stalingrad. This placed the Third Reich in a huge pincers which made its defeat inevitable. The president, of the United States, Franklin Roosevelt, British Prime Minister Winston Churchill, and Soviet leader Joseph Stalin gathered at Teheran in November 1943 for the most significant of the wartime conferences. The Polish position in the war was already very weak. In April 1943 the Germans had discovered mass Polish graves at Katyn and publicly blamed the Soviets for the atrocity. Only after the fall of the Soviet Union did the details of this affair become clear. In March 1940 Stalin and the Politburo had ordered 21,657 Polish officers and civilians to be slain without trial: 4,421 were bayoneted, shot, and dumped in mass graves in a forest near Katyn; 3,620 were murdered in Kharkov; 6,311 were butchered near Tver; and 7,305 died at many other places still not fully reconstructed. In all, the Soviets had murdered much of the elite of the Polish military. The guilty have never been brought to account.

The Soviets insisted that the massacre at Katyn was a German act. Britain and the United States publicly accepted Soviet claims, but they certainly knew better. When the Polish government in exile demanded an investigation be conducted by the International Red Cross, Moscow broke relations with the Sikorski government. The general's whole policy of building a working relationship with Moscow in order to avoid isolating Poland collapsed. It was perhaps merciful that Sikorski died in an air crash at Gibraltar a few weeks later. His replacement, the decent but obscure and unprepossessing politician Stanisław Mikołajczyk, symbolized the fall in Allied esteem for Poland's significance. Sikorski was a respected soldier, a statesman with an established international standing, and a man of impressive bearing; Mikołajczyk was, by comparison, a minor figure.

The break in relations between the government in exile and the Soviet Union transformed the Poles into a nuisance, if not a burden, for the Western powers. Stalin was busy creating alternative future arrangements for Poland. In January 1943 the ironically named Union of Polish Patriots (Związek Patriotów Polskich, or ZPP) was cobbled together in Moscow from a group of Communists and fellow-travelers. It quickly presumed to many of the attributes of a Polish government, issuing declarations about the social and political structure, as well as the foreign policy of a postwar Poland. This putative state was to renounce its eastern territories to the Soviet Union with which it was to conclude a close alliance. The ZPP soon became the political umbrella under which a Soviet-sponsored Polish army was created. Nominally commanded by Colonel Zygmunt Berling, a Polish officer who had deserted from Anders' forces in 1942, this "Kościuszko's Army" was recruited largely from Poles in the Soviet Union. Its officers were almost exclusively Russian although some masqueraded under Polish names. Thus, by mid-1943, the Polish government in exile had an alternative, Soviet-sponsored rival complete with its own army.

In Poland itself Stalin disposed of another political asset, the recently resuscitated Communist movement. The wartime history of Polish communism is lurid. The Polish Communist party, which had been founded in 1918, was dissolved at Stalin's orders in 1938. Those of its members who found themselves in the Soviet Union were executed. In 1942, after the Germans had invaded the Soviet Union, the party was reconstituted in Warsaw by Stalin's order and renamed the Polish Workers' party (Polska Partia Robotnicza, or PPR) in order to avoid the name "communist" which had foul associations in Poland. Initially the PPR busied itself by betraying the leaders of the AK and the government in exile to the Germans, while announcing a passionately patriotic program demanding an immediate rising against the Germans which, in the military circumstances, would have been suicidal. The AK, which had decided to refrain from major military efforts until a propitious moment, was viciously denounced as inert and unpatriotic.

The new Communist party in Poland denounced the government in exile as reactionary and unrepresentative and rapidly expanded its claims to speak for Poland. In December, the PPR, together with a handful of insignificant organizations, proclaimed themselves the National Council of the Homeland. Its chairman was Bolesław Bierut, a Soviet citizen entirely unknown in Poland.

The Polish government in exile was not allowed to attend the 1943 Teheran negotiations. Roosevelt and Churchill even refused to receive Mikołajczyk in advance of the conference to present his views. The fate of Poland was decided without the Poles being present. Teheran thus was to the war era what Munich was to the late 1930s a demonstration of the willingness of the Great Powers to decide the destiny of weaker nations without their consent. Poland's boundaries were redrawn using the Hitler-Stalin Pact of August 1939 to set the eastern boundary of Poland and capriciously providing her with partial compensation in the west by a major amputation of German territory. Thus Poland advanced westward to the line formed by the rivers Oder and Neisse (in Polish Odra and Nysa) and gained East Prussia in the north. However, the Soviets insisted that northern East Prussia, the area around the city of Königsberg today's (Kaliningrad) go to them. Moreover, the principle was acknowledged that the postwar Polish government would be "friendly" to Russia, meaning, in reality, that Poland would be under Soviet control. These facts were purposely omitted from the official protocols of the conference lest they make British and American dealings with the Poles awkward. Roosevelt noted that he had millions of Polish voters in the United States to consider and did not wish any public association with decisions regarding Poland.[13] Churchill was given the unpleasant task of convincing the Polish government in exile to acquiesce in what amounted to the country's fifth partition. Stalin made it clear that should the Polish government in exile not agree, he had alternatives, in other words the ZPP. The fact that this cynical arrangement was accompanied by loud declarations of fighting a war for freedom and democracy made the conference a landmark in diplomatic hypocrisy.

By 1944 the German position in the east was collapsing and the Red Army was moving rapidly toward Warsaw. Both the government in exile and the Polish underground authorities were in the throes of a cruel dilemma. Reports from the east indicated that the Polish underground units that had surfaced to assist Soviet forces entering Polish soil in pursuit of the retreating Germans had been arrested, even massacred. However, any effort to oppose the Soviet advance was obviously impossible: not only would it be suicidal, but it would play into Soviet hands by making the Poles appear to be the allies of the Nazis. Hence, the decision was made to order the AK to launch a major armed effort timed to coincide with the withdrawal or collapse of the German military in Poland. Originally conceived as a series of risings throughout Poland, the plan, named "Tempest" (*Burza*), was designed to make the Poles the liberators of their own country and thus present the advancing Soviets with a fait accompli. This would, it was hoped, give the Poles some bargaining position in the determination of Poland's future if only a symbolic one. Moreover, after almost five years of preparation, the AK was bound to fall upon the Germans at the first indication that their military position was weakening.

The greatest fear was that the Communist underground in Poland would begin a rising to coordinate with the Soviet advance and automatically draw the bulk of Polish forces into the struggle, giving the Communists the moral as well as practical leadership in liberating the country. It was decided to allow the AK commander in Warsaw, General Bór-Komorowski, to make the decision when to launch the Warsaw rising, choosing the precise moment between German withdrawal and Soviet arrival when the Poles might have a chance to retake their own capital. "Tempest" was to be an extraordinarily delicately timed operation. Under the conditions, however, it was doomed to failure. It was doubtful, however, whether the AK had any other serious options to pursue. Perhaps the greatest criticism that can be leveled against the government in exile is their completely unfounded assumption that the rising would gain the serious support of the Western powers who would then come to Poland's aid even if it meant confronting the Soviets in the process. Such a conclusion was utterly contradicted by the obvious tendency of Allied policy and constituted little more than wishful thinking.

Komorowski, a brave soldier but a man of limited ability, was given a daunting task. For weeks the advancing Soviets and local Communists had called on the Poles to rise up and evict the Nazis and had promised their support. Komorowski was well aware that his poorly equipped forces were no match for the *Wehrmacht* should they decided to delay their departure. Further, his knowledge of Soviet military moves and intentions could be only fragmentary, hence his decision for action, on August 1, 1944, was little more than a guess.

The famous Warsaw rising, a nightmare for the Poles, is still the subject of passionate debate. The rising gained only a portion of its military objectives. The Germans, at Hitler's express orders, canceled their evacuation and, heedless of their own strategic interests, concentrated on crushing the Poles. Meanwhile, the Soviets stopped their advance and neither aided the Poles nor allowed the Western powers to do so until all such efforts had no real significance. The result was sixty-three days of street fighting. On October 3, 1944, the last AK insurgent surrendered, and the Germans, though they had fought them with barbarity, granted the defeated the honors of war in tribute to their gallantry. The rising devastated the AK, resulted in massive civilian casualties, probably prompted Hitler's decision for the systematic destruction of Warsaw, and accomplished nothing save proving a legend of heroism in defiance of fate. About 10,000 members of the AK died on the streets of Warsaw, and a staggering 150,000 to 200,000 civilians fell along with them. In a few weeks, the Poles had lost almost the equivalent of the total American casualties of World War II. The Soviets labeled the rising a criminal folly and used it to demonstrate the political incapacity of the last devotees of the Second Republic.

By now the Soviets had prepared a new Polish government. In late July 1944, the ZPP rechristened itself the Polish Committee of National Liberation when they arrived, in the Red Army's baggage train, at Lublin, the first Polish city west of the border set at the Teheran Conference. This new body, which proclaimed itself a virtual government, was later known as the Lublin Committee.

The last months of the war were bitter indeed for the Poles. Polish units fought with conspicuous gallantry in the Italian campaign and across Western Europe after June 6, 1944, D-Day. Polish units played a worthy role at Falaise and later in Belgium and Holland. General Stanisław Sosabowski's elite Parachute Brigade was largely wasted in the fiasco of Arnhem, when allied troops made a bold move to break into north Germany in in operation "Market-Garden" in autumn 1944. These, however, were but episodes in the closing stage of the western front, and they were of no consequence for Poland.

Mikołajczyk, realizing that the Western powers had deserted Poland and that Soviet wishes would decide all fundamental questions, resigned in late 1944 to be followed by Tomasz Arciszewski whose obscurity signaled the arrival of the government in exile at total inconsequentiality. The Yalta Conference, held in February 1945, reflected this low point. As was the case at Teheran, the Poles were not invited to participate in the determination of their country's fate. At Yalta, Roosevelt, Churchill, and Stalin decided that a "Government of national unity" would be created for Poland, consisting of the Lublin Committee, cosmetically enlarged by a few nonentities. The Curzon Line, in other words the 1939 Hitler-Stalin frontier, was to be Poland's eastern border, with vague compensations at German expense in the west. The protests of the government in exile were vociferous and pointless. In Poland, the chief representatives of the AK and underground government, despite Soviet promises of safety, were arrested when they met with Soviet representatives. They were taken to Moscow, tortured, and accused, along with the whole of the AK, of being German collaborators. They were tried and sentenced to various terms of imprisonment.

As the war ended, Mikołajczyk and a few other obscure figures journeyed to Warsaw to join the new expanded Lublin Committee as the Polish Provisional Government of National Unity. Never politically adroit, Mikołajczyk harbored dim hopes of being a force for democracy and a Western orientation in a government otherwise clearly composed of Soviet flunkies. At best he hoped to be able to pursue a cooperative policy toward Stalin without losing his independence and his self-respect. He was deluded. He escaped when reality exposed the foolishness of his anticipations, and Communist control was consolidated in 1947.

In July 1945 the Potsdam Conference made the final determinations regarding Poland's borders. The line of the Oder-Neisse rivers was accepted as Poland's western frontier. In another symbolic demonstration of Poland's new reality, German compensations to Poland were to be settled by the Soviet Union which would allot Poland 15 percent of its own share.

In summer 1945 the triumphant Allies staged a victory parade in London. The Polish government in exile and its armed forces were not allowed to participate. A world away, in San Francisco, the founding conference of the United Nations was convened, and Poland was again absent. For Poland, the war had ended in utter disaster.

The causes of defeat require no elaboration. The Soviet Union did not wish to see Poland emerge from the war either independent or complete with its eastern territories. Both desires were informed by traditional Russian goals, whatever peculiar promptings Stalin's perversity and communism's dictates may have added. That the Soviet preferences proved decisive reflected the Western powers' dependence on Soviet sacrifices to defeat Germany. But this is not the whole of the story. Certainly wartime strategy was paramount in Western policy. But also powerful for London and especially Washington was the vision of a postwar world in which Moscow would be a principal architect of international security, rather than a rival. This desire for harmony did not come to pass. The resulting Cold War was not part of Western designs. The role for Poland in all of these vast schemes was insignificant, if not invisible.

For both Washington and London policy regarding Poland was fundamentally based on ruthless Realpolitik and comported ill with grand declarations of fighting a war for democracy and decency. The struggle against Nazism was cast as a moral crusade rather than a geopolitical struggle and this resulted in a number of awkward issues. Of course, Nazi Germany was repulsive, but the Soviet ally which helped bring it low was little less revolting. By defeating the menace to European civilization threatened by one totalitarian aggressor, Nazi Germany, only to engorge an equally voracious one, Soviet Russia, does not make a compelling case in either geopolitical or moral terms. Poland is at the middle of this paradox.

The war which Britain began in defense of Poland ended in her abandonment. The democracy which the United States claimed to be defending was not protected in Warsaw. Poland gave the Western powers a bad conscience and, as a result, was marginalized even before the conflict had ended. American war propaganda rarely mentioned Poland, and the virtual absence of Poland from the American cinema screen is a striking demonstration of how awkward Poland was for American government and public opinion to confront. Roosevelt's lack of interest in protecting Poland reflected well-established American traditions.

For Poland, World War II also represented the death of serious emigré politics. Since the partitions, the Poles had repeatedly counted on various communities of emigrés, first in Western Europe, and by 1914 in the United States as well, to provide moral and financial support, and on occasion political leadership, in international Polish politics. During World War II, the Polish emigration did not play a significant political role. Poland had a government in exile and did not need ad hoc associations of transplanted patriots. This is especially evident in the case of the United States. A large Polish community, well organized and with considerable assets, did little to influence Washington's policy regarding Poland. Certainly the comparison with the World War I era marks a striking decline in Polonia's ability to influence matters on Poland's behalf. Essentially, Polish Americans by 1941 were so assimilated into the larger American community that they did not act as an emigré lobby but rather as a fundamentally American group which felt constrained to accept the basic dictates of American policy. The bulk of Polonia—organized under the leadership of the Polish National Alliance, and eventually forming the Polish American Congress (PAC)—was unable to gain meaningful concessions from Washington, despite its considerable numbers and enormous efforts.

In simple terms, Polish Americans could not support Roosevelt and champion Poland at the same time. However, this does not mean to say that a Republican alternative existed for them. Roosevelt pursued an American position and it, not the man, was not inclined to Poland's long-range well-being. This realization was the death of illusion for Polonia.

NOTES

1. Wojciech Roszkowski has calculated that 664,000 died as a direct result of German military actions, and an additional 5,384,000 were killed during the German occupation for a total of 6,048,000. In addition, approximately 1.5 million soldiers and civilians were killed by the Soviets, though this number is only an estimate. The combined total of Polish wartime casualties is thus about 7.5 million. Some recent estimates of Polish Christian casualties are lower, and the issue is controversial.

2. The British had issued a "guarantee" of Polish independence in March 1939; Polish-French military and political agreements dated to the early interwar era.

3. Wolfgang Jacobmeyer, "Der Uberfall auf Polen und der neue Charakter des Krieges," in *September 1939: Krieg, Besatzung, Widerstand in Polen*, ed. Christoph Klessmann. (Göttingen, 1989), 16ff.

4. The separate Polish armies were not grouped into "fronts" or "groups" but were directly subordinate to Śmigły-Rydz in Warsaw. Thus when the vulnerable telephone lines (retained due to the costs of conversion to radio) that linked them were cut, not only did the central command lose control of the battle, but each army became unaware of its colleagues' actions.

5. Population figures for the Polish east are controversial. I have followed the argument put forth by Keith Sword in his *The Soviet Takeover of the Polish Eastern Provinces, 1939–41* (New York: 1991), xviii.

6. This figure, admittedly an estimate, comes from Wojciech Roszkowski's *Historia Polski, 1914–1991*, 2d ed. (Warsaw, 1992), 156.

7. *Volksdeutsche*, ethnic Germans imported from the east of Europe, were supposed to replace the ousted Poles. Too few of them were ever imported.

8. Józef Garlinski, *Poland in the Second World War* (New York, 1985), 31.

9. Richard C. Lukas, *The Forgotten Holocaust: The Poles Under German Occupation, 1939–1944* (Lexington, Ky., 1986), 18.

10. The exact number of Polish children thus kidnapped is very con-

troversial; 50,000 is the figure most recently cited in the specialized literature.

11. Regarding Żegota, see the comments in Stefan Korbonski. *The Polish Underground State: A Guide to the Underground, 1939–1945* (New York, 1981), 125.

12. Michael Alfred Peszke, "The Polish Armed Forces in Exile: Part I. September 1939–July 1941" *The Polish Review* 26, no. 1 (1981); 89.

13. Jan F. Karski, *The Great Powers and Poland, 1919–1945* (Lanham, MD and New York, 1985), 476–477.

8

Communism in Poland: The Construction of the PRL, 1945–1970

At the end of World War II Poland was a ruined country. The per capita material destruction was unmatched anywhere in the world. The cost of the devastation was a breathtaking thirteen times the national income for the last prewar year, 1938. Almost 40 percent of the entire productive capacity of the country lay in ruins, and two-thirds of the industrial base at least partially destroyed. In agriculture, livestock numbers had fallen catastrophically: two-thirds of the cattle, half of the horses, and more than 80 percent of the swine were gone; vast farming areas lay in waste; and buildings and supplies were devastated. The transportation system, still primitive in the Second Republic, was virtually inoperable: 80 percent of the railroad cars and engines were gone, the vast majority of bridges and rail lines along with them. Some cities had been virtually leveled: 44 percent of all the buildings in Warsaw had been destroyed, as well as nearly three-fourths of the city center. Many other cities were not much better off, including Gdańsk, Szczecin, Wrocław (the former German cities, respectively, of Danzig, Stettin, and Breslau), and Poznań, to name only the major centers.[1]

Population losses have already been mentioned—over seven million people—but to this number must be added the population of the *kresy*, or eastern borderlands, surrendered to the Soviets, the refugees from

Nazi or Soviet occupation unwilling or unable to return to a Communist land, and those who fell into Soviet hands after 1939 and were scattered throughout Siberia, Central Asia, and the far north. In 1946 Poland comprised fewer than 24 million, a 30 percent decrease from 1938, and this for a country with one of the continent's highest growth rates. This catastrophic demographic setback rivals the Black Plague or the Thirty Years' War in profundity.

Still more drastic was the external and internal reshaping of the country. The eastern territories were gone, ending centuries of Polish history in the *kresy*. They were supposed to be compensated for by gains in the west taken from Germany. However, the balance sheet for Poland in this geographical restructuring is problematical. To be sure, the new borders gained Poland a substantial Baltic coastline with several major ports (chiefly Szczecin and outright control of Gdańsk), which opened up the possibility of Poland's becoming a serious maritime power for the first time in many centuries. Mineral-rich Upper Silesia, now wholly in Poland, was also an obvious asset, and the land-tenure pattern of the western territories exhibited the predominance of fairly substantial farms, rather than the economically marginal dwarf holdings characteristic of the Polish east. The Communist regime was loud and indefatigable in celebrating this territorial acquisition, which it called the "Regained Lands" (*Ziemie Odzyskane*) to emphasize its historic attachment to Poland. The fact that the former German territory had enjoyed a higher level of prosperity also was stressed so that it appeared that the westward shift of Poland actually represented a civilizational advance—a new shape for a new, and presumably better, Poland.

Actually, the first of these claims is dubious and the second involves purposeful misrepresentation. To be sure, some of the lands given to Poland after the war had long connections to Poland and a substantial indigenous Polish population as, for instance, in Silesia. However, much of the territory had only the vaguest and most distant historic links to any Polish state, and the population was almost exclusively German; the region of Western Pomerania around Szczecin is a good example. As for its economic and social superiority, this assumed overlooking the damage done by the war. Some of the most bitter and destructive combat was fought on the Regained Lands, leaving them seriously damaged. After the war, the Soviets exactingly stripped the area of all its most valuable economic assets, bequeathing to the Poles a wasteland.[2] And, of course, the new western lands were far smaller than the lost eastern ones.

This massive redrawing of Polish frontiers, creating a compact, almost square, and much smaller country on the Soviet border, in effect canceled the entire historic experience of Poland by reconstructing the putative borders of the pre-Christian state. Poland, perhaps for the first time, was nationally and religiously homogeneous: the Germans killed the Jews, and the Soviets took the others. After 1945 Poland would be reconstructed on radically different foundations than those that had undergirded the state for a millennium.

The territorial despoiling of Germany would, naturally, produce much resentment toward Poland which, in turn, would require Warsaw to seek protection from the Soviet Union. The Western powers, with a combination of folly and negligence, were tardy and reluctant to recognize the new Polish western borders, although they had accepted Soviet seizure of eastern Poland with alacrity. Thus, in effect, only Moscow guaranteed the territorial integrity of postwar Poland. Thus, quite apart from the creation of a Communist bloc, Poland was drawn into the Soviet orbit by geopolitical necessity. Concomitantly, the Western powers repeatedly left themselves open to the charge of ignoring the most vital matters of Polish security. A profound feeling among many Poles of having been betrayed by the West was a convenient psychological factor for the Communists to exploit.

Between 1945 and 1948, Poland became integrated into the Soviet bloc, which stretched from the Baltic to the Adriatic. Within these several states, a simultaneous process of internal Sovietization—the modeling of the political, economic, and social structure after that achieved by the Soviet Center—soon accompanied by liberal doses of Russification, proceeded apace with international coordination as a protective buffer between Soviets and the West. For almost half a century, these states, including Poland, were removed from full membership in the European community with retardant effects that will take years to overcome. Poland, which culturally identified itself with Western Europe, became the main state of the new Eastern Europe, a term used to designate the Soviet satellites in Europe regardless of their previous historical evolution. Thus, the post-1945 political alignment would also extend retroactively to Poland's past which gradually, at least in the mind of the West, was assimilated into an often undifferentiated Communist bloc. For the Poles, the partition era seemed to have returned.

Internally, Poland was equally transformed. There was a bitter joke long retold after the war that mocked the old Polish tradition of calling a stranger "Pan" or "Sir": "Don't call me 'Pan'—the last of them died in the Warsaw rising," went the retort. This reflects not only the enforced democratization of discourse in postwar Poland, but also the social revolution caused by the war itself apart from Communist policies. Ever since the partitions, Poland had maintained a very traditionalist social ethos, and upwardly mobile Poles through the era of the Second Republic characteristically adopted the manners and habits of the gentry, including their archaically courteous speech. This, it seemed, died for good in the ruins of Warsaw in 1944. The Second Republic had been the last creation of the old Polish tradition, and it had not only failed, but been annihilated. In exile in London sat the successor of the Second Republic and hundreds of thousands of Poles who could not abide the Communist regime's version of modernization. They looked nostalgically, and hopelessly, to those traditions while a new Poland was being built along quite different lines. Millions of Poles abroad, including the huge Polonia of the United States, regarded the new Poland as alien; the link that had bound them to their ancestral homeland had been tainted if not severed.

POLITICS

The first postwar government of Poland had a most unappetizing origin. Negotiations were held in Moscow in the spring of 1945. The Americans were represented by President Franklin Roosevelt's special emissary, Harry Hopkins, whose concern for the Poles was slight indeed, Joseph Stalin agreed that the Lublin Committee would be expanded to twenty-one by the addition of five emigré Poles, but only those who had been approved by the Soviets. Stanisław Mikołajczyk, the former premier of the government in exile, the most prominent of the five, tried vainly to convince the Western powers to regard him as their means of maintaining influence in Poland. Although many of his compatriots in the Peasant party regarded him as a representative of the West, in reality he had no real leverage at all beyond what he could cobble together in Poland. Thus expanded, the Provisional Government of National Unity installed itself in Warsaw. Though supposedly representing five different parties, the Polish Workers' party (PPR) held all the key posts, including the Ministries of Defense and Public Security. Poland began its new history with a government created at the behest of its traditional enemy and staffed by a party that had never enjoyed a popular following.

The initial postwar years of Polish politics are exceedingly complex, though quite simple in outline. In essence, the Communists rapidly monopolized power in the state: opposition parties were preemptively declared illegal, crushed by terror, or subsequently neutralized and absorbed. The ability of the Communists to achieve this position is explained by a combination of a powerful Soviet military force menacingly stationed in the country—300,000 in late 1946—and the abandonment by the West of democratic elements in Poland. The population was demoralized, and most people were willing to accept the rule of the Communists if the resulting civil order would allow them to reconstruct their devastated country.

Hence, the powerful prewar, nationalist movement, or *endecja*: the Christian Democrats; and any other parties that could be classified as politically moderate or right were declared illegal. More open opposition to the Communists was dealt with brutally. Certain elements of the Home Army (AK) and the fanatically nationalist National Armed Forces (NSZ) maintained armed resistance to the new authorities for several years. The numbers involved are very difficult to ascertain, but many thousands were involved at least part-time in guerrilla warfare after 1945. In addition, elements of the Ukrainian nationalist movement continued to act on Polish soil. Their members were similarly hunted down and annihilated, often with the aid of Red Army units. Thus a virtual civil war raged in Poland, especially in its southern and eastern territories where the forests and mountains were a haven to insurgents for years. At least 30,000 Polish casualties, and possibly many more, resulted. This grisly chapter in Polish history still awaits complete elucidation. In any event, the most militant anti-Communists were removed from any legal participation in politics.

This left the political spectrum to a variety of socialists, as well as the peasant parties. Because the peasant parties represented, theoretically, the bulk of the Polish population, Mikołajczyk naively believed that he would be able to use them to gain a powerful non-Communist voice in the new government. His tortuous efforts to win a significant position for his party, the Polish Populist party (Polskie Stronnictwo Ludowe or PSL), were ultimately ineffectual. The first postwar elections, held in 1946 after much delay, were preceded by manipulation and intimidation and were conducted with farcical unfairness. As a result the so-called democratic bloc led by the PPR gained more than 80 percent of the vote, and the PSL won scarcely 10 percent. When seats in the *sejm* were allocated, the PSL was given only 28 seats of 444. This was the death of the party as a political force and left the Communists with no serious organized resistance. The Western powers busied themselves with meaningless protests over this logical culmination of their Yalta arrangements.

The new government elected the PPR's Bolesław Bierut president of Poland, certainly the most insignificant person ever to hold the office. Other leading lights were Władysław Gomułka, who had earlier served in the Provisional Government; the shadowy Jakub Berman, who was virtually a Soviet agent, omnipresent and indispensable; and the fearsome Stanisław Radkiewicz, who was head of the dreaded Security administration. A conveniently flexible interim Little Constitution was adopted, the government was reorganized with an even more obvious preponderance of PPR members, and the PSL was removed from the ruling team. Its membership collapsed, and Mikołajczk, who emerged as either naive or a buffoon, fled Poland in October 1947 with criticism and contempt adhering to him.

After their 1947 electoral "success," the PPR pressured the Polish Socialist party (PPS) into a forced merger, after first insisting that all independent voices be purged from the ranks of the PPS. The result was the 1948 creation of the Polish United Workers' party (Polska Zjednoczona Partia Robotnicza, or PZPR), which was dominated by the Communists. Shortly thereafter the remaining parties reorganized. The various peasant groups became the United Peasant party (Zjednoczone Stronnictwo Ludowe, or ZSL), and the PSL, with many of its leaders having been arrested, was absorbed. A tiny Democratic party (Stronnictwo Demokratyczne, or SD), which appeared shortly thereafter as a transformed version of the several Christian Democratic groups, was composed primarily of urban intelligentsia.[3] Poland was officially a multiparty state; however, two of the three parties were meaningless.

Within the PPR-PZPR two factions contested for predominance. The first, represented by Gomułka, favored a more independent path in the creation of a socialist Poland and opposed slavish copying of Soviet models, especially the collectivization of agriculture. By 1947, however, these "nationalists," as they were derisively called, had been ousted by the "Muscovite" faction, led by Bierut, who were little more than a colonial administration representing Moscow.[4] According to political scientist Jan M. Ciechanowski, "Gomułka and his followers had committed the cardinal sin of refusing to place the interests of the USSR before those of Poland."[5] A massive purge which ensued in the last half of 1948 removed 30,000 nationalists, and Warsaw became an obedient client of Moscow. This was the final step in the process that had begun with the formation of the Lublin Committee in 1944.

RECONSTRUCTION

The most dramatic internal reorganization of Poland was the massive population transfer that was carried out in the years immediately following the war. A large Polish population was expelled from the *kresy* now incorporated into the Soviet Union. As many as 1.5 million were resettled in the Regained Lands in the west where they were joined by several million Poles who had been moved from the densely populated central and eastern regions in an effort to create a better distribution pattern and replace the massive exodus of Germans.

This last phenomenon is extremely controversial. During the final stages of the war, almost 4 million Germans fled before the dreaded Soviet armies. Another 3 million were forcibly evicted after 1945. This exceedingly brutal operation resulted in great hardship and many casualties. For almost half a century, the issue was one of the many blank pages in the history of the Polish People's Republic (PRL) which refused to discuss so ugly an action. Moreover, due to their own conduct during the war, the Germans were incapable of gaining much sympathy for their own hardships in the immediate postwar period, although within Germany organizations of those expelled were not without influence. It is only since the fall of communism that the whole matter has been thoroughly discussed and the cruelty of the Polish treatment of the Germans fully exposed.

On the whole, this resettlement had long-lasting and, within a narrowly defined context, probably beneficial effects on Poland. The western lands were redistributed into potentially prosperous farms. The diminution of the population of eastern Poland allowed a substantial consolidation of dwarf holdings there and created a larger percentage of economically viable farms. In the process much was done to address rural poverty, though that problem has remained serious throughout the century, and it eliminated the estates of the *szlachta*, or gentry class, who now vanished from the Polish scene.

This enormous resettlement program was accompanied by an effort to make the assimilation of the Regained Lands a virtual national crusade. This engendered enthusiasm by Polonizing a vast new territory, making Gdańsk, Szczecin, and Wrocław into truly Polish cities and stimulating a considerable scholarly and popular interest in the Poles' historic and cultural roots in this area. Discerning Poles, however, realized that this was in effect a distraction from the gigantic and irreplaceable losses in the east, an area of incomparably greater historic and cultural significance to Poland.

In rebuilding the economic infrastructure of Poland, the Communists were at pains to reshape Poland into a more industrial and centralized economy. A rapid increase in state control restricted private ownership to small enterprises and petty retailing, so that as early as 1946 the private sector was producing less than 10 percent of the national income. Industry was nationalized by decree as early as 1946, whereas the banking and financial systems, which had not functioned during the war, were simply prevented from starting up again. The first of the several economic "plans" was tentatively unveiled in 1946; more would follow.

This crash rebuilding and restructuring program had mixed results. On the one hand, the rate of recovery to prewar production levels was astonishingly quick: real wages virtually attained their prewar levels by 1948, and the relatively unproductive agricultural population was markedly decreased as the economy became more diversified. Unemployment was largely eliminated by 1949. By that year, 6 million Poles had been settled in the Regained Lands, which had became substantially integrated with the rest of the country. On the other hand, industrialization was often developed unintelligently, emphasizing massive concentrations of heavy industry with already obsolescing Soviet technology. The Soviet fascination with industrial giantism was dutifully and foolishly repeated in Poland. Although it may have given a temporary boost to production figures, it also burdened the Polish economy with looming problems of unwieldy and inefficient industry and caused huge environmental damage. The 1947 decision to collectivize agriculture, though it was rescinded in 1956, was obviously a blow to any possibility of an efficient rural economy.

More immediately striking were the new government's plan to rebuild war-damaged cultural and historic places, quite apart from the economic utility of the effort. Especially significant was the emphasis on the reconstruction of Warsaw, which was enormously popular with all Poles, including the huge overseas population. By ordering the rebuilding of the capital's historic districts, including its churches, with fastidious care and aesthetic devotion, the Communist authorities did much to gain the grudging respect of the population. Here at least, they were seemingly acting as Poles first, regardless of their communism, and they helped convince the population that Poland could recover both materially and culturally from the unprecedented ravages of the war.

Although postwar Poland was almost uniformly Roman Catholic and ethnically Polish—perhaps for the first time in Polish history—the PRL was not without its minority problems. The PRL emphasized that the new Poland was nationally homogeneous, and its positive aspects were compared with the putative weakness and fragility of the multinational Second Republic. Unfortunately for this vision, the new borders did not, in fact, produce a completely "Polish" Poland. The PRL authorities tried to address this at the outset. The Germans were dealt with, as noted, wholesale and crudely, but subsequently the government claimed, mendaciously, that Poland was almost without a German minority. It was only with the fall of communism that a significant German minority was admitted, mostly in the region around Opole (the former German Oppeln) in Silesia. For decades the Polish Germans had been officially nonexistent, and many ethnic Germans passed as Poles.

Another awkward reality was the existence of a fairly large Ukrainian population. There were probably 150,000 Ukrainians and fellow eastern Slavic Lemkos[6] within the 1945 borders of the PRL. Most of them were resettled in the Regained Lands in the west, which conveniently allowed the authorities to scatter them to promote rapid Polonization. Recalcitrant Ukrainians, especially elements of the fanatically anti-Communist Ukrainian Insurgent Army (UPA) were the victims of Operation Vistula (*Akcja Wisla*), a systematic military campaign involving thousands of PRL troops and Internal Security forces. The Soviet role was considerable, but its exact dimensions are still unclear. A large number of Ukrainians were killed, and the whole operation was carried on with singular brutality.[7] For decades the propaganda of the PRL either ignored Operation Vistula or presented it in preposterous terms as a campaign against bandits. It was one of the most lurid of the blank pages that dotted the history of the PRL, and it has only recently received serious, and dispassionate, attention.[8]

A particularly ugly episode regarding the pathetic remnant of the Jewish population raised a number of disturbing questions. On July 4, 1946, in the city of Kielce, forty-two Jews were killed in an anti-Semitic riot.[9] Scattered reports suggest that anti-Jewish outrages were quite common in early postwar Poland as in Hungary and Slovakia, although no thorough, documented studies exist. It was obvious that the anti-Jewish attitudes growing in the Second Republic had not been eliminated by the war, and that the traditional association of Jews and Communism was even more profoundly settled in many minds. In addition, the regime demonstrated its willingness to exploit anti-Semitic prejudice for cynical political ends, a pattern that would be repeated, notably in 1968.

After the Holocaust, the fact that the scrap of Polish Jewry remaining could not resume their lives in security is a tragedy that did much to confirm the notion that Poland was a deeply anti-Semitic country, a conviction which has proven difficult to overcome.

FOREIGN POLICY

The foreign policy of the Communist government was based on a critique of the past and the trumpeting of a program to solve Poland's traditional security dilemma. Even the most virulent critics of the new order had to acknowledge that much of the government's foreign policy rested on a inescapably rational calculation of the Polish raison d'état. The war was the most obvious demonstration that the Second Republic's foreign policy assumptions had been unsound. The two implicit guidelines of Polish foreign policy had been that Poland could survive as a truly independent state without accepting a client status, and that the Western powers ultimately would aid Poland in defending its vital interests. By 1945 both postulates were difficult if not impossible to maintain. The PRL argued that Polish security required a close relationship with the Soviet Union, and the argument had much force. The possibility of German desire for revenge and the obvious indifference of the West to Poland's fate during the war did not suggest that any alternatives existed. Moreover, Soviet protection required the existence of allied, even subservient, Communist authorities in the Warsaw; foreign policy requirements dictated internal politics. Hence, although their visions of a socialist Poland were repulsive to many Poles, the new Warsaw authorities were able to win the cooperation, if not the affection, of much of the population, merely by stressing their irreplaceability.

In international affairs this made Poland a member of the Soviet bloc, which had been created by 1948. This had profound consequences. First, as the Cold War developed in the late 1940s, Poland's association with Moscow caused it to follow the Soviet lead in rejecting participation in the famous Marshall Plan—the 1947 effort by U.S. Secretary of State George C. Marshall to revive the European economy by massive American assistance. This obviously delayed Poland's economic recovery and required it to form a closer relationship with Moscow, which, in the early years, exploited its satellites, including Poland, shamefully. Organized economic plunder masqueraded as Soviet-Polish trade arrangements. Second, bloc membership deflected Polish commercial patterns away from their natural linkage to the West. The fact that Poland's major trading partner both before World War II and after 1994 has been Germany speaks for itself. Poland's integration into the Soviet security system, the Warsaw Pact, formed in 1955 as a counter to West Germany's entrance into the North Atlantic Treaty Organization (NATO), required Warsaw to expend vast resources on its military in order to contribute to Soviet imperial needs. This was obviously an enormous strain on its weak and rebuilding economy.

Polish membership in the Soviet bloc, in long historic terms, however, may well have served Poland's security interests. After the war, Poland was virtually incapable of defending itself, German-Polish relations were officially nonexistent, and the Polish public's attitudes were understandably bitter and fearful. Moreover, the Western powers had repeatedly indicated their indifference to Poland's fate and had quickly integrated West Germany into their military alliance. Hence, without some protection from the Soviets, Poland's postwar existence would have been hazardous indeed. The Warsaw Pact may well appear in historic perspective to have been a temporary shelter behind which Poland was able to regenerate itself. The relative international security Poland has enjoyed since 1991 rests on the integration of Germany, over long decades, into constructive membership in the European community, and the drastic weakening of Russian strength resulting from the dismantling of the Soviet Union. Neither of these conditions could be foreseen in 1945. Given the circumstances, Poland may well have gotten the best available deal, but the costs were tragically high.

Stalinism began in Poland with the consolidation of power by the PPR and the internal struggle against the so-called nationalist dissidents. Gomułka and a number of his most prominent allies were removed from the party and later arrested. The purges in Poland, unlike those in most of the other satellite states, did not result in trials and executions. A cult of Bierut, a provincial copy of the worship of Joseph Stalin in the Center, was encouraged, and his pictures, as well as quotations from his insipid writings, were everywhere displayed.

After 1948 a series of massive purges were carried out within the party and repressive measures rapidly broadened. The armed forces, administration, and even the cultural world were systematically vetted to remove anyone regarded as having a suspect background. The category of undesirables was very broad: anyone associated with the Second Republic, anyone who had relatives in the West, or anyone who had an incorrect (gentry or bourgeois) background. Obviously a large segment of the population was suspect. Thousands of qualified people were removed and were replaced by the more complaint, but often less competent. This ideologically inspired proletarianization of Poland's social system was to have long-lasting effects, and it marked a decided break with the social ethos of the Second Republic. Poland now had involuntary social proletarianization reversing the previous pattern of voluntary social "gentrification."

The security apparatus was greatly expanded, and its operatives penetrated every aspect of Polish society. By the end of 1947, it is estimated that the state security system employed an astonishing 200,000, half of them as a paramilitary force which worked closely with the large contingents of the Soviet Army stationed on Polish soil. At a secret conference of the security forces held in April 1947, Radkiewicz, the head of the security system, explained that since war between the Soviet Union and the West was inevitable, Poland must gird itself for the ordeal by neutralizing all unreliable elements. Waves of arrests and trials followed in which prominent editors, politicians, and veterans of the anti-German resistance were sentenced to long imprisonment or death. Many heroic veterans of the AK were arrested or simply murdered under mysterious circumstances. A series of mock trials were carried out within the military against scores of senior officers who had had long careers in the Second Republic and had later made the mistake of serving the PRL. They were subjected to various charges of espionage or counterrevolutionary activities and tortured; several were executed. Almost 100 penal camps were created to house the "class enemies" who filled them.

A simultaneous effort was launched to make Poland conform more closely to Soviet and Russian norms. Administrative reforms from local to national levels followed Soviet practices, culminating in the 1952 constitution, based on that of the Soviet Union. The parliament (*sejm*) was reduced to a merely formal existence; it enacted virtually no legislation for years. It was in that year that the country was officially renamed the Polish People's Republic (PRL), and in 1950 the judiciary was recast along Soviet patterns. The most visible aspect of this effort was the importation of Soviet personnel to staff key Polish positions. The most prominent of these was Marshal Konstantin Rokossovsky, a veteran of the Red Army, who was conveniently of partial Polish origin. Rokossovsky became a virtual Soviet viceroy in Warsaw laden with an incredible number of posts: marshal of Poland, minister of defense, deputy chairman of the Council of Ministers (i.e., the government), and a member of the PZPR's governing politburo. The Polish armed forces and security administration were soon swarming with Soviet personnel in Polish uni-forms. The mood of the era is represented by the declaration of a high party official: "The Soviet Union is not only our ally. This is the motto of our people. For us, for party members, the Soviet Union is our Fa-therland."[10]

Polish culture was subjected to a concerted drive to reform it according to Marxist lights. The Soviet doctrine of socialist realism became the new aesthetic standard. Many classics of Polish literature were no longer ac-ceptable for "class" reasons or because they were too obviously anti-Russian. Because few Polish works and authors were judged fully acceptable, the PRL was flooded with translations, usually from the Rus-sian, which fulfilled the ideological prerequisites. Marxism-Leninism be-came the ideological touchstone of all intellectual activity, often reaching absurd heights. Education had to be radically recast, with the major over-hauling of certain domains, like history, where the Soviet experience was to be normative. Russian-Polish relations were likewise rewritten, and a never-ending search for heroic working-class examples was undertaken. Soviet texts became mandatory reading in Polish schools, and the works of Lenin and Stalin were issued in huge numbers; 2.5 million copies were printed of Stalin's ten-volume ruminations. This required a wholesale purge of the universities and other educational and cultural institutions. Simultaneously, certain well-established themes and figures had to dis-appear from the curriculum or be reinterpreted in a new light. Józef Piłsudski became alternately excoriated and ignored. Thus was estab-lished the phenomenon of conforming to the party line regarding all issues—a line that constantly changed according to Moscow's whims. Over all poured a never-ending stream of propaganda:

> Ceaselessly repeated were reports about the successes of the USSR and the "Peoples Democracies", or the defeats and failures of the "imperialists" countries. . . . The creation of a war psychosis and spy-mania also served these goals. They tried to promote instinctive reactions, either negative or positive, in relation to phenomena vaguely defined in order to create emotional responses not under-standing. This imaginary world of "newspeak" also had an element of terrorism.[11]

Obviously, the restructuring of Polish culture and values met with opposition from the powerful Roman Catholic Church, to which virtually the entire nation at least nominally belonged. The regime pursued a policy of direct assault, though halting and hesitant, and subversion to unseat the intellectual and social position of the Church. Church land was nationalized, seminaries were closed, religious instruction was ended in schools, religious publications were curtailed and harassed, and many of the social agencies of the Church were discontinued. A virtual ban on construction for Church use was put into effect in 1952. All priests were required to swear an oath of loyalty to the PRL by 1953. The regime then launched a bolder initiative: several prominent clergymen were seized and tried on preposterous charges of espionage. In 1953 even the Primate of Poland, the austere and forbidding Stefan Cardinal Wyszyński, was placed under house arrest and prevented from exercising his office. Five other senior clerics were arrested shortly afterward. These acts no doubt increased the moral authority of the primate and his Church, and they underscore the difficulties the PRL had in dealing with the Church.

Simultaneously, the regime tried to construct a network of priests who would work with the party and cultivated a close relationship with Bolesław Piasecki, a former fascist and a politically malleable leader of PAX, a nominally Catholic social action organization (founded in 1949) which was allowed a broad range of activities and considerable financial resources, in return for collaborating with the regime. Ironically, PAX ultimately became a Frankenstein's monster for the regime as it served more readily as a channel of infiltration of the Church into the regime than the reverse. Groups of so-called patriot-priests were cultivated by the regime to divide the clergy. All the while, the government maintained a propaganda campaign against the Church as the bulwark of reactionary obscurantism and an obstacle to the intellectual and social modernization of Polish society.

This campaign was a failure, and it did little or nothing to reduce the traditional religiosity of the Polish people. Indeed, the fact that the Church was being attacked by so disreputable an institution as the government probably enhanced its status as witness to traditional Polish values. Although the outward activities of the Church were curtailed, all evidence suggests that the secularization of the population was not significantly advanced.[12] Indeed, the fact that postwar Poland had become almost religiously uniform meant that the Church was extraordinarily significant in Poland. In no other country of the Soviet bloc was any independent institution so powerful as the Roman Catholic Church in Poland. This was a daunting reality to the PZPR, and it had long-term consequences for the eventual reemergence of a non-Communist Poland. Because the Church had traditionally regarded itself as the defender of the national heritage, it served as an important element of continuity in Polish history which was otherwise redirected after 1945.

For all of its failings, the initial years of the PRL was suffused with a sense of mission: rebuilding the country and recapturing the western territories. Rapid economic progress gave a gloss of success to these years. However, by the early 1950s, the situation had darkened. Not only was the regime increasingly repressive as the PRL's version of Stalinism developed, but the country's economy was obviously stagnating if not regressing. Food rationing was introduced in 1951, though not for the last time; and real earnings declined abruptly and by 1955 were 36 percent below the 1949 level. The economic plan's goals were not being met, and the failing effort was being maintained only by massive investment of money and labor, creating inefficiencies and long-term difficulties. It was obvious that Communist control of the economy had been characterized by bureaucratization, waste, and mismanagement. The incessant propaganda of success was appearing increasingly ridiculous. There were even sporadic outbreaks of worker protest over economic conditions, notably in Poznań.

The intellectuals, many of whom had been leftist before 1945 when they had found aspects of the Marxist-Leninist doctrine of the PRL at least fascinating, were seriously disillusioned. In 1954 Józef Światło, a high functionary of the state security system, defected and broadcast lurid, and unfortunately accurate, accounts of the realities of PRL politics back into Poland via Radio Free Europe. His revelations, widely heard in Poland, were acutely embarrassing to the regime. In 1955 the Crooked Circle Club was formed in Warsaw and quickly spawned forty branches nationwide. Essentially a forum for discussion among intellectuals, its willingness to dispense with the lifeless formalism of socialist realism led to passionate debates over contemporary problems, which increasingly involved workers as well. The symbol of the era was Adam Ważyk's satiric "Poem for Adults" (*Poemat dla dorosłych*), whose bitter sarcasm and mockery directed at the fraudulence of Polish communism was widely quoted.[13]

Although Stalin had died in 1953, his minions throughout the Soviet bloc were unsure of what line to pursue until new leadership was firmly ensconced in the Kremlin. Because this took until 1956, there was increasing vacillation and chaos in Warsaw as hard-liners and reformers jockeyed for position. In February 1956, Nikita Khrushchev, Stalin's Successor made his famous Secret Speech before the 20th Party Congress in

Moscow, in which he denounced the excesses of Stalin. Bolesław Bierut, then in Moscow, dropped dead.[14]

Khrushchev's speech was almost immediately widely circulated in Poland. The party leadership in Warsaw was sharply divided. The so-called Puławy faction favored a pragmatic accommodation of social grievances, whereas the Natolin group wanted to continue the hard-line and displayed a striking penchant for anti-Semitism. The Kremlin favored the Natolins with whom Rokossovsky was closely associated. A considerable struggle ensued.

Under mounting public pressure, a number of concessions were made by the regime, though no clear policy of liberalization was decided. The worst of the Stalinists were removed, and the security police was reduced in size and their activities were curtailed. In April tens of thousands of political prisoners, predominantly AK veterans, who had long languished in captivity, were pardoned. The *sejm* was allowed, even encouraged, to undertake greater activity. The Church demanded a return to a more active social role. Student organizations became boldly outspoken, and a large number of factory meetings demanded improvements in living standards, as well as release from the iron dictates of the now discredited economic plan.

The PRL was faced with a triple crisis: a faltering economy, revelations of widespread abuse which undermined the prestige of the authorities, and a paralyzing internal debate within the party hierarchy advocating contradictory responses. Thus the regime confronted an amorphous aggregation of discontented workers and frustrated intellectuals. The crisis reached critical mass in June 1956 in the western metropolis of Poznań.

Factory unrest had been brewing for months in Poznań, and the regime's promises of improvement had been dishonest, exacerbating the situation. In late June, a workers' committee called for a general strike and a mass demonstration. Approximately 100,000 gathered on June 28 in the city center where they sang religious and patriotic songs and demanded economic changes. The demonstrators congregated outside party and security headquarters, then burst into the prisons freeing the inmates. Security forces answered with water cannon, then small arms; demonstrators fell. Troops were dispatched to quell what was deemed a "pro-German riot." The shooting lasted until the next day and left 75 dead and 800 wounded. Hundreds were arrested. By blaming the incident on "imperialist agents," the regime further discredited itself in the eyes of the population, already sickened by the brutal suppression. The supposed "workers' government" had killed Polish workers. Not for the last time would the Communist authorities in Poland be embarrassed by the presence of foreigners at an awkward moment. The Poznań riot coincided with the huge annual International Trade Fair in Poznań, and thousands of foreigners, including United Nations Secretary General Dag Hammarskjöld, witnessed the events.

The Poznań riot exacerbated the crisis within the PZPR, which was now virtually paralyzed by conflicting impulses. The Pulawy reformers stressed the growing popular discontent, and the Natolin group was ever more dependent on the Kremlin. Władysław Gomułka, long advertised by the reformers as uniquely placed within the party to placate public distrust because of his earlier punishment for nationalism, was restored to power, replacing the vacillating Edward Ochab, who had filled the small shoes left by Bierut's recent death. Gomułka responded by removing some of the worst Stalinists, including Rokossovsky, and replacing them with his own coterie. The Kremlin was alarmed by the independence of these actions. On October 19, Khrushchev, accompanied by the top Soviet political and military officials, arrived in Warsaw. Simultaneously, Soviet units in Poland marched on Warsaw, and the Soviet Baltic Fleet moved menacingly toward the Polish coast. A violent series of meetings between the Soviet and Polish Communists ensued. Eventually Gomułka and Ochab were able to convince Khrushchev that the new PZPR team in Poland could succeed in regaining public trust and thus restore order. This, in turn, would guarantee continued Communist control in Poland and leave Soviet security structures, including the Warsaw Pact, intact. Khrushchev was persuaded of the wisdom of this argument, and the Soviets soon departed leaving the PZPR to reorganize itself.

Gomułka's tenure began promisingly. He boldly denounced many abuses of the regime and promised reforms, and a number of specific improvements of both real and symbolic importance were made. One-hundred thousand Poles were allowed to return from Siberia where they had languished since World War II. The Soviet economic exploitation of Poland largely ended. The regime ceased its open persecution of the Church and Cardinal Wyszyński was released. A Catholic group, *Znak*, was allowed representation in the *sejm*. And the Club of Catholic Intellectuals (KIK) was allowed to form in a number of cities. (Emerging quickly as a leading light of the KIK was Tadeusz Mazowiecki who later became prime minister of post-Communist Poland.) No longer on the defensive, the Church gradually became a powerful force over the next decades, as communism failed as both an intellectual and practical system. The collectivization of agriculture was ended, never to be resumed.

Socialism thus never established itself in the countryside—Marx's "rural idiocy"—which remained the bastion of traditional Poland. Perhaps most fundamentally, Gomułka enunciated the notion of a "Polish road to socialism," something he had endorsed a decade before and had paid for dearly. This ended, indeed reversed, the increasing Sovietization and Russification under way in Poland. The removal of Russians from many posts, including the despised Rokossovsky, was a symbol of this change.

Most of the concessions proved short-lived, however, and the promised overhaul of the economy never materialized. Even the seeming liberality of the new regime regarding intellectual expression was ephemeral, and Gomułka increasingly showed himself to be a narrow, rather sour philistine and anti-Semite.[15] Thus, the "Polish October" of 1956 is difficult to evaluate, and its significance has altered with lengthening perspective. At the time it appeared to be a modest victory for Polish national sentiment, and Gomułka enjoyed a brief, grudging, but real respect as a "good Pole" who had defended national interests against Moscow. Perhaps more important, his ability to appease the Soviets while pacifying the most passionate dissenters at home allowed Poland to avoid the fate of Hungary, where a more radical protest against communism resulted in Soviet invasion and great suffering in 1956.

However, as time passed, the fact that the regime had managed to maintain untrammeled control of the country and avoid radical reform cast doubt on the real significance of the Polish October. The fact that Gomułka's regime was more authoritarian at its close in 1970 than it had been at its inception made 1956 appear to be pyrrhic victory at best for Poland. However, after the overthrow of communism, 1956 has again taken on a larger significance. It certainly ended the increasingly repressive Stalinist system, and it established the notion that the wishes of the population could not be ignored by the regime with impunity. The Poles had taken to the streets and had, albeit partially and transitorily, influenced the party's decisions. Perhaps Gomułka was really not a patriot in any meaningful sense, but he was widely reputed to be one, and Polish patriotism was shown to have continuing potency.

In 1956 discontent had been widespread but unfocused and unorganized. The intellectuals' unhappiness over the constraints of socialist realism, the workers anguish over poor living conditions, and the Church's bridling under repression did not coalesce into a coordinated movement of resistance with a program for change and a vision for the future. When the various forces of discontent could be focused, the party would be doomed. But, in 1956, international circumstances were certainly not propitious to the overthrow of communism in Poland, regardless of how willing and able the Poles were to attempt it. Moscow was still dedicated to maintaining its Eastern European empire, and as events in Budapest showed (where Soviet tanks crushed a popular rising in November), they were willing to act brutally to do so. The Western powers had long been in the habit of denouncing the evils of the Iron Curtain and bewailing the fate of those behind it, but they were disinclined, and probably unable, to do anything to alter it. Hence, the Poles achieved in 1956 probably as much as they could. More would require changes in both Polish society and the international context.

Gomułka was not a dedicated reformer, and soon after October he became as critical of liberalization as he had been of the Stalinists earlier. The era from 1957 to 1963, known as the Little Stabilization (*mała stabiliizacja*), was a generally uneventful period in which Gomułka was sustained by the goodwill engendered by the initial reforms and the hopes that a "second October" would follow to reorganize the economy and allow greater popular participation in government. Neither hope was fulfilled.

As early as 1957, the impetus to reform within the party had ended, and a renewed hard-line appeared. Over the next months a party purge expelled many so-called revisionists, but there was no wholesale removal of dissidents. The result was a peculiar division between Gomułka and the inner circle, and the rest of the country.

Deep difference about the ends and means of "building socialism" remained under the surface of conformity to the current Party line. The mass media, the universities, the professional organizations, and the intelligentsia remained overwhelmingly reformist at heart, while the party and state bureaucracy, both central and local, continued to be conservative in their sympathies. This harboured the possibility of a future conflict.[16]

In effect, Gomułka was wagering that it was not ideological issues but practical, material improvement that would stabilize the country and win the eventual support of the population for continued Communist rule. Hence, the ability of the PZPR to be a good steward of the Polish economy was central. Unfortunately, Gomułka proved a rather unimaginative traditionalist and an economic illiterate. He reemphasized investment in heavy industry and maintained the clumsy planning fetish albeit with elaborate cosmetic changes. The criticism by Polish economists that a more market-sensitive system, called market socialism in some quarters, must be installed was resisted by Gomułka, and the Polish economy was stabilized largely as a result of considerable loans from the United States, where Gomułka was long regarded as an anti-Stalinist and thus accorded a measure of support. In 1959 ambitious targets were set for a new seven-year plan. Optimistic goals, however, of increased labor productivity failed to materialize; the agricultural sector, which was starved of investment for ideological reasons, declined drastically; and real wages were virtually stagnant. Severe weather in 1962 and 1963 devastated agriculture and ended food exports which, in turn, precluded hard currency earnings. By 1963 the economy was in crisis, again, and the plan had to be largely scrapped. Perhaps the most ominous economic news was the realization that increases in productivity were only being managed by ever greater capital investment, resulting in growing structural inefficiency and an essentially irrational system.

Despite repeated efforts made in the 1960s to salvage the planned economy, the figures continued to be disappointing and the outlook for fundamental improvement bleak. Agriculture was bedeviled by contradictory policies. In 1965 the party decided to increase investment in this sector—reversing its established practice—but soon after Gomułka capriciously decided to end the grain imports essential for livestock feed. The result was a predictable stagnation, punctuated by catastrophic yields in years of bad weather.

In order to maintain high investment rates and find additional capital for modernization, the regime made the politically unwise decision to skimp on spending for consumer needs, housing, and social services. The result was a visible decline in the quality of life, increasing housing shortages, and the virtual stagnation of wages. A last-minute program of radical reforms, cobbled together by Bolesław Jaszczuk at Gomułka's behest, was far too late; by then, Gomułka had squandered the political capital he had amassed in 1956.

As the economy floundered and social frustration grew, the political atmosphere underwent a strange evolution. In the mid-1960s a new hard-line faction emerged with an accompanying resurgence of the security apparatus. These new hard-liners, called the Partisans, combined ruthless persecution of "revisionism" with a strident nationalism featuring martial overtones and an increasingly anti-Semitic rhetoric. Led by Mieczysław Moczar, a veteran of the wartime People's Army (AL) who later served in state security, the Partisans rapidly gained a powerful position within the state and party apparatus, especially the security administration. Moczar, who was minister of internal affairs, used his position as head of the Union of Fighters for Freedom and Democracy (Związek Bojowników o Wolnośc i Demokrację, or ZBoWiD), a veterans' organization, to build bridges to former AK members both in Poland and abroad. Simultaneously he enormously expanded the national auxiliary police, ORMO (Ochotnicza Rezerwa Milicji Obywatelskiej), which became a mass organization with paramilitary trappings designed to embed the Partisan movement broadly in the population. The rise of the Partisans was accompanied by the regime's return to wholesale repression of the intellectuals and the Church which made the late 1960s unpleasantly reminiscent of the Stalinist era a decade earlier.

Already in the mid-1960s there was an obvious stirring among students and young intellectuals, the so-called revisionists, who still expressed loyalty to socialism and phrased their concerns using Marxist terms. In 1965 two Warsaw University graduate students, Karol Modzelewski and Jacek Kuroń, composed an "Open Letter to the Party" in which they argued that however necessary rapid industrialization had been, the result was the creation of a huge, parasitic bureaucracy which now stultified society. They concluded by calling for "absolutely independent" trade unions.[17] Both men were arrested and jailed for three years, but they became the intellectual and moral leaders of the student population. A year later, in 1966, a controversial lecture, given by the prominent philosopher Leszek Kołakowski criticizing the "squandered hopes" of 1956 at Warsaw University, resulted in Kołakowski's expulsion from the PZPR and reprisals against many of the students attending the lecture, including the brilliant student leader Adam Michnik. There was a strong reaction within the faculty and a residue of bitterness.

In March 1968 a performance of *Forefathers* (*Dziady*), a movingly patriotic, openly anti-Russian play written by the nineteenth-century Romantic poet Adam Mickiewicz, was closed by the authorities in Warsaw, touching off student demonstrations which were broken up with violence. Intellectuals and the Church protested as the demonstrations spread to other cities. Thousands of students were arrested, and a major purge of professors was carried out. Far more significant was the regime's explanation for the difficulties: the disturbances were the work of a Zionist conspiracy somehow linked to West Germany. The tiny Jewish population in Poland was held responsible for stirring up unrest, threatening Poland's international position, and a host of other outrages. The Partisans were particularly prominent in the ensuing anti-Zionist campaign, which reached absurd proportions and led to the wholesale removal of Jews from many positions. Gomułka offered to give exit permits for Israel to any Polish Jew who requested one.

Much about this episode remains unclear. There is some evidence that the closing of the performance of *Dziady* was a deliberate provocation by the authorities and the campaign had been prepared in advance. Whereas the Partisans were the principal champions of the Anti-Zionist campaign, Gomułka alternately embraced and distanced himself from the affair. It appears that the Partisans were making a bid for dominance in the party, and Gomułka was forced temporarily to maneuver to maintain his position before regaining the initiative by the end of the year. His ability to resist them rested in considerable degree on the support he enjoyed from Moscow, which appreciated his steadfast loyalty—he had joined the Soviet Union in the invasion of Czechoslovakia in August 1968—and the trepidation in the Kremlin over the implications of the Partisans exploitation of Polish nationalism which inevitably would have anti-Russian, if not anti-Soviet overtones.

The "March events" led to the emigration of the bulk of the tiny remaining Jewish community in Poland, then perhaps 30,000, and gave Poland an international reputation for crude anti-Semitism. The repression that followed further alienated the intellectuals and made Gomułka a despised figure. The revisionist dreams of a humane socialism, which had come to grief in Prague in 1968, had fared badly in Poland as well. The possibility of a reform of the system within a socialist context—making democratic a system founded in Bolshevism—had been dealt a serious, perhaps fatal, blow.

Over the next few years, a large number of discussion groups appeared throughout Poland. All small, some ephemeral, they were spawned by scouting groups, student societies, religious organizations, even hiking clubs. Their ideological coloration was from avowedly Marxist through traditionalist Catholic and even radical *endecja*, or nationalist. In Lublin a theologian argued, "A human community only then has a correct structure when a rightful opposition not only possesses the right of citizenship but is also endowed with the potential for effectiveness needed by the common good and demanded by the right of participation." This common good, theologian Karol Wojtyła (later to become Pope John Paul II), found in "solidarity."[18] The intellectual framework for the emergence of an integrated civil society was being laid.

Equally striking about the 1968 events is the failure of the workers to play any role. Indeed, the evidence suggests that the regime's efforts to portray the students and intellectuals as irresponsible, spoiled hooligans was not without echo among the workers, who largely remained aloof from the protests. It is this reason alone that allowed Gomułka to hang on to power a bit longer.

Gomułka's regime lasted until the end of 1970, when it hastened its own destruction by insensitive economic measures. On December 13, the government announced major price increases on food and other consumer goods just when the population could be assumed to be making their Christmas purchases. Aggrieved by years of privation, the population erupted. Thousands of shipyard workers in the Gdańsk went on strike and staged demonstrations. Police intervention enraged them, and a riot ensued in which the local party headquarters was torched. There were casualties and arrests. Over the next few days, the demonstrations spread along the Baltic coast to Gdynia, Elbląg, and eventually Szczecin. The regime rushed a high-level team of officials to the area and sealed off communications for the whole region. The army appeared in tanks, and the government declared a state of emergency. Party officials tried to intimidate the strikers with threats of Soviet intervention. Strikers who had initially confined their demands to a rollback of the price increases and other economic measures, now added calls for freedom of the press and religion as well as real unions not run by the regime. Significantly, one of the first actions of the workers in Gdańsk was to send a delegation to the local university to apologize to the students for the workers' failure to support them in 1968.

Gomułka, who had become increasingly autocratic with time, declared the workers counterrevolutionaries and refused to conduct any negotiations with them. Sympathy for the Baltic cities spread throughout Poland, and on December 15 Gomułka rejected the idea of a political solution and decided to use force to restore order. (Contrary to a legend later circulated, the then Minister of Defense, General Wojciech Jaruzelski, did not demur and agreed on the deployment of the army against the population.) Obviously convinced that the situation on the coast was gaining momentum, Gomułka turned to the Kremlin for support.[19] This was a momentous decision, and it indicates just how seriously Gomułka viewed the situation—the use of Soviet troops would have had incalculable consequences. Whatever claims Gomułka may have had as a patriotic Pole he squandered in mid-December 1970.

The situation along the Baltic, especially in the so-called tri-cities of

Gdańsk, Gdynia, and Sopot, continued to worsen as strikes, demonstrations, and clashes with police and troops led to further casualties. On the morning of December 17, troops suddenly opened fire on a crowd in Gdynia; a pitched street battle followed leaving scores dead; clashes in Szczecin were also violent. The regime declared the riots, now in the third day, the work of "enemies of Poland and of socialism."

The situation led to a stormy meeting of the PZPR politburo. Gomułka and his closest supporters—in typical PZPR fashion—were given the sole blame for the situation and removed. Edward Gierek, a Silesian miner with a reputation for toughness and managerial competence, replaced him as first secretary. The new leader called for national calm and allowed that the party had lost touch with the workers, which was obvious. He ritualistically promised reforms and denigrated his predecessors. Given the fact that the violent nature of the events along the Baltic was unknown to the bulk of the Polish population, Gierek's seeming moderation and good sense were widely greeted as an improvement. It was only years later that the truth of the events of December were made known. The regime's admission that 45 were killed and more than 1,000 were injured was false: later research disclosed several hundred deaths with many thousands wounded.

In 1956 Gomułka had been returned to power because he was widely regarded as the one Communist who could rally public opinion; fourteen years later, he left because he had unquestionably alienated it. For the first time the Polish public had brought down a PRL regime; it was a lesson not lost.

The Gomułka years brought neither long-term political consolidation nor sustained economic growth. Cultural freedom was more restricted at the end of his tenure than at any time since the depth of Stalinism. Although many of the strategic gains of 1956 were not dismantled, historian M. K. Dziewanowski is perhaps right in characterizing the era as a sustained retreat. The PZPR's Jakub Berman contended that Gomułka was frightened at the very outset of his return to power in 1956 by the "mood of independence [that] had swept the country like a wave" and he "had to stop it because he wouldn't be able to control it and in the end it would sweep him away. Like an ocean."[20]

In retrospect the first quarter century of the PRL produces a mixed but, on the whole, not particularly impressive balance. To its credit must certainly go the virtual ending of illiteracy and the spread of popular education. Social inequality was largely ended by the closing of the gap between rich and poor. Unemployment was eliminated, and the western territories were assimilated and largely repopulated. A modern industrial base was created and wartime devastation rebuilt. Most important, Poland had been granted a generation of peace. However, even this list is subject to qualification. Certainly the social leveling was as much the result of universal impoverishment as better wealth distribution. Even here the senior party loyalists had come to constitute a new class with material perquisites to match their political power. The questionable long-term contribution of PRL economic management has already been discussed.

The Gomułka era saw Poland emerge again from utter inconsequentiality in world affairs. Although the so-called Rapacki Plan for a nuclear-free Europe received no serious attention when it was proposed in 1957, it can be viewed as a step toward European unity and strategic German-Polish cooperation. Indeed, the Polish-German relationship was the central factor in Poland's evolving international position. In 1965 the Polish episcopate issued a "Letter to the German bishops" in which it attempted to advance reconciliation of the two nations by asking and extending forgiveness for historic wrongs, and invited the German episcopate to attend the ceremonies marking the millennium of Poland's conversion in 1966. The regime was outraged, and even many non-Communists were displeased by the bishops' action. However, in retrospect, it reflects the Church's traditional insistence that it acts in the light of Poland's long-range interests, not from the promptings of temporary fashion. Given the centrality of Polish-German amity to Poland's status in Europe in the twenty-first century, the bishops' action appears to have been prescient and perhaps the first significant step to a strategic reconciliation of these two peoples so long bitterly divided.

A few years later, German Chancellor Willy Brandt signed an accord in Warsaw recognizing the immutability of the post-1945 Polish-German border and renouncing all territorial claims. Polish security in the west was historically strengthened. Ironically, this step, the zenith of Gomułka's stewardship of Warsaw's foreign relations, undercut Warsaw's need to rely on Moscow in foreign affairs, the essential claim the Communists used to justify their control in Poland. Gomułka's Poland was a transition stage in Polish history in which the raison d'être of Communist control and Soviet domination were being gradually undermined. It was the preface to the reemergence of a free Poland.

NOTES

1. Kraków, miraculously, was spared destruction when the Germans abandoned the city with unanticipated haste owing to a Russian offensive.

2. Not content to strip the German lands destined for Poland, the Soviets also economically plundered former German lands held by Poland since 1918.

3. The nucleus was the revived version of the 1937 Democratic party (Stronnictwo Demokratyczne.)

4. Gomułka, of proletarian origin from Eastern Galicia, spent the war in Poland. He had long urged cooperation with other left-wing parties to broaden the extremely narrow base communism enjoyed in Poland. Among his closest collaborators were Marian Spychalski, Władysław Bieńkowski, and Zenon Kliszko. All would share Gomułka's disgrace after 1947, as well as his triumphal return in 1956. The Muscovites—Bierut, Hilary Minc, Berman, and Roman Zambrowski—had all spent the war in Russia. As noted by M. K. Dziewanowski, the nationalists boasted of their deeper domestic roots or contacts with the masses and often ridiculed the slavish obedience of their rivals toward the Soviet authorities while, secretly perhaps, envying the Muscovites better contacts with "the Center." While many Muscovites were of Jewish extraction, most natives (i.e., nationalists) were ethnic Poles. See M. K. Dziewanowski, *Poland in the Twentieth Century* (New York, 1977), 163.

5. R. F. Leslie, ed., *The History of Poland Since 1863* (Cambridge, England, 1980), 297.

6. The identification of the Lemkos is controversial. Ukrainian nationalists regard them as part of their nation, but increasingly they are identified as a separate, though certainly kindred, national community.

7. Operation Vistula was not widely publicized at the time. It has been conjectured, however, that even had the Polish population been aware of the outrages, little criticism would have resulted because profound grievances remained toward the Ukrainians as a result of the memories of the Wołyn massacres of the war era. See Tadeusz Andrzej Olszanski, "All About 'Operation Wisla,' " *Ukrainian Quarterly* 2 (Summer 1991). Unfortunately the translation is very poor.

8. During World War II, the Nazis allowed Ukrainian nationalists to massacre Poles in the east. This horrible episode did much to harden Polish hearts to the postwar plight of the Ukrainians. Much mutual recrimination burdens Polish-Ukrainian relations.

9. The circumstances of the events in Kielce are still unclear and controversial.

10. Quoted in Wojciech Roszkowski, *Historia Polski, 1914–1991* (Warsaw, Naukowe PWN 1992), 190.

11. Roszkowski, *Historia Polski,* 212.

12. Particularly valuable in this context is Maciej Pomian-Srzednicki, *Religious Change in Contemporary Poland: Secularization and Politics* (London, 1982).

13. Quoted in Norman Davies, *God's Playground. A History of Poland.* Volume 2, *1795 to the Present* (New York, 1982), 582.

14. The circumstances of Bierut's death are still controversial.

15. This despite his Jewish wife who, it seems, was very sensitive to any reference to her Jewish origins. See Michael Checinski, *Poland: Communism, Nationalism, Anti-Semitism* (New York; 1982), 142–43.

16. Zbigniew Pelczynski, quoted in Leslie, *The History of Poland Since 1863,* 369.

17. The Kurón-Modzelewski "Open Letter to the Party," in Gale Stokes, ed., *From Stalinism to Pluralism: A Documentary History of Eastern Europe Since 1945,* 2d ed. (New York, 1996).

18. Karol Wojtyla, "Toward a Philosophy of Praxis." excerpted in Alfred Bloch, ed., *The Real Poland: An Anthology of National Self-Perception* (New York, 1982), 196ff.

19. Gomułka's negotiations with the Soviets at this point remain unknown.

20. Teresa Torańska *Them: Stalin's Polish Puppets* (New York, 1987), 298–99.

9

Collapse of the PRL, 1970–1990

The events of 1970 brought a new ruling team into power in the Polish Peoples' Republic (PRL), but the changes were more superficial than real. Despite a brief burst of economic dynamism in the years following, the Polish economy soon sank under the weight of the same rigid practices that had doomed it earlier: bureaucratization, irrational pricing and resource allocation, low productivity, and inefficient use of capital. The visible collapse of the economy again demonstrated the incapacity of the Communists to act as wise stewards of the nation's welfare. Failure here left them without any justification for power for they certainly had done nothing to legitimate their authority which rested ultimately on coercion and inertia rather than on popular support. Having long ago exhausted its collection of new ideas, the regime had nothing to offer but the repetition of failed programs launched with the same windy exhortations. By the last quarter of the century communism, which had so long proclaimed itself the agency of the future, was clearly a relic of the past, a reactionary collection of tired phrases repeated insincerely by a fossilized bureaucracy of unimaginative mediocrities.

The periodic crises that vexed the PRL would eventually bring it to ruin, but only at such time as the international situation allowed the regime to fall of its own weight. Communism in Poland failed to root itself in the country, never became essentially *Polish*, and always remained a product of a certain historic moment: the Soviet determination at the close of World War II to consolidate Eastern Europe under its imperial control. Once Moscow lost the ability, or confidence, to maintain the empire, communism in Poland was doomed, and it collapsed with an ease that stunned the world. In its death the PRL retroactively vacated its claim to ever having been the legitimate government of Poland.

The fall of Władysław Gomułka and the advent of Edward Gierek ushered in a protracted struggle for predominance in the Polish United Workers' Party (PZPR). For all of 1971 the party hierarchy was divided among besieged adherents of Gomułka, Gierek loyalists, and a powerful faction of Mieczysław Moczar's Partisans who all jockeyed for position. The Partisans had advocated a tough line regarding the disorders along the Baltic and were highly critical of the Gierek response of negotiations and promised reforms. However, Gierek showed himself to be both a skillful party infighter and a surprisingly adroit politician at winning over dissatisfied workers, and he emerged as the man who defused the crisis without expanded bloodshed and hence enjoyed wide support within the party, as well as the gratitude of Moscow for maintaining stability.

Gierek blamed all Poland's woes upon the Gomułka regime's having "lost touch with the masses," which was undoubtedly true. He had the self-confidence to go directly to the striking factories at the Baltic cities and confront the workers with promises of improved conditions and emotional calls for trust and support. This folksy approach was remarkably successful and rapidly won Gierek the reputation of being someone who was sincerely trying to save a bad situation. These efforts were accompanied by a series of symbolic gestures designed to show that he represented a new, more populist communism sensitive to the concerns of the people, unlike the regime of the ascetic and bad-tempered Gomułka. Although initially opposed, Gierek relented to a rollback of the price increases announced in December 1970 which had touched off the demonstrations. He announced plans to rebuild the magnificent Warsaw Royal Castle (destroyed by the Germans during World War II), an idea Gomułka had rejected as a costly and meaningless gesture. It now became a public relations success cost free to the regime because the whole project was financed by public donations. Gierek also adopted a more friendly attitude toward the Church, including arranging a meeting between premier Piotr Jaroszewicz and Stefan Cardinal Wyszyński.

By the end of 1971 Gierek had consolidated his position within the party and had ended the popular discontent that had brought down his predecessor. The Partisans were defeated and their leader, Moczar, gradually demoted to inconsequentiality. This lull, however, would be only a temporary one unless Gierek could devise bold, new policy initiatives to break Poland out of its deepening economic problems. In many ways Gierek was actually in a weaker position in 1971 than Gomułka had been when he came to power in 1956 when Gomułka had considerable reserves of goodwill upon which to draw and was generally credited with having saved Poland from a catastrophic confrontation with the Soviets. Gierek's position contained far more modest political capital—his critics in the party were in eclipse but still powerful, and the public was far more disillusioned with the promises of the government than it had been years before—and hence he had to gain public confidence with rapid and significant achievements.

Gierek's solution reflected in many ways his predecessor's inclinations: improve the economy and buy the population's gratitude, thereby dulling the spur of privation that drives intellectual discontent. Gierek was, however, a different man. A long-time party boss in industrial Silesia, he was practiced in the arts of winning support through patronage and payoffs. He would now take his experience to the national level. In February 1971 he announced a bold new economic program that combined massive increases in investment with a dramatic expansion of consumption and social spending. In effect, the plan would do everything at the same time and all in a big way. Even these ambitious goals were quickly abandoned, and new, far grander targets were set in 1973 envisioning industrial production to increase by two-thirds, national income to jump by more than half, and investment to leap by almost a quarter annually. At the same time, Poland would undertake major expansion and renovation of the transportation and communications system, increase spending on education, raise retirement income, make substantial investment in agriculture, and, thanks to an agreement with the Fiat Company of Italy, begin production of an automobile sufficiently cheap to allow car ownership to be within the reach of many Poles. It would even produce Coca-Cola by licensing agreement.

These were dazzling plans, and the regime's boast about creating a "second Poland" was not badly chosen. However, the whole project rested on a most precarious foundation. Gierek decided to transform the Polish economy, and save both himself and communism in the process, with money borrowed from the West, and substantially reorient the country's economy toward the capitalist world by creating new trade patterns. Thus communism would mortgage itself to capitalism. The gigantic debt was not admitted to the Polish public which was expected to be grateful for the new regime's ability to produce endless improvements without any visible cost but not to ask awkward questions about how it was being achieved. Inevitably, Gierek's gamble rested on the temporary surfeit of money at the disposal of Western European and American banks, as well as an optimistic anticipation of Poland's ability to penetrate Western markets successfully. Unfortunately for him the willingness of the West to pump money into Poland proved short-lived, and Poland never evolved beyond a minor trading partner for the capitalist world. Efforts made to satisfy consumer demands resulted in huge trade deficits: in 1975 exports had increased an impressive 66 percent over the previous five years, but imports had rocketed 104 percent over the same period. Artificial pricing meant that increased wages—rising at a robust 7 percent per annum in the early 1970s—soon outran supplies, particularly meat, leading to shortages. Moreover, borrowed money was often wastefully invested. By the mid-1970s Poland was alive with rumors of economic boondoggles, waste, and corruption. The observant British journalist Timothy Garton-Ash has referred to the unique feature of Gierek's program being its "breathtaking incompetence." The irrationally gigantic steelworks in Katowice, an economic disaster, became "Gierek's monument."[1] When oil price increases undermined the world economy in the early 1970s, recession in the West caused the flow of money to dry up. Creditors demanded repayment. Gierek had placed Poland in a catastrophic position.

> The planning did not consider matters independent of the regime's will, like the weather or world market conditions, or the needs and possibilities of a budget which had no reserves. As a result difficulties grew and grew.[2]

The economic disaster contrasted bizarrely with the regime's vociferous breast-beating about its success, which continued even after the problems became publicly apparent. Social discontent, which had subsided in the prosperous early 1970s, had returned by mid-decade. Cardinal Wyszyński, in the "Holy Cross Sermons" (*Kazania Świętokrzyskie*), made pronouncements about the rights of the Polish people to live in dignity and justice and denounced the "omnipotence of the state." In moving phrases, Cardinal Wyszyński reminded his countryman that patriotism was the highest value, superseded only by faith in God. A powerful movement that advocated human rights among the lay intelligentsia, which in turn reflected world trends stimulated by the human rights declarations of the "Helsinki Conference on Security and Cooperation in Europe Final Act" of 1975,[3] began to find common ground with the Church and forge intellectual and personal links. Polish society was beginning to coalesce in opposition to the regime.

Throughout the Gierek years a subtle yet increasing growth of Soviet influence was apparent. Within the PZPR hierarchy, the authority of Premier Jaroszewicz, widely regarded as Moscow's agent, waxed continually. In 1973 the school curriculum was overhauled and remade closer to the Soviet model. Personnel and administrative changes in the army and security also reflected increasingly direct Soviet influence. The regime sought to gain closer control over all areas of public life from youth groups to local administration. Even those who still regarded Gierek as having reinvigorated the Polish economy complained that "Gomułka was a better Pole." Unwisely the PZPR was launching a political offensive when its standing in popular esteem was declining, along with the economy.

Matters were quickly brought to a head by the regime's proposed constitutional reforms. Repeating similar developments elsewhere in the Soviet bloc, "there were new references to the socialist character of the state, emphases on the role of the Communist party, and there were inserts about friendship with the Soviet Union."[4] Although none of these changes was a departure from established practices, their inclusion in the constitution was seen by many Poles as a reification of the regime's recent efforts to expand its role in the country and a humiliating public declaration of servility to Moscow.

The episcopate denounced this demonstration of the "totalitarian nature of the Marxist-Leninist ideology of the party and state authorities." An open "Letter of the 59," signed by many prominent intellectuals, demanded that freedom of conscience and speech were irreconcilable with a constitutional positing of a state ideology and a party that monopolizes governing authority. This protest united a broad spectrum of Polish opinion, religious and lay. Other open letters followed. Although a slightly modified series of constitutional changes were adopted in despite of the protests, they had nonetheless galvanized public opposition. Moreover, a very significant principle was established whereby public opinion made it clear that it regarded the constitution as serious, and it was prepared to hold the authorities to the letter of the law. Hence the basis for the legal opposition to the state was laid.

The growing economic discontent and the coalescing intellectual critique came together in the dramatic events of 1976. This year began the continuous, albeit staggering decline of the PRL. In an eerie repetition of the same political and economic insensitivity that had provoked the 1970 riots, the government, without any warning, announced on June 24, 1976, huge price increases, ranging as high as 100 percent on foodstuffs. The irrational and deteriorating economic situation was the cause of the announcement, but only the party's purblindness to the public disposition can explain its manner which showed that, to quote Gierek from 1970, the party had "lost touch with the workers."

Mass strikes and protests greeted the announced price increases. When the strikers appeared in Ursus, the huge factory district adjacent to Warsaw, the authorities cut off communications with the rest of the country. The workers responded by blocking the main east-west rail line across Poland. Street violence led to 300 arrests. In Radom demonstrators burned the party headquarters and virtually seized the city. The authorities recaptured only after great exertions and considerable brutality. Major strikes were also noted in scores of factories across Poland: "75 per cent of the largest industrial enterprises in Poland went on strike."[5] The situation developed more rapidly than it had in 1970. Stunned, the regime rescinded the price increases, but in the next days launched a series of aggressive initiatives. First, they carefully organized supposedly "spontaneous" demonstrations of support throughout the country. The press piously reported a flood of letters and telegrams condemning "troublemakers," and strikers were branded "hooligans." This effort was so obviously contrived that it made the authorities ridiculous in the eyes of the people, but no personnel changes were made in the ruling team. Second, hundreds of strikers were seized and sentenced to lengthy jail terms without serious investigation or fair trials.

The trials were to have profound consequences. Since 1975 students, intellectuals, and the Church had been increasingly united, provoked by the constitutional crisis. Now, the violations of legal practices regarding the workers provoked a groundswell. A number of prominent intellectuals addressed open letters protesting the brutality of the crackdown. Several of the most prominent publicly announced the establishment of the Committee of Workers' Defense (Komitet Obrony Robotników, or KOR) which resulted from contact established between dissident intellectuals and the families of workers brought to trial. Among the founders of the KOR were Jacek Kuroń, Adam Michnik, writer Jerzy Andrzejewski, poet Stanisław Barańczak, socialist scholar Edward Lipiński, scholars Jan Józef Lipski and Antoni Macierewicz, and priest Reverend Jan Zieja. KOR included decorated veterans of World War II, college students, socialists, and Catholics. Both symbolically and practically, the gulf between the workers and the intellectuals had been bridged, and the beginnings of solidarity had been established.

KOR functioned entirely in the open, publishing the names and addresses of its members, which expanded to about two dozen over the next few months. The list of these names represented well-known personalities, but also combined members of both the clergy and the radical left, including former party members. KOR demanded amnesty for those arrested, the rehiring of the fired, and a national investigation of the suppression. It aided the legal defense of the workers and collected money internationally for its efforts. Contributions, which flowed in from Europe and the United States, often from labor groups, were often sent through the intermediacy of the Polish episcopate, thus organizationally linking the Church to the other two elements already joined in KOR. It began the circulation of its own bulletins, a modest beginning to be sure, but in a real sense the first independent press in Poland in more than a generation. A KOR network spread throughout Poland and the exact number of the many friends and supporters is difficult to estimate.

Within a year KOR redefined itself, expanding its goals from defending accused workers to defending the interests of the working class as a whole by articulating an increasingly aggressive program. By this time the authorities admitted that more than two dozen so-called antisocialist groups existed in Poland, including those overtly political and politically right, such as the Confederation of an Independent Poland (Konfederacja Polski Niepodległej, or KPN), which was led by Leszek Moczulski. Something of a profound nature was transforming Polish society, shifting the ground under the PZPR.

The culmination of these developments was the establishment . . . of a democratic opposition among the intellectual community of Poland. Although a small minority among the educated strata, the movement witnessed a rapid proliferation of dissident groups that became the predominant voices in shaping the social thought of the nation through their discourse on the possibilities and directions of change in Poland.[6]

Significantly, the notion of reshaping Poland through reform in the party, dear to the hearts of the 1960s dissidents, was now gone, and the future was increasingly conceived as existing in opposition to the regime. That opposition, however would function legally within the confines of the constitution and by observing the law. The opposition held the regime to a similar respect for the law which, after all, they had crafted.

In many ways what was happening in Poland in the late 1970s was the reclaiming of the intelligentsia of their traditional role in Polish society, long usurped by the party, of guardians of the national patrimony and shapers of the national dialogue, what Garton-Ash refers to as "the romantic version of noblesse oblige [which] is at the heart of the traditional Polish definition of what it is to be an intellectual," whereby you are able to live free spiritually though you exist in prison[7]

The last stand of the revisionist, the pseudo-loyal opposition of the PRL, was the Experience and the Future group which brought approximately one hundred intellectuals together in 1978. Meeting unofficially, but with PZPR blessing, the participants were to analyze the cause of the country's crisis and prescribe remedies. Unfortunately for the regime, the report—which was suppressed rather quickly—painted a damning portrait of a country in structural crisis, a disaffected and demoralized population, and a bleak future. In contrast to this devastating indictment, the remedies were anemic: a series of structural reforms within the ruling elite to reknit the links between the party and the population and a series of equally meaningless bromides. The incompatibility of the solution to the problem was the final proof that the regime could not solve the problems of which it was the principal author.

As the party reflected on the gloom around it, a Pole was elected pope. Karol Wojtyła was elected supreme pontiff in 1978. A brilliant man, respected for his intellect even by atheists, a product of a Communist system who thus understood it better than any pontiff before him, Wojtyła at once became not only the most famous Pole in the world, but the most important one as well. According to British historian R. J. Crampton, "The political situation in Poland was immediately and irreversibly changed. For the majority of Poles the pope was a new national leader operating freely outside the confines of the foreign-dominated national territory."[8]

In the summer of 1979 the pope made a triumphal return to Poland, where he was welcomed by huge crowds with euphoria but also extraordinary dignity and order. He spoke movingly about the right of Poland to its heritage; in Warsaw he condemned the Poles' abandonment by their allies, in Auschwitz he noted that no nation can develop at the expense of another—simple truths but with profound meaning to the Poles' situation. The regime feigned delight at the success of a native son, but seeing that the loyalties of the population were not focused on them; seethed with anger and resorted to petty harassments. In secret instructions to party loyalists, the PZPR noted, "The Pope is our enemy. . . . We must strive at all costs to weaken the Church . . . all means are allowed."[9] In vain: In 1979 the PRL had been defeated by its people; the terms of surrender, however, would take a decade to negotiate.

On July 1, 1980, the regime—which obviously had learned nothing from history—announced price increases. Strikes erupted in many cities. Government efforts to placate the workers or quieten the news of the outbreaks failed as KOR used its network to report developments. Lublin was virtually shut down by a general strike. The regime dispatched a delegation led by deputy prime minister Mieczysław Jagielski, who was able to ease the tension there, but by then the strike movement had spread throughout the country with the focal point the port city of Gdańsk. There the authorities had clumsily dismissed recalcitrant workers, including a crane operator and activist named Anna Walentynowicz, which provoked a mass strike at the Lenin Shipyard. By the end of August, the strike was being led by an electrician, himself fired in 1976, Lech Wałęsa. He had been one of those who had met with Gierek in 1970 and promised to work to save the situation; much had changed in a decade. Short, squat, and poorly educated, the moustached Wałęsa looked like a provincial squire gone to seed, "as unlikely a hero as this nation of heroes has yet produced,"[10] but oddly charismatic and with an infectious humor to go with unyielding courage. Though caught off guard by the strikers' actions, the intellectuals were quick to react. KOR leaders arrived in Gdańsk to advise the strikers, who displayed conspicuous piety and visible attachment to the church. Thus was coalesced the three elements that had repeatedly rocked the PRL: the workers, the intellectuals, and the Church—now acting in solidarity.

Within a few days Wałęsa had convinced his coworkers to continue and broaden the strike which now encompassed two hundred factories in the region and was coordinated by the Interfactory Strike Committee

(Międzyzakładowy Komitet Strajkowy, or MKS), nicknamed Solidarity (Solidarność). By mid-August the strike had taken hold of Szczecin where a similar MKS appeared. The Gdańsk MKS cobbled together twenty-one "demands" they would propose to the authorities which included the right to strike and, most important, the right to form a union independent of the authorities—a proposal briefly bruited in 1970. Other demands covered the freeing of political prisoners, freedom of speech and press, and a series of economic issues including the insistence that the authorities provide the country with honest information about the economy.

The demands had a curious origin. Although several KOR advisors were already on the scene, most of the KOR leadership actually opposed the demands as too radical, especially the call for an independent union. Most prominent among the leaders were Kuroń, Tadeusz Mazowiecki, a Catholic editor and intellectual; and Bronisław Geremek, a historian. It was the workers themselves, however, who pushed the movement forward. Adam Michnik later ironically noted that though the KOR claimed parentage, Solidarity was really an "illegitimate child."[11] In general the role of the workers and the advisors in formulating Solidarity's actions is rather controversial, especially as both contained both moderate and more radical elements. Moreover, there were often differences between strongly Catholic elements in the movement, like Mazowiecki and Wałęsa himself, and the KOR intellectuals who were often irreligious, even former party members. Surprisingly absent from a major role in the heroic first days of the movement was the Church. Cardinal Wyszyński, old and dying, adopted a rather cautious attitude, and the intellectuals from KOR were quicker to come to the workers' support. This only increased the Church's hesitancy given the secular-left background of many KOR activists. The incipient rift between the two was providentially bridged by the overt and obvious religiosity of Wałęsa and other workers whose public piety was a conspicuous feature of the movement.

Gierek rejected the political demands out of hand, but he sent high-level delegations to both Szczecin and Gdańsk to negotiate, following his own example from 1970 and the more recent success of Jagielski in Lublin. However, in an effort to split the opposition, a wave of arrests also netted a number of prominent intellectuals including Kurón, Michnik, and Moczulski. Negotiations were broken off, and a general strike paralyzed the entire Baltic coast. The PZPR was in crisis. A series of rapid personnel changes followed, which indicated a weakening of Gierek, who was now obviously on the defensive. Pressure from Moscow to deal with the deteriorating Baltic situation mounted incessantly.

In the striking cities, tension mounted rapidly as did boldness, and the workers went beyond the advice of their intellectual advisors. News of strikes in many other Polish cities encouraged the Gdańsk workers to maintain their resolve. Negotiations with the regime, now represented by Jagielski, were difficult but moved forward quickly. On the last day of August 1980, Wałęsa and the MKS emerged victorious with acceptance by the PZPR of the right to establish an independent union, giving the party the fig leaf of recognition of its "leading role in the state." Within days strikers at other locations had agreed to end their actions and return to work. It was over.

Gierek suffered a heart attack and was removed from his position as first secretary and was replaced by the corpulent and colorless Stanisław Kania. At its moment of crisis, the PZPR put in place yet another mediocrity. Not surprisingly Kania blamed the difficulties on "errors" and "deformations" and denied any essential differences between the strikers and the government and party.

In many ways the PZPR was already exhibiting signs of a fatal illness. In the late 1970s the appearance of KOR and the subsequent proliferation of opposition organizations had met with a generally feeble response despite the intermittent arrests and harassment. With the establishment of Solidarity, the party began to crumble, stumbling, in the happy phrase of historian J. F. Brown, "from ineffectiveness into impotence."[12] This reflected a twofold process. First, many party members regarded Solidarity as a positive development and abandoned the PZPR for the new movement. A mass exodus of members followed. The remaining loyalists, disheartened by the obvious incapacity of the party to cope with the new situation, became increasingly pessimistic and divided into two antagonistic factions. One faction regarded the emergence of Solidarity as signaling the last chance for the party to rejuvenate itself and recapture some direct contact with the population. Calls for "renewal" (*odnowa*) became the watchword of this liberal faction within the party willing to work with Solidarity or at least tolerate it. The other faction, the so-called hardheads (*twardogłowy*), demanded immediate repression and the reassertion of firm party control over the situation. Although both views had proponents at all levels, the fact that local branches of the PZPR advocated different lines showed the advancing structural disintegration of the party.

Events in Poland developed kalediscopically in September with new unions and regional coordinating committees appearing everywhere. On September 17, in Gdańsk, the burgeoning unions decided to erect a central general union, with regional affiliates given wide autonomy. This was a victory for those who argued the need for centralization in order to oppose the PZPR. Thus was born the Independent Self-Governing Trade Union–Solidarity (Niezależny Samorządny Związek Zawodowy, (NSZZ-Solidarnosc), with Wałęsa as its head. By this time Solidarity already numbered an astonishing 4 million members.

The authorities were understandably overwhelmed by the speed and magnitude of developments, and they reacted by undertaking a series of provocations, isolated arrests, and most important, opposition to the legal registration of Solidarity and several of the similar organizations it had prompted, including Rural Solidarity and student associations. A bizarre relationship developed between the party and Solidarity whereby Solidarity gained its objectives by partial and demonstration strikes and the threat of a general strike that would shut down the entire country. Although the party initially refused and resisted, it gradually conceded to Solidarity's registration, the union's right to issue a mass circulation newspaper and appear on radio and television, and other demands. Each retreat by the party brought it further expressions of outrage from the Kremlin which had described Solidarity as constituting a counterrevolution from the outset.

Whereas the party thus appeared to be in continuous retreat, it was in reality preparing a last counterattack. From as early as late summer a special committee had been commissioned to prepare plans for the repression of Solidarity. The key figure in this group was General Wojciech Jaruzelski, the taciturn soldier who always wore tinted glasses. The committee's plans had to be repeatedly recast and delayed as Solidarity grew steadily in the last half of 1980, reaching almost 10 million members by its peak and presenting the authorities with an ever expanding problem. By early December 1980, Poland was becoming the center of an international crisis of truly gigantic dimensions.

The Kremlin had repeatedly warned the PZPR that it was prepared to use military force to restore order in Poland, and that it was becoming increasingly concerned that Warsaw had lost control of the situation. Evidence of large-scale Soviet troop movements on the Polish eastern border brought direct warnings from U.S. president Jimmy Carter that Soviet military intervention in Poland would bring the most serious consequences. (Here we must consider the influence of Carter's National Security Advisor, Zbigniew Brzezinski, himself born in Poland, and the first expert on Soviet affairs to occupy that position.) Recent disclosures also make it clear that the pope was seriously considering the possibility of returning to Poland to lead the national resistance should the Soviets invade. In light of this, the PZPR's own plan to smash Solidarity with internal forces in order to forestall action by Warsaw Pact units became increasingly considered. The party succeeded in convincing the Kremlin to allow them to make a last effort to reassert control.

Both sides tried to make sense of a paradoxical situation in 1981. On the one hand, Solidarity had won major concessions in August and had garnered further success in the next months; on the other hand, most of these gains remained theoretical and insubstantial. The party had obviously surrendered only under duress and lost no chance to obfuscate, delay, and complicate the changes supposedly already granted. The major crisis occurred over registration and thus legalization of Rural Solidarity, which was interminably delayed by the regime and finally resulted in an ugly incident in which a Solidarity leader, Jan Rulewski, was savagely beaten by the police in Bydgoszcz. Solidarity reacted to this obvious provocation by the regime by threatening a general strike, which was barely averted when the authorities allowed Rural Solidarity to function but still delayed formal registration. This was a victory for Solidarity, which showed both determination in opposing the regime and remarkable discipline in both organizing and then canceling a general strike. The regime's defeat was demonstrated when it finally, and quietly, allowed the farmers to register in May.

In the summer, both the party and Solidarity held national meetings and both demonstrated how much had changed in the past year. The party met first, in July. The rising star was obviously Jaruzelski who had recently been appointed premier. This appointment made Jaruzelski head of both the army and the state, in addition to his powerful party position in the politburo. The party congress was crowded with new people who had been elected by an unprecedented free and secret procedure, thus demonstrating Kania's support for *odnowa*. More strikingly a substantial number of the delegates were also Solidarity members. Although the congress enacted rather dramatic changes in rules and statutes regarding elections and membership, the overall failure of the congress to meet the challenge of the moment was obvious. The PZPR did not reinvent itself but was content to tinker with statutes at a time when the country was in a state of a virtual political revolution.

In early September, Solidarity met for its first national congress, and the contrast with the party affair was remarkable. What was basically at work was a struggle within Solidarity over self-definition: was it indeed a political movement, though still unformed, or was it merely a union? It was clear that the, more radical elements wished it to adopt openly a political program and challenge the PZPR's position directly as well as make pronouncements related to foreign policy. Motions surfaced regarding educational reform, economic restructuring, and many other issues that would have moved far beyond traditional union concerns. On the one hand, with its membership in the millions, Solidarity surely had a broader mandate than the PZPR to shape Poland's future. However, geopolitical realities being what they were, the party's illegitimate, but real, monopoly of power had to be recognized. Thus, moderates like Wałęsa had difficulty in restraining the congress from provocative actions, such as the declaration to other Communist bloc countries of aid in establishing their own version of Solidarity, the implications of which for the Kremlin were all too clear.

Kania was caught between Soviet anxieties and pressure from the hardheads within Poland who had recently taken on an organizational form as the Katowice Forum, and the increasing aggressiveness of Solidarity. He resigned his party leadership in October and was replaced by Jaruzelski, who seemed destined to occupy every significant post in the PRL. Matters were heading for a dramatic denouement. Solidarity began showing signs of losing control of its members as more radical elements, especially Kuroń, called for a confrontational approach and urged a showdown with the PZPR over who really governed Poland. Certainly public opinion was on the side of Solidarity; an opinion poll showed the Church and Solidarity had the support of almost the entire nation; the party had virtually none.[13] Meanwhile, the new Jaruzelski government was exhibiting signs of resolve by interfering with Solidarity meetings and breaking up a strike in Warsaw by brute force in early December. It seemed that the PZPR was finally responding to Solidarity's provocations, but Jaruzelski had actually been planning a coup against the opposition for months and had been implored to act by the Kremlin which regarded the situation in the most extreme light.

In a tense atmosphere, Solidarity's leaders held a meeting in Radom at which speakers openly called for revolt and expressed confidence that the army would not support the regime. Happily for Jaruzelski, the meeting, which was electronically bugged, provided a perfect justification for the declaration of martial law—in PRL parlance, a "state of war"—on December 13, 1981.

During the night of December 13–14, virtually all Solidarity leaders were arrested; Wałęsa was interned; the organization's offices were seized and documents confiscated; communications between Poland and the outside world were cut; and police and army units appeared on every street. A few points of resistance, like the miners in Silesia, were besieged and forced to capitulate by Christmas. Jaruzelski, in full uniform and with great solemnity, addressed the nation early on December 13 and explained that "anarchy" was threatening the nation and he was forced to transfer all power to a Military Council of National Salvation (Wojskowa Rada Ocalenia Narodowego, or WRON), which was composed of about two dozen senior officers led by himself. Jaruzelski explained that he had not staged a "military coup d'état" nor had he imposed a "military dictatorship," although he had obviously just done both.

Essentially Jaruzelski's postcoup regime presented two contrasting elements. It had been carried out with extraordinary precision and professional competence, stunning the population and virtually precluding serious opposition. Its initial actions showed resolve and preparation. For the next few days after the coup, the country was bombarded with declarations: all labor unions were closed, all meetings were banned, as were artistic and sporting events, a curfew was imposed, almost the entire press (save a few government organs) was suspended, censorship was imposed, radio and television was severely restricted, and most factories were militarized and their staffs placed under army discipline. The population was exhorted to observe peace and order and work hard to revive the faltering economy. The whole was liberally undergirded with dire threats in the case of disobedience. Appeals to patriotism were entwined with veiled but unmistakable references to the possibility of Soviet invasion which the coup, ostensibly, had averted but still impended should the situation not radically improve. Lest these admonitions not be credited, the military authorities arrested several thousand people over the next several days—which they menacingly reported in the press—and dealt with any resistance with crushing force.

However, as expert as was his mounting of the coup, equally incompetent was Jaruzelski's strategy of solving the crisis. His efforts to save the PZPR's rule in Poland effectively doomed it from the outset. Jaruzelski basically created a military dictatorship without reference to the party or the constitution; his WRON effectively wiped out a generation of admittedly ineffectual efforts by the PZPR to legitimize itself in Poland. Jaruzelski's coup was as much against the party as it was against Solidarity since it deprived both of a claim to power. According to David

Ost, an American political scientist, when the party did begin to reappear in 1982, "[T]here was never any question that it could run things by itself. That notion had been discredited forever."[14] Now what would be put in place, and what would be the basis of its claim to rule?

Ultimately Jaruzelski's regime required three victories to survive, let alone consolidate a new political system. First, it had to convince the Kremlin to support its efforts by massive economic aid to bail out a floundering economy and purchase the population's goodwill. Second, it had to neutralize the opposition by decapitating its leadership and, more important in the longer run, weakening its popular support. This goal required a carrot-and-stick approach to economic stability and threats of dire consequences—Soviet invasion—should the opposition not be silenced. Third, the regime had to revive the economy, a perennial task of new PRL regimes and a challenge they inevitably failed to met.

The tailspin of the economy, which had done much to fuel the rise of Solidarity, was accelerating after 1979. National income actually fell in 1980 by 6 percent and a horrifying 12 percent further in 1981. At the same time, investment in economic growth also declined steeply, thus mortgaging the possibility of future improvement. Jaruzelski's coup did nothing to improve matters because the economy fell a further 8 percent in 1982. Threats and exhortations to increase production could not overcome systemic inefficiencies and the aging plants dilapidated by inadequate investment. Living standards declined drastically—in 1982 by 32 percent—wiping out years of slow progress for the average Pole. Desperate efforts made to stop the slide from 1983 to 1988 only exhausted remaining reserves and virtually ended investment. In most economic categories Poland ended the decade behind where it had been in 1978. Moreover, Poland's debt was becoming huge, reaching $40 billion by 1988. The economy was devouring itself. Given the centrality of economics to the Communists' claim to lead Poland this dismal performance must rank as a central indictment of their years in power.

Jaruzelski tried hard to convince Moscow to aid Poland's economy, and he did achieve some measure of success. However, as recently released Soviet documents demonstrate, the Kremlin was increasingly reluctant to bail Poland out economically because of their own mounting financial difficulties, as well as a conviction that Jaruzelski was being manipulative and exploiting his political difficulties to extract money from them. Ultimately, Jaruzelski would have to fix Poland by himself, including the ruined economy, Moscow concluded.

This raises the second fundamental question of Moscow's support for

Jaruzelski. Certainly the evidence is clear that the Kremlin was alarmed by Solidarity and viewed its series of successive confrontations with the party as indicative of the bankruptcy of the Gierek, then Kania, team. By comparison, Jaruzelski's determination to act with boldness helped restore their confidence that Communist rule in Poland could survive. Although direct military action was considered, the Kremlin rejected it as far too costly an enterprise; Poland's size and martial traditions made it an incomparably more daunting proposition than Hungary had been in 1956 or Czechoslovakia in 1968. Besides, in those earlier times, Moscow itself had been more politically resolute and less economically hard pressed than it was in the final days of Soviet leader Leonid Brezhnev's lifeless rule or the chaotic era of transition that followed.

Jaruzelski's ability to silence political opposition went through a rapid evolution. Initially, he paralyzed Solidarity, and only a handful of leading activists escaped the dragnet. So overpowering was the initial show of force by WRON that even the new cardinal, Józef Archbishop Glemp, who replaced Wyszyński after his death in 1981, seemed overawed. He released a rather timid statement urging his countrymen to bow to overwhelming forces. However, the regime's predominating position soon began to erode. The creation of the Patriotic Movement for National Revival (PRON), Jaruzelski's effort to harness public support under an umbrella organization to siphon off supporters of the banned Solidarity, turned out to be an embarrassing failure because it attracted few members and virtually all of them from the ranks of the party or its allies. The regime failed to establish a base of support and thus the field lay open to the opposition.

Despite its efforts, the regime did not capture all of the Solidarity leadership. Activist Zbigniew Bujak built up a so-called Underground Solidarity which became a series of small local organizations. The goals of this movement were seemingly modest, to avoid confrontation, while building a network of alternative structures for Polish social life. By spring 1982 a clandestine national coordinating body had emerged, the Solidarity Temporary Coordinating Commission (Tymczasowa Komisja Koordynacyjna or TKK). More radical splinter organizations, including Fighting Solidarity (Solidarność Walcząca) advocated virtual guerrilla warfare against the regime, but they attracted few followers. An illegal opposition press flourished with dozens of titles and a circulation that soon reached seven figures. A great galaxy of political factions, spanning the political spectrum, appeared over the next years. Simultaneously, the church harbored many artists and writers and allowed them to continue their activities, which included "flying universities" where taboo topics of recent history were discussed. At the same time, spontaneous strikes, demonstrations, and rallies continued throughout Poland, catching both Jaruzelski and the TKK off guard.

Jaruzelski had hoped to win over the moderate elements in Solidarity to some collaboration with the regime, but martial law polarized society and isolated WRON as a despised dictatorship—though, in reality, it was a rather lax regime after its initial repression. Simultaneously Jaruzelski hoped to reach some accommodation with the church and Cardinal Glemp. Essentially, the regime adopted a policy of unprecedented liberality regarding the Church, eventually allowing permits to construct almost 1,000 new churches and even providing government funds. The Church was also allowed increased access to the mass media. In return, Jaruzelski saw in Glemp someone who would regard stability as the strategic good of Poland and work with him to stifle social radicalism. Whether this was a complex game in which both were using each other, or a convergence of patriotic impulses, although from disparate sources, is an intriguing question. Unquestionably, both wanted peace to return— the questions were at what price, and who would gain the truly strategic concessions. Glemp's dislike for many of the KOR and Solidarity activities, whom he rightly regarded as leftist secularists, undoubtedly played a role in his actions. Perhaps he did not see the challenge mounted to the regime in the early 1980s as one he could wholeheartedly support.

Jaruzelski began a policy of strategic retreats, accompanied by threats of renewed repression in an effort to move toward a controlled and gradual normalization. In December 1982 he suspended martial law and released Wałęsa from internment. Nonetheless, harassment of the Solidarity leaders continued, and the official press maintained a steady campaign of abuse denouncing Solidarity as antisocialist and a menace to Polish security. In July of the following year the WRON was dissolved. Ironically this should be seen as a demonstration of confidence by Jaruzelski who was convinced that he had pacified Poland and could now dismantle the ad hoc machinery of repression. Wałęsa was awarded the Nobel Peace Prize in October, 1983. This was a great morale boost for Solidarity and forced Jaruzelski to make further concessions.

Jaruzelski entered the most complex phase of his career in the mid-1980s; his motives and goals make fascinating speculation, and he is, without compare, the most intriguing leader produced during the life of the PRL. This is best demonstrated by the lurid and complex Popiełuszko affair. In 1984 Father Jerzy Popiełuszko, a fiery patriot and beloved

Warsaw priest whose monthly "Mass for the Fatherland" was of national importance, was murdered by agents of the regime's security apparatus, though by whose orders still remains unclear. All of Poland was outraged. Glemp regarded Popiełuszko as a firebrand and an obstacle to smooth relations with the regime and Jaruzelski doubtlessly despised the priest; nevertheless, both were visibly shocked by his grisly murder. According to Gale Stokes, an American analyst of Eastern Europe, Popiełuszko's murder was the precipitating event in Jaruzelski's efforts to move from sham pluralism to a real pluralism, which ended with the negotiated collapse of the PRL.[15]

Jaruzelski allowed a public trial of the security forces responsible for the priest's murder, thus demonstrating his acceptance of the demands of public opinion. Simultaneously, he began purging the hard-liners from the party and undertook a major dismantling of the security apparatus. In effect, Jaruzelski was moving toward accommodation with Solidarity because they would not move toward him. In the summer of 1986 Jaruzelski granted a full amnesty to all those arrested as a result of martial law. On the opposite front, Wałęsa responded by publicly announcing the establishment of a Solidarity Provisional Council (Tymczasowa Rada Solidarności, or TRS), composed largely of recent prisoners, but the underground TKK continued to function, casting a surreal light on Polish politics of the era, as both sides undertook complex maneuvers and the alignments blurred.

Jaruzelski next suggested the creation of a consultative council with participation of oppositionists to debate issues openly. He also drastically relaxed censorship, giving Poland a virtually free press. Marxist-Leninist phraseology, which had been the rhetorical rituals of the government for a generation, became conspicuous by their absence. Poland was not a free country, but whether it was still a Communist country was problematical. The influence of the ascent of Mikhail Gorbachev in the Soviet Union in 1985 and his proclamation of glasnost—a policy allowing freedom of discussion—is certainly reflected in Jaruzelski's actions, but internal Polish dynamics seem to have played the major role. And here the continuing collapse of the economy and Jaruzelski's utter inability to address the issue were crucial. Poland may have been politically paralyzed in the late 1980s, but economically it was terminal.

Events now moved quickly to a conclusion as both sides lurched toward accommodation. Perhaps the chief impetus was the odd referendum staged by Jaruzelski in 1987 in which he asked the population whether it would support a radical restructuring of the economy, which would entail sacrifices for the immediate future to salvage the situation. Though the issue carried with a considerable majority, the government admitted that the voter turnout had been low and hence the majority of the nation had not demonstrated any willingness to support the measures. This self-castigating honesty, regardless of its intentions (which still remain mysterious), had a profound effect on Poland where the issue before the nation seemed to be: Poland is in crisis; can its most prominent representatives cooperate in its salvation? Calls for a "historic pact" between Jaruzelski and Wałęsa appeared in the opposition press.

As though obedient to an inevitable foolishness, the last regime of the PRL had to repeat eerily and literally the mistakes of its predecessors. In February 1988 the government announced a 40 percent rise in food prices. Strikes broke out everywhere, and when they were suppressed or bought off by wage or price concessions, they only erupted later elsewhere. Solidarity had not organized or led the strikes, which now responded to their own inner dynamic. After almost a decade, Solidarity was alive more as a symbol of national unity and resolution; its real control over events was about as feeble as the party's. In reality, it was the birth of post-Communist Poland in all its rich diversity which no organization, even one as amorphous and respected as Solidarity, could represent and control.

After months of frustration, the government surrendered and agreed to open, direct talks with Solidarity over the national crisis; the only condition was that Wałęsa end the strikes, a tall order because he had neither started nor run them. In perhaps his greatest moment, Wałęsa boldly agreed to the condition and then, with prodigious effort, restored labor peace. This demonstrated his enormous power in the country and forced the government to open the talks in which they would face an incomparably strengthened Wałęsa: the regime had conjured the force that would destroy it.

For several months the government tried desperately to wriggle out of its predicament by postponing, sabotaging, or manipulating the negotiations. Much of the blame for this sorry performance goes to Mieczysław Rakowski, the last PRL prime minister,[16] whose early reputation as a "liberal communist" was permanently ruined by these actions. Jaruzelski pressed for the rapid commencement of the talks, even threatening resignation to overcome intransigence in the regime.

The negotiations, conducted around a round table, finally began in February 1989 and lasted two months. There were about sixty principal participants, with the Church, Solidarity, and the regime (with separate delegations from government and party) the chief factions, though many others were represented; including the politically meaningless Peasant and Democratic parties which the regime had created at its inception, now attended its wake; the ridiculous PRON, and a number of independent agents. As a result, Solidarity was legalized and soon reappeared with its press network; the structure of the Polish government was overhauled: there would be a bicameral legislature, recreating the Senate from the Second Republic. Elections to this upper body would be free; the lower house, the *sejm*, would be chosen according to a curious formula which basically "fixed" the election: 65 percent of the seats would be contested exclusively by the PZPR; the remaining 35 percent would be elected in open competition. This parliament would be transitional. After four years (in 1993), new elections would be completely unfettered. The Senate could veto *sejm* actions by a two-thirds vote, and both houses, in joint sessions, would elect the president, whose powers would be considerable.

Despite many predictions that the party would use its stranglehold on the media, and its limitless powers of patronage, the elections were a stunning victory for Solidarity which won all 161 contested seats in the *sejm* and 99 of 100 seats in the Senate. Most of the senior PZPR candidates were humiliatingly defeated. It was the first real referendum on the PRL, and it had been thoroughly rejected by the Polish people. The result was a state of political disorientation: the party was unable to comprehend the magnitude of its defeat; Solidarity was unprepared for the consequences of so overpowering a victory. What followed was a demonstration of almost preternatural political wisdom on the part of Solidarity, particularly Wałęsa, who demonstrated a combination of tactical adroitness and strategic sensitivity to the country's position which deserves great credit.

After much behind-the-scenes maneuvering, it was decided that only Jaruzelski would run for the presidency, and parliament duly elected him by a single vote and thanks only to the support of Solidarity deputies. Jaruzelski resigned all his high party posts upon becoming president. This step, which outraged many longtime foes of the regime, was a brilliant stroke by which the PRL was politically dismantled gradually without destabilizing lurches, allowing Marxism-Leninism to stroll, rather than be hustled, to the dustbin of history. A noteworthy aspect of the parliamentary vote was the action of the Peasant and Democratic parties which, for the first time since they were created to provide props for the regime's claim to being "democratic," showed their independence by opposing Jaruzelski's candidacy.

The deal to elect Jaruzelski gave the Communists titular control of Poland, but far more important was the bitter struggle over the composition of the government. Jaruzelski advanced the candidacy of his closest lieutenant, General Czesław Kiszczak, who had played a large role in the round-table talks, for prime minister, but Kisczak was unable to form a government. Wałęsa then stunned the PZPR by arranging a coalition uniting Solidarity with the PZPR's former lackeys, the Peasant and Democratic parties, which enjoyed a parliamentary majority. After some desperate thrashing about, Jaruzelski caved in and asked Solidarity's Tadeusz Mazowiecki, whose status as a prominent Catholic intellectual made him more attractive to the Church than Kuroń or Geremek, also considered by Wałęsa, to form a new government. In the Kremlin, Gorbachev decided to let Polish events take their own course.

In August, Mazowiecki became Poland's premier and communism in Poland died. He fainted at his swearing in. In a dizzying rush, the crown, which had been removed during the PRL; was returned to Poland's national emblem, the White Eagle; the ancient name *Rzeczpospolita Polska* (the Polish Republic) replaced the PRL; and the leading role of the party was constitutionally abolished and it withered away. Poland led the way in the dismantling of communism in Eastern Europe and the Soviet Empire which had created and maintained it. Forty-five years of PZPR rule in Poland ended without a shot being fired. Gorbachev was quoted as calling the PZPR "crap,"[17] a fitting epitaph.

The British historian Lytton Strachey once lamented that he could not write the history of the Victorian Age because he knew too much about it. It is thus far too soon to assess the meaning of the PRL because its effects are still too ambiguous to be clearly seen and evaluated. Certainly, as is the case with so much in Polish history, it has bequeathed a paradoxical heritage. The most obvious feature of the regime was its utter failure to legitimize itself in the eyes of the Polish people. It remained what it was at its birth, an essentially foreign implantation, sustained by the threat of force. When that threat disappeared, the system it had supported collapsed. Thus the end of the PRL and the sapping of Soviet, nay Russian, power in the world are inseparably combined. To its credit, the PZPR grasped early in its life that to become something beyond an occupation regime it would have to demonstrate to the population that, at the very least, it could further the nation's economic well-being. But here it failed, and centrally, and its other failures merely exacerbated this more fundamental one. The almost predictable regularity of PRL economic crises is a trenchant indictment of both the flaws of the system and the mediocrity of its devotees.

Bierut, Gomułka, Gierek, Kania, and Rakowski are all almost absurdly small figures. For all of their flaws, the patriarchs of the Second Republic—Piłsudski, Dmowski, Paderewski, Sikorski, even, Mościcki, Beck, and Śmigły-Rydz—are giants by comparison. Poland like France finds it difficult to live without *la gloire* and none attaches to the fatuous PZPR gang, the complex and intelligent Jaruzelski forming a category apart.

However, the near half-century of the PRL cannot be consigned to the category of historic aberration, an interruption in the integrated development of the national story. Many aspects of the PRL conform to profound themes in the Polish past, and during its life it was sustained in large part by its ability to assimilate elements of Polish political traditions and to reflect the demands of the country's structural security dilemma.

From the outset, the PZPR insisted that, in Jakub Berman's formulation, "Poland can't float in the air"[18]; in other words, political geography being what it is, a truly free Poland cannot exist between Germany and Russia without dependence on one of them. This argument was not original or unique to the Communists. Dmowski posited it at the turn of the century and it was not new even then. By 1945 it had become a grudging postulate in much Polish thinking about strategic questions. Post war Poland closely replicated Dmowski's model: virtually nationally homogeneous, the Jews gone, the multinational eastern territories abandoned, and close cooperation with the Russians the face of a hostile confrontation with the Germans. To be sure, Dmowski did not endorse communism and atheism, but even here the difference is perhaps not so great. The PZPR's insistence on a strong state echoed Dmowski's criticisms of the Polish tradition of weak central authority and popular distrust for government. As for religion, Dmowski's *endecja*, or nationalism, originally regarded the church as reactionary and backward and accommodated it only because of its obvious hold over the population, much like the PRL leadership was forced to do. Thus in some ways the groundwork for the PRL was set a generation before by the *endecja*, ironically the party of the right. Both shared a fundamental hostility to the past, especially the Polish past, which they wished to overcome and excise from the national conscience. Had the PRL leadership not been composed of such a pack of scoundrels, had it not been so shamelessly sub-servient to Moscow, though here we must blame Stalin and Russian megalomania chiefly, it is not inconceivable that the PRL might have worked, or at the very least, it may not have failed so utterly to graft itself onto the nation's life.

But if Berman—and *mutatis mutandis*, Dmowski—are to be proven wrong, for Poland to exist, in sovereignty, and not as a dependency of either neighbor, a change had to be worked in the international system whereby such geopolitical possibilities could arise. In other words to liberate Polish domestic politics we first had to witness the transforma-tion of the European scene. And we have. It is the world of the Third Republic.

Here we confront another Polish political tradition. In the last months of his rule, Jaruzelski authorized public remembrance of the deeds of Piłsudski, even allowing the stirring "March of the First Brigade," Piłsudski's theme song, to be played.[19] The General doubtless felt in-creasing kinship with his soldier predecessor. He too carried out a coup d'état at the prompt of what he regarded a menacing international scene, and arrested his critics, tried to create a umbrella organization to unite supporters under a nonpolitical banner and failed in the process, alien-ating the public in the bargain. There are many similarities in the two Polish soldiers. But Jaruzelski was no Piłsudski, however, for the former always regarded national independence as the only real end, and na-tional dignity as the only acceptable means. Piłsudski, with typical blunt-ness, once explained that he became a revolutionary because he refused "to live in the toilet" of Russian domination; Jaruzelski spent his life as a latrine orderly.

Hence, it was not Jaruzelski, but Wałęsa who more closely approxi-mated the tone and style of the Marshal, and thus the new Poland would not break with the past, but chose which version of the past to in-form it.

The PRL oddly maintained and strengthened one of the most profound of all Polish political traditions: public hostility toward governing au-thority. Strong government was conspicuously absent from the old Com-monwealth, and the century of partition bred into Poles the notion that authority was by definition alien and hostile. This became a great burden for the Second Republic, and the *sanacja* was a clumsy effort to respond. Obviously the occupation regimes of World War II only exacerbated this divide between rulers and ruled. The PRL, however, with its indelible stain of foreignness, deserves dubious credit for the institutionalized alienation of the Polish population. Paradoxically, it was this feature that forced the opposition to take the form it did, the grassroots organization of a civil society which eventually overcame and supplanted the party, thus ending the historic divide between government and nation in Poland. The Third Republic thus rests on a firmer basis of popular identification than any perhaps in all Polish history. It was the Communists' greatest and most inadvertent service to Poland.

NOTES

1. Timothy Garton-Ash, *The Polish Revolution: Solidarity* (New York, 1983), 14–15.
2. Wojciech Roszkowski, *Historia Polski, 1914–1991* (Warsaw, 1992). 320.
3. A resolution adopted by many countries, including the United States and the USSR, which committed the signers to respect human rights.
4. Jakub Karpinski, *Countdown: The Polish Upheavals of 1956, 1968, 1970, 1976, 1980 . . .* (New York, 1982), 184.
5. Jan Jozef Lipski, *KOR: A History of the Workers' Defense Committee in Poland, 1976–1981* (Berkeley, Calif., 1985), 39.
6. Jack Bielasiak, ed., *Poland Today: The State of the Republic* (Armonk, NY, 1981), xiv.
7. Timothy Garton-Ash, *The Uses of Adversity* (New York, 1990), 105–6.
8. R. J. Crampton, *Eastern Europe in the Twentieth Century—and After*, 2nd ed (London, 1994), 365.
9. Quoted in Gale Stokes, *The Walls Came Tumbling Down: The Collapse of Communism in Eastern Europe* (New York, 1993), 33.
10. J. F. Brown, *Eastern Europe and Communist Rule* (Durham, NC, and London, 1988), 183.
11. Stokes, *Walls Came Tumbling Down*, 37.
12. Brown, *Eastern Europe*, 186.
13. Crampton, *Eastern Europe*, 374.
14. David Ost, *Solidarity and the Politics of Anti-Politics* (Philadelphia, 1990), 151.
15. Stokes, *Walls Came Tumbling Down*, 114.
16. Jaruzelski had voluntarily stepped down in 1985. He was followed as premier by Zbigniew Messner, who failed to avert or manage the economic crisis and was, in turn, replaced by Rakowski.

17. Stokes, *Walls Came Tumbling Down*, 130.

18. Cited in Gale Stokes, *From Stalinism to Pluralism* (New York, 1996), 48.

19. The "March" begins with a bitter refrain about being unappreciated. Jaruzelski must have found it ironically comforting.

10

The Third Republic

At the close of the twentieth century the position of Poland was better than it had been at any time in more than three centuries. This reflected a combination of a decade of stable democratic domestic politics, a rapidly expanding economy, and an unprecedentedly favorable constellation of international forces. The twentieth century began with Poland's being a virtually forgotten cause, it witnessed the nation's most agonizing trauma, and it ended with the country's dazzling recovery.

THE POLITICAL SCENE

Tadeusz Mazowiecki's government simultaneously had to dismantle the Polish People's Republic (PRL) and construct the new Third Republic. Comprehensive reforms in many fields quickly made Wojciech Jaruzelski's presidency appear both anachronistic and irrelevant, and he left office prematurely—and anticlimactically—in late 1990. A striking and radical economic restructuring had begun within a matter of weeks when Finance Minister Leszek Balcerowicz unveiled a bold strategy to create capitalism in Poland by shock therapy: a series of sudden, high-risk changes. No Communist economic system had ever been dismantled, and this aggressive approach was widely criticized as both politically incautious—as it would lead to almost immediate economic hardship for many Poles—and based on dubious theoretical foundations.

Jaruzelski's resignation precipitated a struggle within Solidarity—the so-called war at the top—which pitted Mazowiecki's caution against Wałęsa's increasing interest in revenge against the Communists: Solidarity split into two major factions. The result, late in 1990, was a complex, three-cornered, national presidential election in which Mazowiecki finished a weak third, a humiliating performance for one of the most attractive of the Solidarity leaders. Wałęsa emerged victorious, but not until after a second round of voting when he defeated an insurgent candidate, a Canadian-Peruvian emigré named Stanisław Tyminski, whose irresponsible campaign was an embarrassment to Poland, especially for Mazowiecki. After his election, Wałęsa installed Jan Krzysztof Bielecki, a liberal, free-market advocate, as premier.

The struggle between Mazowiecki and Wałęsa and the presidential election that followed ushered in an era of political instability in the early 1990s which gave observers pause to reflect whether Poland would be able to build a stable democratic system. The first truly free parliamentary elections were held in 1991 under a cumbersome and bewilderingly complex system of parliamentary apportionment. A myriad of parties, resulted in a confused election and a splintered *sejm* echoing the worst features of the Second Republic. Given so unstable a base, it is not surprising that governments followed one another with great speed. Bielecki lasted ten months. He was followed in January 1991 by the dour rightist attorney Jan Olszewski, whose chaotic ministry lasted only five months, giving way to the impressive Hanna Suchocka, the first woman ever to hold the top governmental position in Polish history. She proved an energetic and capable leader, but the 1993 parliamentary elections brought about a dramatic turn in Polish politics.

The Polish United Workers' Party (PZPR) had dissolved itself in 1990 but reformed as the Social Democracy of the Polish Republic, the chief element of a left coalition called the Democratic Left Union (Sojusz Lewicy Demokratycznej, or SLD). The SLD scored a surprising victory in 1993, profiting from widespread unhappiness at the cost of economic restructuring, and formed a coalition with the reborn Polish Populist Party, the PSL. This alliance toppled the Suchocka government and replaced it with one led by the PSL's taciturn and diffident Waldemar Pawlak. Though the stronger partner, the SLD gave Pawlak the premiership to avoid galvanizing the splintered anti-Communists. Whereas this was certainly a prudent decision, the mumbling, colorless Pawlak embodied the worst defect of traditional Polish peasant politics, narrow class provincialism without any broad, integrating national program. The result was a conflict between the president, Wałęsa—who became increasingly aggressive in power—and a collection of former Communists, peasants, and the faint-hearted who thought Balcerowicz's crash introduction of capitalism was too abrupt a transformation of the Communist welfare state: "shock" to be sure, his critics concluded, but little visible "therapy." Although Poland's international creditors were willing to forgive or reschedule much of the country's massive indebtedness, the costs of transformation were staggering: unemployment, inflation, and plummeting production with promises of future improvement quickly losing their appeal. By 1993 Poland was exhibiting signs of a political crisis with voter apathy, parliamentary gridlock, and a constant parade of bickering factions who were bringing discredit to democratic politics. With the left dominating parliament, Wałęsa increasingly viewed himself as the lone champion of unalloyed anti-Communism, and he fought his parliamentary opponents ruthlessly, acting, by his own admission, with dubious legality.

In the presidential election of 1995, Walesa lost the presidency after a particularly rough and brutal campaign. The winner, the SLD's Aleksander Kwaśniewski, was a former Communist who combined a politically unsavory past with an offensively glib personal style and often played fast and loose with the truth. His victory, coupled with the left's 1993 parliamentary success, seemed to some to threaten the seemingly unimaginable: the Communists returning to office, this time legally and democratically. Wałęsa's defeat, which was the final shattering blow to a Solidarity already divided into quarreling groups, threatened to undo the accomplishments of the past decade. In reality, this fear was unjustified.

Kwaśniewski and his party repeatedly eschewed a return to the political or economic policies of the Communist era. Indeed, their supporters were a collection of those who feared too rapid a plunge into an unknown future and a growing number who feared that Wałęsa and his allies had become morbidly consumed with the politics of revenge, punishing the former leaders of the PRL, rather then concentrating on charting a direction for Poland's future. Moreover, the SLD had adroitly captured considerable support from the growing secularist middle class in Poland—ironically, a group fast increased by the introduction of capitalism—which saw Wałęsa's close association with the Church as heralding a conservative social agenda and a powerful clerical role in political affairs. The fact that many of Wałęsa's most vociferous proponents were neo-*endecja* anti-Communist radicals played into the hands of the SLD. By 1995 Solidarity was the past, and its goals fit ill with a Poland that had already passed through de-Communization—at least psychologically—and wished to consider the next phase in Polish history. In a practical sense, the SLD had a great, but temporary, advantage over its rivals on the right: it was an experienced political team, whereas their opponents were amateurs only recently come together when partisan politics was reborn in Poland. While the SLD focused the forces of the left, by contrast the right, probably a larger proportion of the voters, was divided among numerous factions. The result scattered the center-right vote and netted it relatively few seats in a parliament in which the left was over-represented and the right underrepresented. Obviously, this advantage for the left would last only until their opponents learned the art of electoral politics.

In 1997 the right, after interminable wrangling, achieved sufficient unity to gain an electoral following more reflective of their support in the country. The chief ingredient in this was the organization of a post-Wałęsa Solidarity which became the nucleus of a right-center coalition by refocusing the movement back to union goals and away from the amorphous political role it had played for several years; in other words, Solidarity returned to where it began before natural political differences fragmented it. The chief architect of this transformation was Marian Krzaklewski who assembled a center-right coalition of more than thirty parties into the Solidarity Electoral Alliance (AWS). Meanwhile, Balcerowicz, the architect of Poland's economic rebirth who had been virtually driven from government in 1994 by popular outrage over his austerities, reemerged as a powerful though controversial political actor. He took over the feckless Freedom Union party (Unia Wolności, or UW) and showed consummate skill in reorienting it into a more conservative direction while still maintaining its devotion to secular politics and economic liberalism. The UW had emerged as the most dynamic party in Poland by the late 1990s. Both the AWS and the UW were careful to stress their plans for Poland's future and minimize the need for recriminatory considerations of the PRL. As the center-right forces solidified, the SLD's advantages waned, and its coalition partner, the PSL, remained essentially an agricultural lobby without a national agenda, and it finally collapsed under the uninspired leadership of Pawlak.

The elections of 1997 resulted in a center-right victory in the *sejm* and the formation of a new government based on a AWS-UW coalition.

Though the AWS's Jerzy Buzek was prime minister, his cabinet was dominated by the forceful Balcerowicz who, as deputy premier and holder of the finance portfolio, again had broad authority to structure the Polish economy. By 1999 the better organized UW was quickly overtaking the AWS as the dominant partner in the governing coalition.

In a larger sense, the 1997 election stabilized Polish politics. Fears about a neo-Communist takeover, never really serious, gradually disappeared, as the SLD, during its years in power, piously endorsed the main elements of post-PRL reconstruction: a market economy, a pluralist democracy, and a Western alliance in foreign policy symbolized by seeking membership in the North Atlantic Treaty Organization (NATO). Future victories for the left would not threaten the essential basis of the state. There would be no radical challenge from the left. Post-Communist Poland had achieved a national consensus.

THE ECONOMIC SITUATION

If the PRL was perpetually unstable as the result of an ever reappearing economic gloom on the horizon, the increasingly brightening future of the Polish economy after 1990 has much to do with the stabilization of Polish politics in the Third Republic. This occurred in several short and dramatic phases. The Mazowiecki government inherited an economy in serious, perhaps catastrophic, decline. Rather than take tactical measures, to improve the situation, Mazowiecki gambled on the radical solutions proposed by Balcerowicz who announced a package of reforms to begin at once, his so-called shock therapy approach. Government subsidies to inefficient industries were cut or eliminated and price controls were ended, but Western nations leery about the stability of the new system invested little. The larger Russian market and the seemingly more sound economies of Hungary and even the Czechoslovak Republic (after 1993 the Czech and Slovak Republics) were attracting the lion's share of foreign investment. The result was a severe recession, a staggering surge in inflation, and massive unemployment, which caused the fall of the first Solidarity government and criticism of Balcerowicz by many Poles as a heartless captive of free market dictates oblivious to social needs. On the other hand, his efforts—which were slowed but not reversed by his successor, Grzegorz Kołodko in the SLD-PSL coalition years—did a great deal to lay the basis for the Polish economic resurgence that began in the mid-1990s. Poland's trade was largely reoriented to the West, away from the crumbling trading partners of the Commonwealth of Independent States (CIS) in fact, by 1996, Poland had replaced Russia as Germany's principal eastern commercial partner. Although privatization was slower than anticipated—and lagged especially in the SLD-PSL years—the bulk of the statist economy was dismantled, and even Balcerowicz admitted to being stunned by the vigor and enterprise of the private sector which quickly became the engine of economic expansion.

Two factors deserve special attention in explaining the Polish economic resurgence. First, Poland was able to arrange the cancellation of billions of its foreign debt in 1994, largely due to Kołodko's efforts, thus removing an enormous burden from the economy. Whereas this was an indubitable achievement, a second feature is more controversial. Kołodko has argued that the last years of the Jaruzelski regime saw considerable restructuring of the economy and hence allowed Poland a head start on capitalism. Critics of Balcerowicz, and there are many, point to this, rather than credit his dramatic efforts, which they condemn as having caused much needless destabilization, as the basis for Polish recovery. The origins of the Polish economic success remain controversial.

Nonetheless, by 1994, the economy had begun to register serious jumps in annual growth of the gross domestic product (GDP), averaging almost 6 percent per annum for the rest of the decade and making Poland one of the fastest growing economies in Europe, the "tiger of the emerging markets" according to the international financial press, and the most conspicuous success story of the post-Communist states. In the latter part of the decade, Hungary and the Czech Republic, which had earlier forged ahead of Poland by more cautious restructuring strategies and the influx of a greater Western investment, began to falter and suffered through years of sluggish or negative growth. These Poland avoided. Even more impressive, the Poles were able to escape largely unscathed from the collapse of the Russian economy in 1998 which had serious effects in much of Europe and was catastrophic to the CIS nations. Warsaw was increasingly regarded by 1997 as the economical capital of the post-Communist east. Foreign investment surged, and Poland became the leading locus for foreign capital in the region by the late 1990s, attracting 10 billion dollars annually. Warsaw's main street, Nowy Świat, long a dreary collection of eclectic and indifferent architecture, had become by 1998 the busiest commercial street on earth.

Yet more impressive than the isolated figures of sustained GDP growth are the simultaneous drop in inflation, which dipped to 7 percent in 1999 and continued to shrink thereafter, and the steady fall in unemployment at roughly the same rate. Poland was expanding the economy while dampening inflationary pressure. Moreover, developments in key economic areas were extraordinary: investment was increasing at more than 20 percent per annum-(triple the GDP growth rate), leading the Organization for Economic Cooperation and Development (OECD); industrial production stood at more than 10 percent; consumption was rising at better than 7 percent; investors doubled their volume yearly, reflecting and stimulating profound optimism. The Polish financial press boasted that the country enjoyed, in Balcerowicz and Hanna Gronkiewicz-Waltz, the "best finance minister in Europe" and the "best national bank president," respectively—boasts certainly reflecting great self-confidence regardless of their accuracy.

This achievement is especially striking when it is placed in an international context. Poland's economic surge came against the background of a general lackluster performance of the European economy, erratic growth by its fellow ex-Communist neighbors, the collapse of the CIS, and the lingering Asian and South American downturns of the 1990s. Only tiny Estonia and Slovenia enjoyed similar levels of success. Western interest in Poland visibly evolved from doubt, to fascination, to praise. Poland's bond rating improved steadily after 1995: in late 1998, Reuters reported that Poland was regarded as the most attractive locus for capital of any emerging market. This was reflected in the reports of the annual *Economic Freedom of the World*, which showed Poland advancing forward many places yearly.

In 1998 Balcerowicz unveiled a bold vision for Poland's economic future which probably over-optimistically called for a sustained strategic growth of over 6 percent, inflation rates of about 5 percent, and unemployment to stay below 8 percent. This would be accomplished by accelerating the remaining privatization of the economy through a mass privatization program (MPP) which would involve the entire adult population of the country in the purchase of shares in enterprises being privitized. The MPP was a rapid success, attracting 95 percent of all eligible investors. Early in 1999, analysts unveiled strategic projects for the Polish economy which anticipated growth rates of from 5 to 6 percent to continue for the first two decades of the next century, almost triple the anticipated Western European average. Both the government, and with less caution, the population began to speak about a Polish economic "miracle." The press was filled with prognostications about exactly when Poland would overtake various Western states, with the first major success predicted for about 2020. Poland was, it seemed, finally leaving the backward east to which it had been for so long confined.

By the end of the 1990s, however, Poland was confronted with a question whose answer was not obvious. The severe recession in many Asian and South American economies, plus the virtual collapse of the CIS states, led directly to a stunning shrinkage of Western investment in so-called developing economies, a decline of 90 percent in just a few years. Poland was regarded by many in the West as being an exception, but it was dangerously included in the weak and volatile "emerging" world in the minds of others. Would Poland escape from a dangerous category or be damaged by affiliation? Signals were mixed by the end of the century, but an unexpected GDP drop in late 1998 was unsettling, albeit transitory. Most conjectured that NATO membership and rapid acceptance into the European Union (EU), anticipated for 2003, would make any downturn in the Polish economy a short-lived one.

This economic transformation had a profound effect on Polish life as the country began to take stock of the changes around it. Some commentators were deeming the economic and political success of the 1990s one of Poland's greatest victories, allowing the nation to regain its self-respect and reassert a claim to being regarded as a worthy member of the European community, not just a poor and primitive relation. Hopes to stage the Olympic games in Poland early in the twenty-first century; to make Warsaw an important center of modern art by the construction of huge galleries; to modernize the road, railway, and air systems to make Poland a major European link—all these reflect this mood of national pride and self-confidence. Warsaw, long a dreary metropolis, at only 3 or 4 percent of the national population a small capital by European standards, was emerging at century's end as second only to Berlin as the most dynamic city in Europe. To be sure, problems remain. Poland is still poor by West European standards, and the recent economic surge has been unevenly felt, exacerbating the gap between rich and poor. As Poland moves towards union with Europe, some sections, like Warsaw and the Western provinces, are transforming far more quickly than eastern Poland. Rural areas and Polish farmers generally—at least a quarter of the population—have benefited little from the socioeconomic transformation. Thus, there are many problems still to address.

INTERNATIONAL AFFAIRS

In March 1999 Poland, formerly the cornerstone of the Warsaw Pact, joined NATO which symbolized the revolutionary transformation of Poland's international position. The birth of Third Republic was attended by changes in the structure of Europe more profound than those that enabled the rebirth of the Second Republic eighty years earlier. In a few years, the Soviet Empire had collapsed, independent states emerged or re-emerged in Belarus, Ukraine, and the Baltic; Germany was reunited. Each of these events had huge significance for Poland; all of them together have worked a geopolitical revolution.

Poland's security dilemma had been created long ago by a slow but inevitable decline in the country's strength in relation to that of its neighbors. The history of the Second Republic was essentially a vain search for some escape from this dilemma, which the PZPR clung to as the permanent justification for its rule. The communists could make a case for this in 1945; fifty-years later, their arguments were irrelevant.

German unification in 1990 initially suggested an overpowering threat from the West for a staggering Poland. Poland's participation in the "Two plus Four" unification negotiations, however, resulted in two fundamental political accords with the new Germany. The first, concluded in November 1990, resulted in the new state's recognition of the Oder-Neisse (Odra-Nysa) line as the frontier between the two countries. Second, seven months later, Warsaw officially recognized the existence of a German minority within its borders and allowed it to organize a network of political and social organizations. This was accompanied by Polish acknowledgment of a sizable German population within the country, perhaps as many as between 300,000 and 400,000, though the exact figure is problematical.

Germany quickly emerged as the principal sponsor of Poland's entrance into the political, military, and economic structures of integrating Europe. Warsaw made it clear that the fundamental goals of its foreign policy were, in the 1992 words of Foreign Minister Krzysztof Skubiszewski, "integration with West European structures and institutions" with a "strategic objective in the security sphere . . . to join NATO."[1] Initially the new Polish authorities sought to enter Europe via French sponsorship but found Paris a reluctant advocate. Germany's Chancellor Helmut Kohl endorsed the main goals of Polish policy and pledged German support of Polish efforts to seek membership in the European Community (EC). In 1999 the new chancellor, Gerhard Schröder, reiterated this position. Germany's steadfast support of Poland reflects the transformation that has made Germany the principal proponent of European unity and continental stability. To be sure, an underlying sense of guilt plays a role in German actions toward Poland, but the overpowering advantages brought by reconciliation between France and Germany after 1945 is doubtless the factor that has played the stronger role. Moreover, Germany sees in a stable and prosperous Poland a guaranty of its own eastern security. Poland's NATO membership has integrated it into a European security system as Berlin's ally.

The German minority has not become the contentious issue many Poles had feared. Two factors seem to be at work. First, the tiny German minority represents no threat to internal stability, whereas during the Second Republic, millions of Germans formed dominating elements in the western frontier region of Poland. Second, the German minority is a sensitive issue in direct proportion to the tension between Warsaw and Berlin. In the present era this tension is low.

German economic power has also failed to assume the menacing proportions feared. Here the resurgence of the Polish economy has played a major role. The Germans have found in a robust Poland a lucrative trading partner and an attractive place for investment. The economic assimilation of the former German Democratic Republic (or East Germany) has been enormously costly to Germany and has soaked up much of the investment money at Berlin's disposal. This, in turn, allowed the Germans less opportunity to expand to the east in the first vulnerable years of post-Communist transition. Poland's full membership in the EC will further stabilize the economic relationship between the two countries.

This is not to say that there are no possibilities of a renewal of Polish-German frictions, only that any comparisons with the interwar period are fundamentally invalid. Currently the large structures, NATO and the EU are shaping events in a cooperative rather than confrontational direction. A catastrophic breakdown in political or economic stability in either country would obviously pose serious problems, but even in such a case, the larger context is more propitious for peaceful solutions than had been the case previously.

Poland's relations with Russia, the other traditional antagonist, have been less auspicious. The cause of the difficulties may be found largely in the east. The collapse of the Soviet empire, the political and economic instability of Russia, the anomalous structure of the CIS, the weakness of Ukraine, and the virtual collapse of Belarus's bid for national independence in the 1990s have all made Poland's vision of the east understandably troubled. Obviously a reconciliation with Russia similar to that being worked out with Germany would be the ultimate gain in Polish security. However, this is largely out of Poland's hands, and it presumes a stable and prosperous Russia which did not exist at the end of the twentieth century.

Essentially Poland's eastern policy is a combination of relations with its immediate neighbors and direct relations with Moscow. Beyond question, it is of fundamental importance to Poland to see secure and independent regimes established in Ukraine, Belarus, and Lithuania. Poland, which was the first country to recognize Ukrainian independence in 1991, has pursued, on the whole, an enlightened policy toward its eastern neighbors. In the early 1990s Polish-Lithuanian relations were repeatedly strained by a hostile Lithuanian policy demanding apologies for perceived wrongs suffered at Polish hands in the past. Moreover, the large Polish minority in Lithuania, which has suffered some discrimination at Lithuanian hands, threatened to provoke further strain in relations between the two countries. Poland adopted a conciliatory policy toward the Lithuanians by refusing to champion the Polish minority about which the Lithuanians are sensitive. The Poles seem, on the whole, quite aware of Vilnius's vulnerabilities and wisely have not tried to exploit them for temporary advantage at the expense of regional stability. Here we may see this as an analogy to Polish-German relations with Warsaw adopting the role of Berlin. By the late 1990s Polish-Lithuanian relations had been considerably repaired, and Lithuania now counts on Poland to act as its champion in Lithuania's efforts to join NATO and perhaps the EC.

This reflects Warsaw's principal advantage in dealing with the eastern states. As Poland moves toward European integration, it becomes the model for its neighbors; this increases Warsaw's stature and prompts neighboring states to strike a cooperative attitude. Here a good example is the steady evolution of Ukraine's position on Polish NATO membership, which began with hostility, but by the late 1990s was characterized by open declarations of support with the reminder that the Poles should help ease the role of the Ukraine as it follows the path blazed by Warsaw.

The relationship between the Ukraine and Poland has been problematical. First, the Ukraine has had a rocky road to political and economic reconstruction after the collapse of the Soviet Union. Its economy fell steadily over the decade of the 1990s, and the gap between the Polish and Ukrainian economies has become dramatic: within a decade, the per capita GDP went from virtual parity to a Polish advantage of almost 4 to 1. With severe demographic problems, which threaten to decrease the population by hundreds of thousands annually, the Ukraine faces a grim future, despite its huge size, generous endowment of resources, and strategic location. The great fear of both Poland and Ukraine is that continued instability in Ukraine will prompt emulation of the Belarussian example, which is a sort of national suicide in which the country has gradually surrendered itself to reintegration with Russia and control from Moscow. This would be a disaster for Poland almost as great as for Ukraine, and the realization of this has caused the Poles to adopt a positive policy toward Ukraine. With the Polish minority in Ukraine reduced to insignificance, and the Ukrainian presence in Poland only slightly more, the traditional minority frictions have been attenuated if not eliminated. However, Poland's ability to assist Ukraine is minimal and until greater economic and political order prevail there, this will remain an area of much concern for Warsaw.

Belarus is obviously a grave disappointment for Poland. Belarus, essentially eastern Poland for a longtime, was systematically denationalized by the Russians. The Belarussian national movement, which made a fragile appearance at the beginning of the century, never succeeded in rooting itself broadly or deeply in the land. As a result, powerful Russian influence, plus the close integration of the local economy with that of Soviet Russia, made the independence of Belarus a virtual fiction by the end of the 1990s. This is particularly galling to the Poles as it makes manifest the Russian ethnographic victory at Polish expense over the last two centuries which have made such historic Polish centers as Grodno, Brześć, and Lida—now east of Poland's border in Belarus—Polish no more. Whereas the loss of Wilno and Lwów have been painful to Poland, recognition of their loss is essential to the creation of harmonious relations with Lithuania and Ukraine, a vital concern for regional security. By contrast Belarus has not emerged as an independent state, and the Polish territorial losses here have accomplished nothing other than diminishing Poland. Belarus's president, the unstable Aleksander Lukashenka, opposed Poland's entry to NATO, lamented his lack of nuclear warheads, and called for Russia to organize an anti-NATO coalition.

A particular challenge to the Poles is how to develop close and mutually beneficial relations with these eastern states without alarming Russian fears of Polish imperial desires encroaching on what they still regard as their preemptive sphere of influence. Poland cannot be indifferent to the fate of the Baltic, Belarus, and Ukraine, nor can it risk developing relations with this area in a manner provocative to Moscow. This problem for Poland is the more perplexing, because it is largely a matter of Russian sensitivities over which the Poles exercise very little influence.

In May 1992 Wałęsa paid a state visit to Boris Yeltsin the president of the Russian Federation. This was the first time the head of a truly independent Polish state had ever been received in the Kremlin. Wałęsa adopted a policy widely criticized at the time in Poland by demanding no symbolic concessions from the Russians but concentrated instead on pressing practical issues, especially the speedy removal of Russian troops from Polish soil, which was accomplished over the next year. The Poles even agreed to pay the costs of cleaning up the ecological problems left by the departing Russians. This was obviously a concession to Moscow's continuing great power vanities, but it also avoided beginning this new phase in Polish-Russian relations with bitterness and confrontation.

Over the next several years, Polish-Russian relations have been dominated by Poland's determined effort to join the economic and security systems of Western Europe and thus abandon any shadow of Russian control. This has provoked a long and occasionally bitter effort by the Russians to assert their rights to some ill-defined influence over the former Soviet empire. As Poland's quest for NATO membership gradually garnered support in the West, Moscow stepped back, recognizing its declining leverage in international affairs. When Poland joined NATO in March 1999 Russian's symbolic influence over Poland ended, but the central problem of Polish-Russian relations was merely redefined. Warsaw was regarded by Moscow as trying to intrude in its traditional sphere of influence by supporting Lithuanian and Ukrainian efforts to join the West.

A separate but quite significant irritant in Polish-Russian relations is the problem of Kaliningrad, which threatens to cause difficulties in the future. The Russians insisted on retaining this slice of east Prussia, the former Königsberg area, during World War II and subsequently made it into a major naval base and imported a considerable population. After the fall of communism, there was some speculation that the territory would become a free trade zone for Russia and perhaps fall under effective German economic control. Neither of these happened probably because of Russia's economic difficulties.

Kaliningrad is an anomaly. Its small population, with a low birthrate and a high mortality rate, is demographically ailing. A center for illegal arms and its drug trade, Kaliningrad, notorious for crime, has the highest AIDS rate in Europe. Its Russian population regularly supports extreme nationalist candidates. The only part of Russia to border Poland, Kaliningrad is a potential point of friction between Warsaw and Moscow. If Belarus is again swallowed by Russia, Kaliningrad will pose an awkward issue between Poland and Russia, in some ways disturbingly reminiscent of the role played by East Prussia as a point of friction between Poland and Germany before World War II.

Obviously, Poland would gain immeasurably by a reconciliation with the Russians to complement that being forged with the Germans. However, this does not appear probable in the immediate future. First, Germany is one of the great postwar economic success stories. Simultaneously, the new Germany has shunned its former passionate quest for continental dominance which so disordered the twentieth century and, instead, is the leading proponent of European integration—including the post-Communist states with Poland in the forefront. In other words, Germany has successfully redefined its European mission in a manner that is immensely beneficial to both itself and the continent.

By comparison, Moscow, by the end of the century, had arrived at the depths of a profound crisis of self-definition without a clear strategic vision of its role in the world. Its economy visibly declining, a political system only occasionally characterized by democratic practices, Russia is a singular combination of vast military power and a floundering economy. Until Russia emerges as a healthy, constructive member of the European community, Poland's only recourse is to look to its own security and avoid provocative actions in the east. Poland's quest for NATO and EC membership has been a response to the enigma of Russia as much as it has been an effort to avoid confrontation with Germany.

So overarching has been the significance of Poland's relationship with Russia and Germany that the links with its neighbors to the south, the Czech and Slovak Republics and Hungary, have been, by comparison, less important. This, too reflects the interwar period. Initially, the Third Republic attached considerable significance to the so-called Visegrad Triangle a regional coordination of Warsaw, Prague, and Budapest, expanded after 1993 to include Bratislava. However, the Czechs showed little support in the mid 1990s, regarding the link to the Poles as hindering rather than promoting rapid integration into Europe. By the late 1990s the Visegrad group seemed to be revitalizing, but with three of the four states entering NATO in 1999, the Visegrad combination has a problematical future.

PONDERING THE FUTURE

In 1950 Poland with a population of 22 million, was about twice the size of Hungary, and 150 percent that of Czechoslovakia. Ukraine to the east was 50 percent larger. Spain, which Poland had surpassed in the

1930s to become the fifth largest European country, exceeded Poland's population by a wide margin. Italy, England, and France were all twice Poland's size. Half a century later, thanks to sustained high birth rates, Poland had four times Hungary's population, and more than 250 percent of the combined population of the Czech and Slovak republics. It has caught Spain, again, and is close to 70 percent of the size of the three large West European states. The population gap with Ukraine is closing at perhaps 500,000 annually, suggesting parity within a generation. Even though Russia, with more than 140 million is better than triple Poland's size, this is an incomparable smaller gap than the almost eight to one disparity between Poland and the Soviet Union a generation ago, and the gap is closing. Poland is by far the most important country in the region. In short, it has overcome the biological nightmare of World War II and has worked a significant change in its relationship with the other members of the European community, a change of historic dimension as Poland's current rapid economic success is now multiplied by a far larger factor, thus magnifying its relative weight in Europe. This demographic vigor has also neutralized minority problems and lessened dramatically likelihood of frontier revision. When the history of this century is written a generation later, Poland's surge to success will be linked inextricably to its demographic expansion since 1945.[2]

A second major fact explaining Poland's happy conclusion of what was otherwise a most difficult century was the high degree of religiosity. This almost uniform Roman Catholic loyalty gave the country a cohesion rare in Europe and almost unique in the region. The degree to which Polish Catholicism inhibited the PRL regime, or possibly even stayed the hand of the Kremlin at crucial moments, is a fascinating, though ultimately conjectural, exercise. Nonetheless, the Church certainly and in a very real sense acted as the "shield of the nation."

Closely associated, but deserving special attention, is the historical significance of John Paul II, the Polish pope. His patriotism, personal loathing of anti-semitism, and magnanimity were an inspiration of how Poles could maintain their oldest traditions and yet confront the modern world with confidence and faith. He has been an example of the best features of the Polish national character and has inspired his countrymen to emulation.

The pope has played a central role in combating the lingering taint of anti-semitism in Poland. Both as pope and as a Pole, Karol Wojtyła has championed reconciliation between Catholic Poles and the Jewish community. During his pontificate, more has been done to advance Catholic-

Jewish relations than in any other similar period in Church history. This is of enormous significance to Poland, the site of the extermination of Europe's Jewish community. At the end of the 1990s, a rebirth of Jewish life is visible in Poland, though of a most unusual sort. The Jews of Poland are but a handful, but the community has shown renewed vigor. The world Jewish community has also rediscovered its Polish roots and has done much to stimulate interest in the culture and history of this vital component of Poland's past. Belatedly, many non-Jews in Poland are discovering Polish Jewry for the first time, not, alas as a living community, but as a heritage of rich complexity that helped shape the national past.

Whereas it may be speculated that other former Communist states emerged with their independence without either the demographic vitality or the Catholic fervor of the Poles, this omits a crucial factor: without Poland would the Soviet Empire have fallen and in the manner in which it did? Was not Poland, because of its size and strength, the anchor for the survival and reemergence of independent states in Central Europe? In other words, did not a free Czech Republic require the prior existence of a free Poland?

Third, Poland reemerged as a version of itself; a conscious effort was made to reknit the rent fabric of historic continuity. The Solidarity era's chantlike song "Żeby Polska byla Polska" ("So that Poland might be Poland") is symbolic. The emotional energy behind the dissident movement was not to create something new but to reassert something old: the right of Poland to be a country according to its own lights, informed by its own history, and faithful to its own values.

Fourth, is the geopolitical context forming around the Third Republic. Scattered evidence seems to suggest the reemergence of Poland as a point of coalescence for the peoples between Germany and Russia, the leadership of the area once associated with the Jagiellonians. As the leader in the movement toward reintegration with Europe, politically and economically, Poland seems in many ways to be returning to an old role. If in a fast-integrating continent, Poland emerges playing the largest role in Central Europe, this will vindicate the lasting value of many of the most generous aspects of the Jagiellonian tradition while rejecting the Dmowskiite view of Poland which has brought but problematical gains, and much loss.

Finally, Poland in the year 2000 has regained considerable ground in the esteem of the world which it had lost over the preceding two centuries. Poland was a name associated with failure for much of modern

European history. The partitions were an indictment of the Polish past; the failed insurrections were a further demonstration of national incapacity. The Second Republic seemed, by its brevity and crushing conclusion, but renewed failure. The history of the PRL was a half-century of fecklessness, punctuated by episodes of anti-semitism and economic clownishness. The West had gradually come to see Poland as something between the inconsequential and the ridiculous.

At century's end, Poland is rapidly emerging as a respected, though still struggling, member of the European community with many victories already to its credit. Economic success, political stability, international prudence, and the support of its neighbors are fashioning a new Poland for the world's consideration. In so doing this newly furbished Poland will prompt a retrospective reconsideration of the national past, in which the greatness of Poland will emerge alongside and perhaps overpowering the folly.

Two hundred years ago, when Tadeusz Kościuszko fell gravely wounded, he was believed to have said, "This is the end of Poland." The quotation is apocryphal but not inaccurate. A century later, the novelist Joseph Conrad, a Pole, could not even speak of Poland, so convinced was he that its resurrection was impossible. At the beginning of the twenty-first century, Poland is prosperous and secure. It is too soon to take the measure of so much so fast. The return of Poland and the rapid movement of Europe toward unity recall Mickiewiczian predictions of Poland's resurrection which would herald a new day for Europe. This is, perhaps, national Romanticism; it is also, perhaps, the truth.

NOTES

1. Quoted in Richard F. Staar, ed., *Transition to Democracy in Poland* (New York, 1993), 238–39.

2. The decline in the Polish birthrate over the last years has understandably worried many analysts.

Notable People in the History of Poland

Anders, Władysław (1892–1970). Soldier of the Second Republic. Anders fought with distinction in the war with the Bolsheviks (1919–1921) and in the September Campaign (1939). Captured by the Soviets, he commanded the Polish forces in the Soviet Union after 1941 and led them to the Middle East in 1942. As commander of the Second Corps, Anders achieved a brilliant record in North Africa and Italy, notably in the action at Monte Casino. Politically controversial, he feuded with Władysław Sikorski and became the last commander of the Polish forces in exile at the end of World War II.

Balcerowicz, Leszek (1947–   ). Economist and statesman. His controversial shock-therapy economic transformation (1989–1991) resulted in serious dislocation, and he was forced out of his position as minister of finance. His views were later vindicated by the resurgence of the economy, and he returned to government in 1997. One of the most adroit politicians of the Third Republic, he refashioned the Freedom Union party into a powerful force.

Batory, Stefan (1533–1586). Transylvanian prince elected king of Poland in 1576. His brilliant victory over the Russians in the Livonian wars made the Commonwealth the dominant military power in the east. His promising reign was cut short by his mysterious death in 1586.

Beck, Józef (1894–1944). Soldier and statesman of the Second Republic. A legionnaire, he became Józef Piłsudski's trusted lieutenant regarding foreign policy after 1926 and served as foreign minister from 1932 to 1939. Often criticized for abrasively overplaying a weak diplomatic hand and naiveté regarding Germany, Beck faced a virtually impossible task. He died in exile in Romania in 1944.

Bierut, Bolesław (1892–1956). Polish People's Republic (PRL) politician. A Comintern official before World War II, he was the leader of the Muscovite faction of the Polish Workers' party. He served as head of the state, the government, and especially the party (1948–1956). He was a colorless, insignificant patriarch of the PRL.

Bolesław I (967?–1025). Piast duke and first king of Poland (1025). His campaigns against the Germans, Russians, and Czechs made Poland a major power in Central Europe. His establishment of Gniezno as an independent archbishopric assured the independence of the Polish church from the Holy Roman Empire with important consequences for Poland.

Czartoryski, Adam Prince (1770–1861). Statesman. Scion of one of the most powerful aristocratic families, Czartoryski served Alexander I of Russia in opposition to Napoleon whom he profoundly mistrusted. A major influence behind the Congress Kingdom, Czartoryski was able to preserve much of the Polish culture in the *kresy* by serving as head of education in so-called western Russia. A major figure in the abortive November Rising (1830), he later led Polish emigré conservative politics from Paris.

Dmowski, Roman (1864–1939). Ideologue and statesman. Author of a root and branch critique of the Polish political tradition, Dmowski is the father of modern Polish nationalism. Dmowski led the Polish National Committee during World War I and represented Poland at the Paris Peace Conference (1919). His active political career was brief, but his nationalism became the dominant ideology of post-1919 Poland.

Gierek, Edward (1913–   ). Polish People's Republic (PRL) leader. Gierek spent much of his youth in Western Europe and later became the party "boss" of Silesia. He replaced Władysław Gomułka in 1970 and led a disastrous economic restructuring that prompted the crisis of the mid-1970s. Solidarity led to his downfall and his replacement by Stanisław Kania.

Glemp, Józef (1929–   ). Religious leader of the Polish People's Republic (PRL) and Third Republic. He became the primate of Poland after Stefan Wyszyński's death in 1981. A homely, awkward man, Glemp had been criticized for his excessive accommodation under the PRL and his tactless political statements afterward, especially regarding Polish-Jewish relations. His historic position will suffer from his unfortunate juxtaposition between the giant figures of Wyszyński and Karol Wojtyła.

Gomułka, Władysław (1905–1982). Polish People's Republic (PRL) leader. He served as the Polish Workers' party first secretary, from 1943 to 1948, but was purged for supposed nationalism. He reemerged in 1956 during Polish October and led the party until he was replaced by Edward Gierek in 1970.

Haller, Józef (1873–1960). Soldier and statesman of the Second Republic. Haller was a legionnaire, though not a Piłsudskiite. He became head of the Polish army raised in the West (1917–1918) and played a major role in the Bolshevik war. Associated with the opposition to the Piłsudskiite regime, Haller played a brief role in the World War II exile government. Politically inept, his military talents did not extend beyond battlefield command.

Jadwiga d'Anjou (1374–1399). Granddaughter of Piast Kazimierz III and wife of Jagiello (1386–1399) and thus the link between the two dynasties. She is remembered for her virtual restoration of the University of Kraków and other educational and charitable activities. She was recently canonized.

Jagiełło (1350?–1434). Grand duke of Lithuania (1378–1401). Jagiełło married Jadwiga d'Anjou in (1386) and began the dynasty that ruled until 1572. This union resulted in the conversion of Lithuania to Catholicism and the Polish-Lithuanian victory over the Teutonic Knights at Grünwald in 1410.

Jaruzelski, Wojciech (1923–   ). Polish People's Republic (PRL) soldier and politician. Soviet-trained, he rose rapidly to become minister of defense (1968). He later served as prime minister (1981–1985) and first secretary of the Polish United Workers' Party (PZPR), (1981–1989), replacing Stanisław Kania. He declared martial law in 1981 but eventually was forced to deal with Solidarity and negotiate the end of Communist rule. He served as the president of Poland, from 1989 to 1990, during the transition from the PRL to the Third Republic. Intelligent and complex his motives and actions remain controversial.

Kazimierz III ("Wielki") (1310–1370). Last and perhaps greatest king of the Piast line. Ruling from 1333 to 1370, he more than doubled the size of Poland, especially to the southeast, while pursuing successful diplomacy with the Teutonic Knights. His foreign policy successes were accompanied by the foundation of the first Polish University (1364) and the codification of the national laws. His tolerant policy toward the Jews encouraged their large-scale movement to Poland.

Korfanty, Wojciech (1864–1939). Leader of Silesian Poles in German parliament before World War I. He led the Silesian risings (1919–1922). An opponent of the *sanacja* regime, he joined Ignacy Jan Paderewski and Władysław Sikorski in creating a political opposition group called the *Front Morges*.

Kościuszko, Tadeusz (1747–1817). Soldier and statesman. Kościuszko fought with distinction in the American Revolution and returned to Poland to lead an insurrection against Russia, attempting to avert the Third Partition (1794). His victory at Racławice was notable, but the rising ended in disaster. A radical republican, Kościuszko tried to refashion Poland along modern lines, but he was unable to conduct war and reorganize Poland politically simultaneously. His defeat sealed the end of old Poland. A national hero of unequaled stature, Kościuszko is revered for both his patriotism and his almost saintly personal goodness.

Kuroń, Jacek (1934–). Polish People's Republic (PRL) dissident and Solidarity activist. Kuroń was a renowned critic of the PRL from the early 1960s, at first from a Marxist perspective. He cofounded the Committee of Workers' Defense (KOR) and was an early adviser to Solidarity. He played a major role in the roundtable negotiations that ended the PRL. Kuroń has served in several Third Republic governments, but his efforts to win the presidency have failed badly. Kuroń is one of the major figures in the birth of the Third Republic.

Kwaśniewski, Aleksander (1954–   ). President of Poland since 1995. Kwaśniewski was a prominent PZPR official and joined the SLD after the fall of Communism. Clever, charming, and flexible, he defeated Lech Wałęsa for the presidency in 1995 and emerged as the most effective former communist politician in Poland.

Lelewel, Joachim (1786–1861). Historian and politician. Lelewel was one of the founders of Romantic historiography, which evinced a radical democratic interpretation of the Polish past. Active in the November rising (1830), he later led the radical camp in Polish emigré politics.

Mazowiecki, Tadeusz (1927–   ). Catholic intellectual member of the Polish People's Republic (PRL) *sejm*, and one of the principal early advisors to Solidarity. He became first prime minister of the Third Republic in 1989. His feud with Lech Wałęsa, and his government's shock-therapy economic transition, led to his fall from power and a humiliating defeat in the 1990 presidential election.

Michnik, Adam (1946–   ). Polish People's Republic (PRL) dissident and intellectual. A student leader, Michnik played major roles in both the Committee of Workers' Defense (KOR) and the advisory committee to Solidarity. Although he served briefly in the *sejm* of the Third Republic, Michnik has concentrated on making his newspaper, *Gazeta Wyborcza*, the most widely read and respected journal in Poland. Michnik has combined a fundamentally secular disposition with a sympathy for Polish religious traditions. He is perhaps the most influential intellectual figure in Polish politics today.

Mickiewicz, Adam (1798–1855). Poet and philosopher. Mickiewicz is the most significant of the Polish Romantic poets of the early nineteenth century. His profound, mystical patriotism, combined with great poetic talent, resulted in the creation of works which have proven to be remarkably influential though little known and virtually incomprehensible outside of the Polish cultural ambit. With Mickiewicz begins the role of the national bard who preserves Polish tradition during eras of national subjugation.

Mikołajczyk, Stanisław (1901–1966). Politician of the Second Republic and leader of the government in exile. Mikolajczyk was a prominent Populist party politician before the war and led the party in exile after

1939. He replaced Władysław Sikorski as premier of the exile government after the general's death in 1943. He resigned his post and returned to Poland to join the Polish Workers' party (PPR)-dominated coalition government in 1944 but was forced to flee in 1947. A weak and unimpressive figure, his decision to return was well intentioned but unwise.

Moczar, Mieczysław (1913–1986). Polish People's Republic (PRL) politician. One of the most disreputable of the Polish United Workers' party (PZPR) leaders, Moczar spent his early career in the security apparatus and became minister of the interior in 1964. He was the leader of the so-called Partisan faction, which combined crude often racist patriotism with anti-Semitism in an effort to suppress dissent within the PZPR and society as a whole. His motives still remain mysterious, but his tactics were disreputable and damaged Poland's international standing.

Norwid, Cyprian (1821–1983). Poet, playright, and artist. Norwid's complex and original writings have gained in esteem throughout this century.

Paderewski, Ignacy Jan (1860–1941). Pianist, composer, and statesman. Paderewski was the most celebrated concert artist of his day. He used his celebrity status to raise money and support for Poland during World War I, and eventually he was widely recognized, especially in the United States, as the leader of the Polish cause. With Western support, he became Poland's first prime minister in 1919. An incompetent administrator, he soon left politics and spent the rest of his life in Switzerland where he was associated with the opposition to the Piłsudskiite regime, the *Front Morges*. He briefly served in the government in exile during World War II. A patriot nonpareil, Paderewski was also vain and unsteady.

Piłsudski, Józef (1867–1935). Revolutionary, soldier, and statesman. The patriarch of Polish socialism, he was the charismatic head of the Polish legions and served as the first head of state of reborn Poland (1918–1923). He was the victor in war against the Soviet Union and (1919–1921) and retuned to power from 1926 to 1935. A symbol of Polish patriotism, he is associated with federalism and the Jagiellonian conception of Poland's place in Europe.

Poniatowski, Stanisław August (1732–1798). Last king of Poland. This controversial monarch began his reign as a Russian puppet and later championed the reforms that culminated in the May 3rd Constitution. Highly cultured, Poniatowski ruled at a time of enormous difficulties for Poland which he was unable to master.

Popiełuszko, Jerzy (1947–1984). Priest and patriot. He emerged as a fiery defender of national and human rights during the martial law era (1981–1989). He was kidnapped and murdered by the security apparatus of the Polish People's Republic (PRL). The subsequent trial of his assailants undermined the regime's authority and forced it to recognize the power of public opinion. Widely regarded as a national martyr, Popiełuszko has been suggested as a candidate for beatification.

Sienkiewicz, Henryk (1846–1916). Writer and winner of the Nobel Prize in literature in 1905. His gigantic *Trilogy* has played a large role in the formation of modern Polish culture. Set during the innumerable wars of the mid-seventeenth century, the *Trilogy* paints a picture of Polish chivalry, magnanimity, and patriotism which stirred a nation increasingly in despair over the dismal prospects of partitioned Poland at the end of the nineteenth century.

Sikorski, Władysław (1881–1943). Soldier and statesman. He fought in the legions from 1914 to 1918 and saw distinguished service in the war against the Bolsheviks from 1919 to 1921. Politically he opposed Józef Piłsudski and later the colonels' regime. He served as premier of the government in exile from 1939 to 1943. He died in a controversial air crash off Gibraltar. His death meant the collapse of the exile government's status in the war. Sikorski combined broad vision and commanding personality with vanity and petty jealousy.

Słowacki Juliusz (1809–1849). Romantic, messianic poet. Słowacki is traditionally regarded as one of the greatest of all Polish writers.

Śmigły-Rydz, Edward (1886–1941). Soldier and statesman of the Second Republic. He served as a legionnaire and was a prominent commander in the war against the Bolsheviks (1919–1921). Józef Piłsudski's most trusted lieutenant, he became the first soldier of Poland after Piłsudski's death (1935) and increasingly influential. His performance as commander in the 1939 September campaign was deeply flawed. He left Poland in September to much criticism, but he returned and died in 1941. His political ineptitude and disastrous leadership in 1939 have overshadowed his very impressive earlier military career.

Sobieski, Jan (1629–1696). King of Poland. A military hero, Sobieski was elected king and tried to rejuvenate the Commonwealth after decades of ruinous warfare. Although he won a great victory over the Turks in Vienna in 1683, he was unable either to arrest Poland's strategic decline or to solidify the dangerously weak monarchical authority. He is remembered as the last great leader of pre-partition Poland and an incomparable battlefield commander.

Suchocka, Hanna (1946–   ). Stateswoman of the Third Republic. Suchocka, a lawyer by training, served in the *sejm* of the Polish People's Republic (PRL) and briefly in that of the Third Republic. She became Poland's first female prime minister in 1992 and proved an effective administrator. Her ministry fell when the 1994 elections brought a combination of the Democratic Left Alliance (SLD) and the Polish Populist Party (PSL) to power, but she returned to prominence in 1997 with the coalition of the Solidarity Election Alliance (AWS) and the Freedom Union (UW) made her minister of justice. Her ability to combine Catholic loyalties with a progressive socioeconomic policy has made her one of the most successful and highly regarded politicians of the Third Republic.

Traugutt, Romuald (1826–1864). Principal political leader of the January rising (1863). A fiery patriot and radical democrat, he was captured and publicly executed by the Russians.

Wałęsa, Lech (1943–   ). Labor organizer. A worker of humble origin, he emerged as a leader of the 1980 strikes and eventually of the Solidarity movement. He won the Nobel Peace Prize in 1983. In his dealings with the Polish People's Republic (PRL) regime, he showed wisdom and resource, but after he was elected president (1990–1995), his leadership was riven with controversy over his administrative incompetence and high-handedness. In the late 1990s he tried to restore his image as an elder statesman. Charismatic and irascible, he played a central role in bringing down the PRL.

Witos, Wincenty (1874–1945). Most significant Polish populist leader of the twentieth century. Witos held the premiership twice in the 1920s. A political opponent of the Piłsudskiite regime, he was imprisoned in 1930 and later went into exile. To many, Witos is the symbol of peasant power; to others, he is a wily and unscrupulous politician.

Wojtyła, Karol (1920–). Intellectual, writer, bishop of Rome. Wojtyła was a prominent cleric (Archbishop of Kraków, 1963–1978) and intellectual before his elevation to the papacy as John Paul II in 1978. His powerful character, intellectual stature, and fervent patriotism have made him a national hero. Even non-Catholics regard his becoming Pope John Paul as having an incalculable significance in undermining the Polish People's Republic (PRL) and rallying the nation.

Wyszyński, Stefan (1901–1981). Dominant religious figure of the Polish People's Republic (PRL). Wyszyński became primate of Poland in 1948. Interned by the Communists in the 1950s, Wyszyński enjoyed great moral authority in Poland. His policy of alternating bold initiative (for example, the 1965 letter to the German bishops) with conciliation made his role complex and controversial. Though a powerful advocate of Polish tradition, he never risked inciting direct conflict with the PRL authorities. Some regard him as the most significant actor in the history of the PRL.

Glossary

blank pages

Significant issues and ideas that could not be discussed, or could be discussed only circumspectly, in the Polish People's Republic (PRL) and are now openly examined.

Centrolew

The left-center parliamentary coalition in the Second Republic.

Commonwealth

Translation of the Polish term *Rzeczpospolita*—now more frequently translated as "republic—it was the name given to the Polish state after 1569.

Congress Kingdom

The central provinces of Poland granted limited autonomy under Russian rule by the Congress of Vienna, 1815. Formally abolished in 1831, the name remained for Russian Poland minus the *kresy*.

endecja

The nationalist political movement. The name is derived from the first letters of National Democracy (*Narodowa Demokracja*).

Galicia	The portions of Poland gained by Austria in the partitions. It is virtually synonymous with Austrian Poland.
General Gouvernement	German-occupied central Poland (1939–1945) Western Poland was attached directly to the Reich.
inteligencja	Virtually indefinable term, traceable to the mid-nineteenth century, referring to a class of people who were sufficiently educated and conscious of Polish national aspirations to regard themselves as a having a special responsibility to preserve and defend the national tradition and function as the conscience of the nation.
Jagiellonian	Name of Polish ruling dynasty, 1386–1572. By extension it refers to a Polish policy which emphasizes the importance of the east: Lithuania, Belarus, and Ukraine.
kresy	The eastern borderlands of Poland.
Kulturkampf	German persecution of Roman Catholics and ethnic minorities inaugurated in 1872.
liberum veto	Constitutional requirement for parliamentary unanimity.
Lublin Committee	Popular designation of the Polish Committee of National Liberation, established in Lublin in July 1944 as the nucleus of a future Communist government for a Soviet-dominated Poland.
Operation Vistula	Persecution and resettlement of Ukrainians in the Polish People's Republic (PRL).
PAX	Group of Catholic laity begun in 1947 in close but still mysterious connection with the Communist regime. It disintegrated in 1989.
Piłsudskiite	A follower of Józef Piłsudski, or someone who supports his conception of Polish history and foreign policy.

Polish Corridor	That portion of Poland separating East Prussia from the rest of Germany in the interwar era.
Polish October	Events of 1956 which led to liberalization.
Polonia	The Polish community outside of Poland; all people of Polish birth or origin living abroad.
Polonize	To assimilate to Polish culture.
Regained Lands	The territories gained by Poland from Germany after World War II; in Polish, *Ziemia Odzyskane*.
Roundtable	1989 negotiations among the Communist government, the Solidarity-led opposition, and the Church which allowed the peaceful transition to a post-Communist government.
sanacja	The post-1926 Piłsudskiite regime's policy of government without corruption, patriotism, and civic virtue; by extension, the regime itself.
Second Republic	The independent Poland recreated in 1918. After the fall of Poland in 1939 its government was reassembled in exile.
sejm (sejmiki)	The national parliament (regional assemblies).
szlachta	The gentry class.
"Tempest"	Code-name for the Home Army's (AK's) anti-German insurrection of 1944 of which the Warsaw rising was the central element.
Third Republic	Today' post-Communist Poland.
Visegrad Triangle	Cooperation among Poland, Hungary, and Czechoslovakia after 1989. After Czechoslovakia's separation into the Czech and Slovak republics, the still evolving relationship is occasionally referred to as the Visegrad Quadrilateral.
War at the top	1990 conflict between Lech Wałęsa and Tadeusz Mazowiecki which splintered Solidarity.
Warsaw ghetto rising	Jewish insurrection against the Germans in 1943.

List of Abbreviations

AK	Armia Krajowa—Home Army
AL	Armia Ludowa—People's Army
AWS	Alians Wyborczy Solidarność—Solidarity Electoral Alliance
BBWR	Bęzrpartyjny Blok Wspólpracy z Rządem—Nonpartisan Bloc for Cooperation with the Government
GG	German General Gouvernement, 1939–45
KIK	Klub Intelektualistów Katolickich—Club of Catholic Intellectuals
KNAPP	Komitet Amerykanów Polskiego Pochodzenia—Committee of Americans of Polish Descent
KNP	Komitet Narodowy Polski—Polish National Committee
KON	Komitet Obrony Narodowej—National Defense Committee

KOR	Komitet Obrony Robotników—Committee of Workers' Defense
KPN	Konfederacja Polski Niepodległej—Confederation of an Independent Poland
KTSSN	Komisja Tymczasowa Skonfederowanych Stronnictw Niepodległościowych—Provisional Commission of Confederated Independence parties
MKS	Międzyzakładowy Komitet Strajkowy—Interfactory Strike Committee
MPP	Mass Privatization Program
NKN	Naczelny Komitet Narodowy—Supreme National Committee
NSZ	Narodowe Siły Zbrojne—National Armed Forces
NSZZ-Solidarność	Niezależny Samorządny Związek Zawodowy—Independent Self-Governing Trade Union–Solidarity
ORMO	Ochotnicza Reserwa Milicji Obywatelskiej—Volunteer Reserves of the Citizens' Militia
OZON	Obóz Zjednoczenia Narodowego—Camp of National Unity
PAC	Polish American Congress
POW	Polska Organizacja Wojskowa—Polish Military Organization
PPR	Polska Partia Robotnicza—Polish Workers' party
PPS	Polska Partia Socjalistyczna—Polish Socialist party
PRL	Polska Rzeczpospolita Ludowa—Polish People's Republic
PRON	Patriotyczny Ruch Odrodzenia Narodowego—Patriotic Movement for National Revival

PSL	Polskie Stronnictwo Ludowe—Polish Populist party
PZPR	Polska Zjednoczona Partia Robotnicza—Polish United Workers' party
RP	Rzeczpospolita Polska—Polish Republic
SD	Stronnictwo Demokratyczne—Democratic party
SLD	Sojusz Lewicy Demokratycznej—Democratic Left Union
TKK	Tymczasowa Komisja Koordynacyjna Solidarności—Solidarity Temporary Coordinating Commission
TRS	Tymczasowa Rada Stanu—Provisional State Council (1917); also, Tymczasowa Rada Solidarności—Solidarity Provisional Council (1986)
UW	Unia Wolności—Freedom Union
WRON	Wojskowa Rada Ocalenia Narodowego—Military Council of National Salvation
ZBoWiD	Związek Bojowników za Wolnośc i Demokrację—Union of Fighters for Freedom and Democracy
ZPP	Związek Patriotów Polskich—Union of Polish Patriots
ZSL	Zjednoczone Stronnictwo Ludowe—United Peasant party
ZWC	Związek Walki Czynnej—Union of Armed Struggle

Bibliographic Essay

GENERAL STUDIES

To begin with general histories, Norman Davies's massive *God's Playground* (two vols., New York, 1982) is written with great flair; it is also replete with errors and controversial interpretations. His one-volume *Heart of Europe: A Short History of Poland* (Oxford, 1984) attempts a highly unusual reverse chronological approach with mixed results. Though P. S. Wandycz's *The Price of Freedom: A History of East Central Europe from the Middle Ages to the Present* (London, 1992) covers the whole region, its comments about Poland are important. A good one-volume account is the lively and beautifully illustrated *The Polish Way* (New York, 1987) by Adam Zamoyski, which admirably attempts to include a discussion of cultural matters. Hans Roos's *A History of Modern Poland* (New York, 1966) covers a restricted period and is now dated but it is a good introduction. The same could be said for M. K. Dziewanowski's *Poland in the 20th Century* (New York, 1977). Among widely available older works, Oskar Halecki's famous *Poland* (New York, 1943) is really a sustained personal essay interpreting Polish history. The volume was posthumously revised and updated in 1977. The *Cambridge History of Poland* (two vols., New York, 1941–1950) contains some still useful essays, although they are now largely obsolete. In many ways, the volumes edited by J. K. Fedorowicz, *A Republic of Nobles: Studies in Polish History to 1864* (Cambridge, 1982) and R. F. Leslie, *The History of Poland since 1863* (Cambridge, 1980), constitute a valuable new edition of this work. An extraordinarily readable multivolume essay on Polish history by Paweł Jasienica is available in English as *Piast Poland, Jagiellonian Poland, and The Commonwealth of Both Nations* (Miami, 1985–1992).

A number of important studies and essential documents in English translation are available in M. B. Biskupski and James S. Pula, eds., *Polish Democratic Thought* (New York, 1990). The revised edition of *For Your Freedom and Ours: Polish Progressive Spirit from the 14th Century to the Present*, edited by Krystyna M. Olszer (New York, 1981), contains several valuable documents. W. J. Wagner's edited collection *Polish Law Throughout the Ages* (Stanford, California, 1970) covers broad themes. A handy reference is Jacek Jędruch's *Constitutions, Elections and Legislatures of Poland, 1493–1977* (Washington, D.C., 1982). A useful though sentimental history of the *kresy* is found in Adam Żółtowski's *Border of Europe: A Study of the Polish Eastern Provinces* (London, 1950). Jewish life in old Poland is engagingly presented in Bernard D. Weinbryb's *The Jews of Poland: A Social and Economic History of the Jews in Poland from 1100–1900* (Philadelphia, 1972). A broader survey is available in an important collection edited by C. Abramsky, M. Jachimczyk, and Antony Polonsky, *The Jews in Poland* (Oxford, 1986).

For the cultural history of Poland, there are several basic volumes, including Czesław Miłosz's idiosyncratic *History of Polish Literature* (Berkeley, California, 1983) and the lavishly illustrated volume by Bogdan Suchodolski, *A History of Polish Culture* (Warsaw, 1986).

Pre-Partition Poland

For the earliest period in Polish history, there is a translation of the synthetic essay by Tadeusz Manteuffel, *The Formation of the Polish State: The Period of Ducal Rule, 963–1194* (Detroit, 1982) and a rather flawed translation entitled *Boleslaus the Bold and Bishop Stanislaus* by Tadeusz Grudziński (Warsaw, 1985). Paul Knoll's *The Rise of the Polish Monarchy* (Chicago, 1972) is important. The crucial years which follow are presented by the work edited by Thaddeus Gromada from the manuscript of his mentor, Oskar Halecki, *Jadwiga of Anjou and the Rise of East Central Europe* (New York, 1991). It is now rather dated but retains its importance owing to the author's astounding erudition. There are two significant volumes on the Renaissance era: the collection edited by Samuel Fiszman, *The Polish Renaissance in Its European Context* (Bloomington, Indiana, 1988) contains several excellent essays; and Harold B. Segel's *Renaissance Culture in Poland: The Rise of Humanism, 1470–1543.* (Ithaca, New York, 1989) is concerned largely with literature. Halecki's *From Florence to Brest* (New York, 1958) is vital to understanding the Polish east and the religious structure of the Commonwealth. The ethos of the dominant *szlachta* of old Poland is superbly captured in *Memoirs of the Polish Baroque: The Writings of Jan Chryzostom Pasek* (Berkeley, California, 1976). Religious toleration, an important theme not well known in the West, is well presented in Janusz Tazbir's compact *A State Without Stakes* (New York, 1973). The only study of the vital 1569 reorganization of the Commonwealth is Harry Dembkowski's *The Union of Lublin* (New York, 1982). Robert I. Frost's *After the Deluge: Poland-Lithuania and the Second Northern War, 1655–1660* (Cambridge, 1996) is most impressive. A stimulating discussion of the ethnic and structural problems of pre-partition Poland, involving Oswald P. Backus, Oskar Halecki, and Joseph Jakstas, is reprinted in Donald W. Treadgold, ed., *The Development of the USSR: An Exchange of Views* (Seattle, Washington, 1964), pp. 275–319. A handy collection of essays on a variety of economic and social issues is found in Antoni Mączak, Henryk Samsonowicz, and Peter Burke, eds., *East-Central Europe in Transition: From the Fourteenth to the Seventeenth Centuries* (Cambridge, 1985).

Unfortunately, the era of the Cossack wars still has not produced a major synthesis though there are some valuable essays in the volume edited by Peter J. Potichnyi, *Poland and Ukraine: Past and Present* (Edmonton, Canada, 1980). Jerzy Łukowski's *Liberty's Folly: The Polish-Lithuanian Commonwealth in the Eighteenth Century, 1697–1795* (London, 1991) is thorough. A new study of the partition era is Łukowski's *The Partitions of Poland, 1772, 1793, 1795* (London, 1998). Herbert H. Kaplan's *The First Partition of Poland* (New York, 1962) is solid; Robert H. Lord's *The Second Partition of Poland* (Cambridge, Massachusetts, 1915) is valuable despite its age; and Lord's brief "The Third Partition of Poland" (*Slavonic Review*, vol. 3 [1924–1925] also retains much value. A useful popular study is Adam Zamoyski's *The Last King of Poland* (New York, 1997). There is much engaging material on social history in the poorly tilted *Child-Rearing and Reform: A Study of the Nobility in Eighteenth-Century Poland* by Bogna Lorence-Kot (Westport, Connecticut, 1985).

POLAND'S LONG CENTURY, 1795–1914

Piotr S. Wandycz's *Lands of Partitioned Poland* (Seattle, Washington, 1975) is an outstanding compendium, but it is very densely written. The initial chapters of R. F. Leslie's *History of Poland since 1863*, already noted, are pertinent to this period. Adam Bromke's *Poland's Politics: Idealism vs. Realism* (Cambridge, Massachusetts, 1967) suggests a problematical yet stimulating methodology for analyzing politics which is also relevant to later periods. A brilliant and stimulating work is Jerry Jedlicki's *A Suburb of Europe: Polish Nineteenth Century Approaches to Western Civilization* (Budapest, 1999). Stefan Kieniewicz's *The Emancipation of the Polish Peasantry* (Chicago, 1969) is useful concerning the oft-overlooked peasantry. Andrzej Walicki's works on Polish political thought are essential and correct many established stereotypes. Particularly valuable are his *Philosophy and Romantic Nationalism: The Case of Poland* (London, 1982) and *The Enlightenment and the Birth of Modern Nationhood: Polish Political Thought from Noble Republicanism to Tadeusz Kościuszko* (Notre Dame, Indiana, 1989). Rett R. Ludwikowski's *Continuity and Change in Poland: Conservatism in Polish Political Thought* (Washington, D.C., 1991) deals with a significant and neglected aspect. Henryk Wereszcyki's "Polish Insurrections as a Controversial Problem in Polish Historiography" (*Canadian Slavonic Papers*, vol. 9 [1967], pp. 98–121), is stimulating.

There is no English-language account of Napoleon and the Polish Question, but two works cover this as well as the subsequent generation: Marian Kukiel's now dated *Czartoryski and European Unity, 1770–1861* (Princeton, New Jersey, 1955) and W. H. Zawadzki's *A Man of Honour: Adam Czartoryski as a Statesman of Russia and Poland, 1795–1831* (Oxford, 1993). An engaging memoir, though unreliable, is the strikingly illustrated *Memoirs of a Polish Lancer: The Pamiętniki of Dezydery Chlapowski* (Chicago, 1992). Given the paucity of readily available English-language materials, a volume by Jan Pachoński and Reul K. Wilson, *Poland's Caribbean Tragedy: A Study of the Polish Legions in the Haitian War of Independence, 1802–1803* (New York, 1986), is an important contribution to Polish affairs in the Napoleonic era.

The early nineteenth century in Russian Poland is treated in a well-researched study by Frank Thackeray, *Antecedents of Revolution: Alexander I and the Polish Congress Kingdom, 1815–1825* (New York, 1980). The November Rising is the subject of R. F. Leslie's *Polish Politics and the Revolution of November 1830* (London, 1956); he also wrote an account of the January Rising, *Reform and Insurrection in Russian Poland, 1856–1865* (London 1963); both are rather unsatisfactory. Peter Brock's *Polish Revolutionary Populism* (Toronto, 1977) is useful regarding agrarian politics. There remain very serious gaps in English-language scholarship regarding Poland.

Stanislaus A. Blejwas's *Realism in Polish Politics: Warsaw Positivism and National Survival in Nineteenth Century Poland* (New Haven, 1984) is an important study, as is a biography by Kazimiera Janina Cottam, *Bolesław Limanowski, 1835–1935: A Study in Socialism and Nationalism* (New York, 1978). Two accounts of the radical left in Russian Poland are a weak volume by Lucjan Blit, *The Origins of Polish Socialism: The History and Ideas of the First Polish Socialist Party, 1878–1886* (Cambridge, 1971), and the more impressive one by Norman Naimark, *A History of the 'Proletariat': The Emergence of Marxism in the Kingdom of Poland, 1870–1887* (New York, 1979). The first years of the twentieth century in Russian Poland are dealt with in an important study by Robert E. Blobaum, *Rewolucja: Russian Poland, 1904–1907* (Ithaca, 1995).

The Poles under Austrian rule await their historian. A very brief introduction is found in Piotr S. Wandycz's "The Poles in the Habsburg Monarchy," reprinted in a volume edited by Andrei S. Markovits and Frank E. Sysyn, *Nationbuilding and the Politics of Nationalism: Essays on Austrian Galicia* (Cambridge, Massachusetts, 1982), pp. 68–93, which also contains several other useful studies on Polish-Ukrainian topics.

Useful introductions to the German partition include William Hagen's *Germans, Poles, and Jews: The Nationality Conflict in the Prussian East, 1772–1914* (Chicago, 1980) and Lech Trzeciakowski's *The Kulturkampf in Prussian Poland* (New York, 1990), a translation of the work by the prominent Polish specialist. John J. Kulczycki's *School Strikes in Prussian Poland, 1901–1907: The Struggle over Bilingual Education* (New York, 1981) is broader than the title and raises important questions.

WAR AND INDEPENDENCE, 1914–1918

The Polish question during World War I has no recent history in English, but Titus Komarnicki's badly dated *Rebirth of the Polish Republic: A Study of the Diplomatic History of Europe, 1914–1920* (London, 1957) is a useful introduction. Wiktor Sukiennicki's encyclopedic *East Central Europe During World War I: From Foreign Domination to National Independence* (two vols., New York, 1984) is a mine of information. Both works are also useful for the next era as well.

There is, disappointingly, no biography of Roman Dmowski, although Alvin Marcus Fountain's *Roman Dmowski: Party, Tactics, Ideology, 1895–1907* (New York, 1980) is a start. Adam Zamoyski's *Paderewski* (New York, 1982) is a reliable popular account and supersedes older works by Charles Phillips (1934), Rom Landau (1934), and Charlotte Kellogg

(1956). An abbreviated English version of Ignacy Jan Paderewski's recollections, up to 1914, appeared as *The Paderewski Memoirs* (London, 1939); it is, like its author, charming and unreliable. There are two recent biographies of Józef Piłsudski; neither is satisfactory. The first, written by an admirer, is infelicitous in style and organization [Wacław Jędrzejewicz, *Piłsudski: A Life for Poland* (New York, 1982)]. The translation of Andrzej Garlicki's Józef *Piłsudski, 1867–1935* (New York, 1995) is impressively researched but militantly hostile and unpersuasive.

Western diplomacy regarding Poland's rebirth is recounted in an important unpublished study by Paul Latawski, "Great Britain and the Rebirth of Poland" (Ph.D. diss., University of Indiana, 1985). The forthcoming *The United States and the Rebirth of Poland* by M. B. Biskupski is very thorough. There is no study from the French side. The collection edited by John Micgiel, *Wilsonian East Central Europe: Current Perspectives* (New York, 1995) is valuable for this period and the next as is a volume edited by Latawski, *The Reconstruction of Poland, 1914–23* (New York, 1992). A rather revisionist view of Woodrow Wilson is presented in several works by M. B. Biskupski of which the most detailed is "Re-Creating Central Europe: The United States 'Inquiry' into the Future of Poland, 1918" (*International History Review* 12, no. 2 [1990]. Though there is no study of Polish emigré politics in France or Russia, activities in the United States have prompted a great deal of writing. An attempt to evaluate and synthesize is made in M. B. Biskupski's "Paderewski as Leader of American Polonia, 1914–1918" *Polish American Studies* 18, no. 1 [1986].

WARS, EXPERIMENTS, AND FRONTIERS, 1918–1921

Kai Lundgreen-Nielsen's massive study *The Polish Problem at the Paris Peace Conference* (Odense, Denmark, 1979) is impressively researched, though its interpretations are not always convincing. M. K. Dziewanowski's quasi-biography of Piłsudski, *Joseph Piłsudski: A European Federalist, 1918–1922* (Stanford, California, 1969) is useful in this context. The best study of the Polish-Russian war is P. S. Wandycz's *Soviet-Polish Relations, 1917–1921* (Cambridge, Massachusetts, 1969). The war itself is recounted with much verve, though occasional lapses in fact and judgment, by Norman Davies in his *White Eagle Red Star* (New York, 1972) and by Adam Zamoyski in his *The Battle for the Marchlands* (New York, 1981). A British diplomat, Lord d'Abernon, wrote a dramatic account, *The Eighteenth Decisive Battle of the World, Warsaw, 1920* (London, 1931), whose title tells all. Piłsudski has left a virtually unique memoir and analysis of the war in his *The Year 1920* (New York, 1972). Unfortunately, there are virtually no biographical studies of many of the major figures of the era.

THE SECOND REPUBLIC, 1918–1939

This is a subject badly neglected in English-language historiography. A useful introduction, stronger on domestic than foreign policy problems, is Antony Polonsky's *Politics of Independent Poland, 1921–1939* (Oxford, 1972). The popular account by Richard Watt, *Bitter Glory: Poland and Its Fate, 1918–1939* (New York, 1979) is well written. The appropriate sections of Joseph Rothschild's *East Central Europe Between the Two World Wars* (Seattle, 1974) are well worth reading. A good introduction to the economic situation is found in Ferdynand Zweig's *Poland Between Two Wars* (London, 1944), although it is now badly dated as is Jack J. Taylor's *The Economic Development of Poland, 1919–1950* (Ithaca, 1952). A translated work by Zbigniew Landau and Jerzy Tomaszewski, *The Polish Economy in the Twentieth Century* (New York, 1985), is based on more recent scholarship, but it is rapidly becoming obsolete owing to the researches of post-PRL scholars. Readers are advised to consult works published since 1991 such as Wojciech Roszkowski's *Landowners in Poland, 1918–1939* (New York, 1991) and Jan Kofman, *Economic Nationalism and Development: Central and Eastern Europe Between the Two World Wars* (Boulder, CO, 1997).

Regarding politics, Olga A. Narkiewicz's *The Green Flag: Polish Populist Politics, 1867–1970* (London, 1976) is disappointing, although it is the only history of the populists. Joseph Rothschild's *Piłsudski's Coup d'Etat* (New York, 1966) is outstanding and delivers more than the title suggests. The Piłsudskiite Colonels regime is well handled by the detailed account of Edward Wynot given in *Polish Politics in Transition* (Athens, Georgia, 1974). Given the large role of the military in the Second Republic, M. B. Biskupski's "The Military Elite of the Polish Second Republic, 1918–1945" (*War & Society* 14, no. 2 [1996] is useful.

Regarding the important minorities question, there are two volumes by Ezra Mendelssohn, *The Jews of East Central Europe Between the World Wars* (Bloomington, Indiana, 1985) and *Zionism in Poland: The Formative Years, 1915–1926* (New Haven, 1981), but both are highly critical. Celia S. Heller's *On the Edge of Destruction: Jews of Poland Between Two World Wars* (New York, 1977) is polemical. An important work is Antony Polonsky, *Jews in Independent Poland, 1918–1939* (London, 1997), as is the older Edward D. Wynot " 'A Necessary Cruelty': The Emergence of Official Anti-Semitism in Poland, 1936–39" (*American Historical Review* 76, no. 4 [1971]: 1035–58. Richard Blanke's *Orphans of Versailles: The Germans in Western Poland*, 1918–1939 (Lexington, KY, 1993) is valuable concerning the Germans. For the Belorussians, the older work by Nicholas P. Vakar, *Belorussia: The Making of a Nation* (Cambridge, Massachusetts, 1956), is still useful though flawed and dated. There is no major work on the important Ukrainian minority. Stephen Horak's older *Poland and Her National Minorities: 1919–1939* (New York, 1961) is unsound. Far better, though rather narrow in focus, are Bohdan Budorowycz, "Poland and the Ukrainian Problem, 1921–39" (*Canadian Slavonic Papers* 25, no. 4 [1993]), and Alexander J. Motyl's "Ukrainian Nationalist Political Violence in Inter-War Poland (1921–1939)" (*East European Quarterly* 19, no. 1 [1985]).

Two overviews of foreign policy issues are available. Roman Debicki's *Foreign Policy of Poland, 1919–39* (New York, 1962) is very sketchy and now much dated, but it is a good introduction. The much more detailed work by Jan F. Karski, *The Great Powers & Poland, 1919–1945* (Lanham, Maryland, 1985), is uneven and disappointing. A brilliant synthesis is the brief essay by Piotr S. Wandycz, *Polish Diplomacy, 1914–1945: Aims and Achievements* (London, 1988). Anna M. Cienciala's *From Versailles to Locarno: Keys to Polish Foreign Policy, 1919–1925* (Lawrence, Kansas, 1984) does not cover the whole era, but it is an important reference with an exhaustive discussion of the literature. Josef Korbel's *Poland between East and West: Soviet and German Diplomacy Towards Poland, 1919–1939* (Princeton, 1963) is a useful synthesis. The crucial question of relations with France are handled by Piotr Wandycz's two volumes, *France and Her Eastern Allies, 1919–1925* (Minneapolis, 1962) and *The Twilight of French Eastern Alliances, 1926–1936* (Princeton, 1988). A good overview of Polish-German relations is found in Harald von Riekhoff's *German-Polish Relations, 1918–33* (Baltimore, 1971). Regarding the United States we have a fine work by Neal Pease, *Poland, the United States, and the Stabilization of Europe, 1919–1933* (New York, 1986). Anna Cienciala's study of Beck's diplomacy, *Poland and the Western Powers, 1938–1939* (Toronto, 1968), is a masterpiece. Anita J. Prażmowska's *Britain, Poland and the Eastern Front, 1939* (Cambridge, England, 1987) is a valuable analysis of British policy, but it is very weak regarding Poland.

WORLD WAR II, 1939–1945

Military aspects of the September Campaign are competently presented in Steve Zaloga and Victor Madej's *The Polish Campaign, 1939* (New York, 1985); Nicholas Bethell's *The War That Hitler Won* (London, 1972) places the campaign in a diplomatic context. The only overall account of Polish military activities throughout the war is found in Michael Alfred Peszke's oddly titled *Battle for Warsaw, 1939–1944* (New York, 1995), which is uneven but a mine of information otherwise inaccessible in English. Naval combat is covered in Peszke's volume as well as in M. B. Biskupski's "A Prosopographical Account of the Polish Naval Officer Corps" (*Journal of Slavic Military History*. 12, no. 1 [199]; 166–179). There is valuable material in the appropriate chapters of Jerzy Cynk's *History of the Polish Air Force, 1918–1968* (Reading, England, 1972).

A good overall account of the Polish question in the war is found in Józef Garliński's *Poland in the Second World War* (New York, 1985). International diplomacy regarding Poland has produced an enormous literature. A useful start is an older work by Edward Różek, *Allied Wartime Diplomacy* (New York, 1958), and a more recent volume by Antony Polonsky, *The Great Powers and the Polish Question, 1941–1945* (London, 1976). Anna Cienciala has produced a series of important essays relying often on recent revelations from former Soviet archives. Chief among these are "The Question of the Polish-Soviet Frontier in British, Soviet, and Polish Policy in 1939–1940" (*Polish Review* 33, no. 3 [1988]; 295–323); and "General Sikorski and the Conclusion of the Polish—Soviet Agreement of July 30, 1941: A Reassessment" (*Polish Review* 41, no. 4 [1996]; 401–434). Sarah Meiklejohn Terry's *Poland's Place in Europe: General Sikorski and the Origin of the Oder-Neisse Line, 1939–1943* (Princeton, 1983) is broader than the title and important. Richard C. Lukas's *The Strange Allies: The United States and Poland, 1941–1945* (Knoxville, 1978), is fundamental regarding Polish-U.S. relations. Prażmowska's *Britain and Poland, 1939–1943* (Cambridge, England, 1995) is badly flawed and disappointing. Now dated, though still useful, on the same theme is George V. Kacewicz's *Great Britain, the Soviet Union and the Polish Government-in-Exile, 1939–1945* (The Hague, 1979).

German-occupied Poland is the subject of Richard C. Lukas's *The Forgotten Holocaust: The Poles Under German Occupation* (Lexington, Kentucky, 1986), a valuable account though marred by its polemical tone regarding Jewish issues. An equally controversial, and flawed, volume from the opposite perspective is David Engel's *In the Shadow of Auschwitz:*

The Polish Government-in-Exile and the Jews, 1939–1942 (Chapel Hill, North Carolina, 1987). The extraordinary story of the Polish Underground State still lacks its historian. A brief introduction by a participant, Stefan Korbonski, *The Polish Underground State: A Guide to the Underground, 1939–1945* (New York, 1981), is a valuable reference. The Warsaw uprising has produced a well-done entry by Jan M. Ciechanowski, *The Warsaw Rising* (Cambridge, England, 1974), which argues that the rising was an avoidable mistake, a thesis rejected as untenable by current scholarship. J. K. M. Hanson's *The Civilian Population and the Warsaw Uprising of 1944* (Cambridge England, 1982) adds the social dimension. A valuable memoir account is Tadeusz Bór-Komorowski's *The Secret Army* (London, 1951), which is worth consulting to gain an understanding of the Home Army's (AK's) view. Two of the couriers to the underground have left memoirs: Jan F. Karski, *The Story of a Secret State* (Boston, 1944), an established classic; and Jan Nowak, *Courier from Warsaw* (Detroit, 1982), valuable and compelling reading.

The Jewish fate in German-occupied Poland has produced an enormous literature. Particularly useful are Lucjan Dobroszycki, *The Chronicle of the Łódź Ghetto, 1941–1944* (New Haven, CT, 1984); Yisrael Gutman, *The Jews of Warsaw, 1939–1943: Ghetto, Underground, Revolt* (Bloomington, IN, 1982); and Emanuel Ringelblum, *Notes from the Warsaw Ghetto* (New York, 1958). Jewish-Polish relations in the era are the subject of Władysław Bartoszewski's massive *Righteous Among Nations* (London, 1969); Bruno Shatyn, *A Private War* (Detroit, 1985); and Nehama Tec, *When Light Pierced the Darkness* (New York, 1986). The already mentioned works by Engel, Lukas, and Heller may also be consulted. All works on the Holocaust, understandably, devote considerable space to the fate of Poland's Jewry.

Little is yet available regarding Soviet-occupied Poland. Keith Sword, ed., *The Soviet Takeover of the Polish Eastern Provinces, 1939–41* (New York, 1991), is especially valuable, as is his companion volume, *Deportation and Exile: Poles in the Soviet Union, 1939–1948* (New York, 1994), which covers a broader period. Jan T. Gross's *Revolution from Abroad: The Soviet Conquest of Poland's Western Ukraine and Western Belorussia* (Princeton, 1988) is still useful though rapidly becoming obsolete in light of new scholarship. The Katyń massacre still lacks a thorough study. Janusz K. Zawodny's *Death in the Forest: The Story of the Katyn Forest Massacre* (Notre Dame, Indiana, 1962) is the best available. A new synthesis based on post-Soviet revelations is badly needed. A unique survivor's account of the Soviet arrest and trial of sixteen Polish underground leaders is found in Zbigniew Stypułkowski's *Invitation to Moscow* (New York, 1962).

There is no thorough biography of Władysław Sikorski, which is a major gap. The brief collection edited by Keith Sword, *Sikorski—Soldier and Statesman* (London 1989), may be noted, but Sarah Terry's work, mentioned earlier, is the most important title, and the recent entry by Leon J. Waszak, *Agreement in Principle: The Wartime Partnership of Wladyslaw Sikorski and Winston Churchill* (New York, 1996), is of note, as are the recent essays by Cienciała, already mentioned. There are a number of important memoir accounts by generals Władysław Anders (*An Army in Exile*, 1949), and Stanisław Sosabowski, *Freely I Served* (London, 1960), the diplomat Edward Raczyński (*In Allied London*, London, 1962), and the underground leader Stefan Korboński (*Fighting Warsaw: The Story of the Polish Underground State*, New York, 1956) all are particularly valuable.

COMMUNISM IN POLAND: THE CONSTRUCTION OF THE PRL, 1945–1970

Though brief and not devoted exclusively to Poland, an excellent summary is Joseph Rothschild's *Return to Diversity: A Political History of East Central Europe Since World War II* (New York, 1989). This supersedes a number of older studies of which the best is Richard F. Starr's *Poland, 1944–1962: The Sovietization of a Captive People* (Baton Rouge, 1962). Participant or eyewitness accounts, including Stanisław Mikołajczyk's *The Rape of Poland: The Pattern of Soviet Aggression* (New York, 1948) and American diplomat Arthur Bliss-Lane's *I Saw Poland Betrayed* (Indianapolis, 1948), give a feel of the period, but they are not particularly reliable. Regarding the larger Soviet context, Zbigniew Brzeziński's *The Soviet Bloc: Unity and Conflict* (Cambridge, Massachusetts, 1960) is a classic. Still the best history of the Polish Communist party is found in M. K. Dziewanowski's *The Communist Party of Poland: An Outline of History* (Cambridge, Massachusetts, 1968), even though now it is obviously hopelessly dated.

Major themes in PRL history include Andrzej Korboński's *Politics of Socialist Agriculture in Poland, 1945–1960* (New York, 1965), regarding agriculture; Maciej Pomian-Śrzednicki's *Religious Change in Contemporary Poland: Secularization and Politics* (London, 1982), regarding religiosity; and the famous *The Captive Mind* (London, 1953) by Czesław Miłosz, concerning intellectual freedom.

Important for the Soviet takeover of Poland at the end of the war are Krystyna Kersten's *The Establishment of Communist Rule in Poland, 1943–1948* (Berkeley, 1991) and Antony Polonsky and Bolesław Drukier, eds., *The Beginnings of Communist Rule in Poland: December 1943–June 1945* (London, 1980). The patriarchs of the PRL are revealed in all their mediocrity in the indispensable *"Them": Stalin's Polish Puppets* by Teresa Torańska (New York, 1987). The events of 1956 still await a comprehensive analysis based on much fresh material. The old collection of Paul E. Zinner, *National Communism and Popular Revolt in Eastern Europe* (New York, 1956), is still of value but its interpretations are obsolete. The PRL's foreign relations in the early years are deftly handled in Richard C. Lukas's *Bitter Legacy: Polish-American Relations in the Wake of World War II* (Lexington, Kentucky, 1982).

There are very few major studies of PRL figures; therefore, Nicholas Bethell's *Gomułka: His Poland, His Communism* (London, 1969) is important, though the subject was, like most of the PRL leadership, a gray figure indeed.

COLLAPSE OF THE PRL, 1970–1990

A sophisticated analysis of the development of the movement for a civil society and the origins of Solidarity is found in Michael H. Bernhard's *The Origins of Democratization in Poland* (New York, 1993). *Background to Crisis: Policy and Politics in Gierek's Poland*, edited by Maurice D. Simon and Roger E. Kanet (Boulder, Colorado, 1981) includes several solid essays. An outstanding collection that explains the origins of Poland in the 1980s is found in Stanisław Gomułka and Antony Polonsky, eds., *Polish Paradoxes* (London, 1990). Jan Józef Lipski's important history of the Committee of Workers' Defense (KOR) has been translated into English as *KOR: A History of the Workers' Defense Committee in Poland, 1976–1981* (Berkeley, 1985). David Ost places Polish developments in a rather elaborate framework in his *Solidarity: The Politics of Anti-Politics: Opposition and Reform in Poland Since 1968* (Philadelphia, 1990). An indispensable translated document indicting Gierek's PRL is Jack Bielasiak, ed., *Poland Today: The State of the Republic* (Armonk, New York, 1981). The perceptive journalistic account by Timothy Garton Ash, *The Polish Revolution: Solidarity, 1980–82* (London, 1983) is probably the best of the many contemporary books inspired by the events of 1980. Jadwiga Staniszkis's *Poland's Self-Limiting Revolution* (Princeton 1984) is a sociological account of Solidarity by a participant. Many valuable insights are embedded into highly jargonized prose. A particularly useful collection of documents and studies was edited by Leopold Labedz as *Poland Under Jaruzelski* (New York, 1983). *A Way of Hope*, Lech Walesa's autobiography (New York, 1987), is of interest, though, like its author, neither graceful nor reflective.

THE THIRD REPUBLIC

Obviously, the Third Republic has not yet stimulated a large literature. Ray Taras's *Consolidating Democracy in Poland* (Boulder, Colorado, 1995) is a useful outline though already dated. Foreign policy matters are the subject of a useful collection edited by Ilya Prizel and Andrew A. Michta, *Polish Foreign Policy Reconsidered* (New York, 1995). The Polish viewpoint is presented, with admirable frankness, in Barbara Wizimirska's *Yearbook of Polish Foreign Policy, 1998* (Warsaw, 1998). Darcy O'Brien's *The Hidden Pope* (New York, 1998) is a readable account of recent Polish-Jewish relations, although the author's knowledge of Polish history is limited. A superb essay on Polish-Jewish relations, a perennially sensitive topic, is Piotr Wróbel's "Double Memory: Poles and Jews After the Holocaust" (*East European Politics and Societies*, 11, no. 3 [Fall 1997]).

Index

About the Author

M. B. BISKUPSKI is Professor of History at St. John Fisher College in Rochester, New York.

Other Titles in the
Greenwood Histories of the Modern Nations
Frank W. Thackeray and John E. Findling, Series Editors

The History of Japan
Louis G. Perez

The History of Israel
Arnold Blumberg

The History of Spain
Peter Pierson

The History of Germany
Eleanor L. Turk

The History of Holland
Mark T. Hooker

The History of Nigeria
Toyin Falola

The History of Brazil
Robert M. Levine

The History of Russia
Charles E. Ziegler

The History of Portugal
James M. Anderson

The History of Mexico
Burton Kirkwood